Daughters of the Moon

When have I last looked on
The round green eyes and the long wavering bodies
Of the dark leopards of the moon?
All the wild witches, those most noble ladies,
For all their broom-sticks and their tears,
Their angry tears, are gone.
The holy centaurs of the hills are vanished;
I have nothing but the embittered sun;
Banished heroic mother moon and vanished,
And now that I have come to fifty years
I must endure the timid sun.

W.B. Yeats, *Lines Written in Dejection*

Daughters of the Moon

Edited by
Shakrukh Husain

Illustrated by
Liane Payne

Faber and Faber
BOSTON · LONDON

First published in the United States in 1994 by Faber and Faber, Inc.,
50 Cross Street, Winchester, MA 01890. Originally published in the
United Kingdom in 1993 by Virago Press Limited, 20–23 Mandela Street,
Camden Town, London NW1 0HQ

Library of Congress Cataloging-in-Publication Data

Daughters of the Moon : witch tales from around the world /
[edited by] Shahrukh Husain.
p.   cm.
ISBN 0-571-19856-2
1. Witches.   2. Witchcraft.   I. Shahrukh Husain.
GR530.D36   1994
398.21—dc20   94-3332
                                                                                    CIP

Jacket design by Lorna Stovall
Jacket photograph by Merlyn Rosenberg

Printed in the United States of America

To Christopher Shackle,
my husband

Contents

Acknowledgements   viii
Introduction   ix

1. Alluring Women and Ailing Knights

Indravati and the Seven Sisters   3
Finn's Madness   9
The Nixy   11
The Maiden on the Loreley   15
Coonlagh Ruadh and the Fairy Maiden   17
The Marriage of Sir Gawain   20

2. Wise Old Women

I Love You More Than Salt   27
The Tale of the Merchant, the Crone and the King   33
The Four Gifts   36
Habetrot   44
Unfortunate   48
Biddy Early's Flying Magic   58

3. Witches in Love: Possessive Women and Devoted Wives

The Morrigu	63
The Painted Skin	66
Lilith and the Blade of Grass	70
Daughter of the Moon, Son of the Sun	71
The Loving Fox	76
The Story of Aristomenes	77
Ala and the Old Hag	85
The Queen's Ring	87

4. Transformations

The Grinning Face of the Old Woman	93
The Red Woman	95
The Woman Who Turned Her Husband Into a Snake	99
Kertong	100
The Boy and the Hare	105
Roland	107
The Snake Wife	111
The Old Woman in the Wood	112
The Leopard Woman	115
The Three Crones	117

5. Guardians of the Seasons and Elements

The First People and the First Corn	123
Mistress of Fire	126
Anancy and the Hide-Away Garden	129
Johnny, Draw the Knife	134
The Snow-Daughter and the Fire-Son	136
Mother Holle	139

6. Witchy Devices: Cauldrons, Broomsticks, and Trysts with the Devil

Hooch for Skye!	145
The Cauldron-Born	153

The Witches' Sabbath	157
The Birch Besom	159
The Broom is Busy	163
The Horned Women	165
The Goodwife of Laggan	168
Baba Yaga	172

8. Hungry Hags: Cannibals and Blook-Suckers

Vikram and the Dakini	177
The Old Eagle-Hawk Woman	182
The Two Children and the Witch	184
My Sweet Witch	186
The Curse	189
Two Children and a Witch	191
El-Muzayyara	194

8. Trials and Contests

The Bewitched Churn	199
Rabbi Joshua and the Witch	201
The Witchmaster's Advice	204
The Son of Seven Queens	205
The Caellie Bheur	213
Hag-Rog	215
Biddy Early, the Priest and the Crow	217
Petie-Pete Versus Witch Bea-Witch	219
Notes	223

Acknowledgements

My grateful thanks to Pat Ryan, Linda-May Ballard, Jill Laidlaw and my brother Aamer Hussain for their help in finding sources; to my editor Ruth Petrie for her consistent support and for occasionally tightening the reins to keep me on track, also for including me in those parts of publishing that other authors never reach; to Teresa Lonergan for uncomplainingly clearing up the debris and detritus generated by this book and for still being here to keep me tidy; to Natalie Brady and Philippa Briggs for kicking off the book with the photocopying of stories; to my son Monty for acting as critic with remorseless honesty – his advice was a valuable mixture of the freshness and cynicism that colours a ten-year-old's attitude to fairy tales; to my daughter Samira for listening hungrily and pointing out repetitions with all the wisdom and mental agility of her five years – also for sharing my unconditional passion for witches. And above all to my husband Christopher Shackle, not only for his unstinting practical help and research, but also for building up for me nearly single-handedly a comprehensive library of witch literature; to my dear friend Carol Topolski for listening patiently and reacting stimulatingly (like Christopher) to my theories about the psychological function of witches in fairy tales. This book has benefitted from the uniqueness of each contribution. Finally, thanks to all my friends and colleagues who encouraged my efforts and shared my excitement at various stages of its compilation.

Permission to reproduce these stories is gratefully acknowledged to the following:
Wilhelm Stollfuss Verlag for 'The Maiden on the Loreley' from *Legends of the Rhineland* by August Antz, translated by Kathlyn Rutherford

copyright © Wilhelm Stollfuss Verlag; Pat Ryan for 'Coonlaugh Ruadh and the Fairy Maid' copyright © 1985 Pat Ryan; Beaver Books for 'The Marriage of Sir Gawain' from *The Tale of Sir Gawain* by Neil Philip copyright © 1987 Neil Philip; Duncan Williamson for 'I Love You More than Salt' from *Tell Me a Story for Christmas* copyright © 1987, published by Canongate Publishing Ltd., for 'Hooch for Skye!' from *The Genie and the Fisherman* by Duncan and Linda Williamson copyright © 1991 Duncan Williamson, published by Cambridge University Press; Penguin Books Ltd. and A.P. Watt Ltd. for 'Habetrot' from *A Dictionary of Fairies* by Katharine Briggs copyright © 1976 Katharine Briggs, 'The Story of Aristomenes' from *The Golden Ass* translated by Robert Graves copyright © 1950; Magnet Books for 'Unfortunate' and 'The Queen's Ring' from *A Book of Curses and Enchantments* by Ruth Manning-Saunders copyright © 1976 Ruth Manning-Saunders; The Mercier Press Ltd. for 'Biddy Early's Flying Magic' and 'Biddy Early, the Crow and the Priest' from *In Search of Biddy Early* by Edmund Lenihan copyright © 1987 Edmund Lenihan; William Collins Sons and Co. Ltd. and Doubleday, a division of Bantam Doubleday Dell Publishing Group, Inc., for 'Lilith' from *Jewish Folktales* by Pinhas Sadeh, translated by Hillel Halkin, English translation copyright © 1990; Canongate Publishing Ltd. for 'Daughter of the Moon' and 'Mistress of Fire' from *The Sun Maiden and the Crescent Moon: Siberian Folk Tales* by James Riordan copyright © 1989 James Riordan; Heinemann Educational Books Ltd. for 'Ala and the Hag' and 'My Sweet Witch' from *Myths and Legends from the Congo* by Jan Knappert copyright © 1971 Jan Knappert; Pantheon Books, a division of Random House, Inc., for 'The Loving Fox' and 'The Grinning Face of the Old Woman' from *Japanese Tales* by Royall Tyler copyright © 1987 Royall Tyler, 'The Leopard Woman' from *African Folktales* by Roger D. Abrahams copyright © 1983 Roger D. Abrahams, 'Baba Yaga' from *Russian Fairy Tales* by Aleksandr Afanas'ev, translated by Robert Guterman copyright © 1947, copyright © renewed 1973 by Random House Inc.; Harcourt Brace Jovanovich, Inc., for 'The Three Crones' and 'Petie-Pete Versus Bea-Witch' from *Italian Folktales* by Italo Calvino, translated by George Martin, English translation copyright © 1980 Bruce Jovanovich, Inc.; The Smithsonian Institution Bureau for American Ethnology, Bulletin 98 for 'The Woman Who Turned Her Husband into a Snake' from *Tales of the Cochiti Indians* by Ruth Benedict copyright © 1934; Houghton Mifflin (U.S.A.) and The Bodley Head Press for 'Kertong' from *Sweet and Sour Tales from China* retold by Carol Kendall and Yao-wen Li copyright © 1978 Carol

Kendall and Yao-wen Li; The Ulster Folk and Transport Museum for 'The Boy and the Hare' by storyteller Thomas Cecil from *Tape Archive C79.29* copyright © 1979 by Thomas Cecil and for 'Johnny, Draw the Knife' by storyteller Thomas Cecil from *Tape Archive C79.33* copyright © 1979 by Thomas Cecil; Indiana University Press for 'The Snake Wife' from *The Yanagita Kunio Guide to the Japanese Folk Tale* edited and translated by Fanny Hagin Mayer copyright © 1986; Thomas Cecil; Henry Holt (U.S.A.) and Walker Books Limited for 'Anancy and the Hide-Away Garden' from *Anancy-Spiderman* by James Berry copyright © 1988 James Berry; *Ulster Folklife* for 'Johnny, Draw the Knife' from *Seal Stories and Belief of Rathlin Island* by Linda-May Ballard copyright © 1983 Linda-May Ballard and Thomas Cecil, Ulster Folk and Transport Museum; The Aquarian Press for 'The Cauldron-Born' from *The Song of Taliesin* by John Matthews copyright © 1991 John Matthews; University of Chicago Press for 'The Witches' Sabbath' from *Folktales of Norway* by Reidar Christiansen, translated by Pat Shaw Iverson copyright © 1964 by The University of Chicago, 'El-Muzayyara' from *Folktales of Egypt* by Hasan El-Shamy copyright © 1980 by The University of Chicago; Aberdeen University Press for 'The Birch Besom' from *The King of the Black Art and Other Folk Tales* by Sheila Douglas copyright © 1987 Sheila Douglas; Graywolf Press for 'The Broom Is Busy' from *The Woe Shirt: Caribbean Folk Tales* by Paulé Bartón as translated by Howard A. Norman copyright © 1980 Howard Norman; Routledge and Kegan Paul Ltd. for 'The Goodwife of Laggan' from *Nine Lives: Cats in Folklore* by Katharine M. Briggs copyright © 1980 Katharine M. Briggs; Sun Books for 'The Old Eagle-Hawk Woman' from *Aboriginal Myths and Legends* by Roland Robinson coypright © 1968 Roland Robinson; Wayne State University Press for 'The Curse' from *100 Armenian Tales*, collected and edited by Susie Hoogasian-Villa, copyright © 1966 Susie Hoogasian-Villa; David Goldstein for 'Rabbi Joshua and the Witch' from *Jewish Folklore and Legend* David Goldstein copyright © 1980 David Goldstein; Columbia University Press for 'The Witchmaster's Advice' from *Ozark Superstitions* by Vance Randolph copyright © 1947 Columbia University Press.

Every effort has been made to trace the copyright holders in all copyright material in this book. The editor regrets if there has been any oversight and suggests the publisher be contacted in any such event.

Introduction

No collection of fairytales is complete without a tale or two about a witch. There is a proliferation of scholastic studies and encyclopedias on witchcraft but apart from the odd anthology of tales for children I know of none devoted to witches – to the celebration of the sheer magnitude of a what a witch represents, from a wild and terrifying creature of evil to a sedate and canny helper. Whichever form she comes in, she is a woman who is true to herself, using her magic and her foresight to maximise her own experience of life, even if she pays heavily for it in the end.

Witches have been a part of every known culture since the dawn of time, casting spells, healing the wounded and spinning fate. Even before recorded time, they became identified almost immutably with death and evil. The first extant mythology (circa 3000 BC) found on Sumerian tablets tells of an exiled witch-goddess – stern, cold and pitiless – ruling the Underworld like her later counterparts such as Demeter. Yet stories – be they myth, folklore or fairytale – abound in equivocal, sometimes benevolent, representations of witches in all their forms. They come from many traditions – myth, history, theology, literature and oral culture: some are the focus of story-clusters, or comprise a convention of their own, others are nameless, mere stereotypes providing insight into folk-belief and the horrific phantasms that lurk in the human mind.

European classics and oral Indian lore alike include the *femme fatale* witch – a woman so ravishing in demeanour that she can bewitch any man. Ruthlessly she changes form, abducts men or petrifies the objects of her desire to bring them to heel. While Persian and Indian fairies of Middle Eastern descent abduct and imprison their lovers, the Celtic fairy-woman has her own form of enchantment – she possesses her man with her great beauty, so that bent upon being with her, he can no longer function in his own society. Juxtaposed with these are the hideous Gorgons, the snivelling, crawling bloodsuckers and corpse-eaters effecting their lowly magic to do little more than fill their bellies and calm their raging libidos.

All oral traditions and folklores have their nature hags living in water, cave and mountain, controlling and protecting their environment and its flora and fauna, destroying anyone who threatens the natural order of life. Many of these are familiar, terrifying hags and sprites, enticing, tricking, snatching their human quarry to death or oblivion.

Violent witches are perhaps the most familiar ones in all cultures. Often portrayed as ugly hags, they eat humans, particularly children, and suck the blood of the dead and the living. The provenance of the cannibal-witch is ancient and two-fold. On the one hand she is connected to the fertility rituals of the primal nations of the South Seas, Australia and New Zealand where child-eating represents the natural cycle of planting, reaping and regrowth. Among the indigenous tribes of North and South America she is sometimes represented by the vagina in many modes, including the dreaded dentate. On the other hand, the actions of Mesopotamian-born Lilith, the first created woman, resonate through her activities: openly lascivious, she consorts with demons and devils, wantonly sapping the male vitality of mortal men to produce monsters.

The depletion of male strength is another motif internationally associated with witches. In Chinese tales certain formless spirits take possession of humans in order to drain them of their life energy. In most of these stories the possessing spirit is female, her victim almost invariably male. Often too, the spirits of the dead reach out from magical spheres to help and protect their loved ones. These benign and haunting witches are in some elusive yet indisputable way distinct from ghosts. In fact, there is some question about the status of these and other witches – are they mortal or constant, human or indestructible? Energy and semen-draining witches are clearly not mortal, nor, as their name makes clear, are the inhabitants of the Land of the Ever Young. Nature-witches too, regenerate themselves with seasonal cycles or remain permanently in their inherent element – water, air, trees – emerging only when called upon or disturbed.

Some witches, on the other hand, are undoubtedly mortal, living within families in the village communities of countries as far apart as the United States, Africa, Britain and India, furtively plying their trade for good and evil. The witches of some West African regions may return after death, head up their covens and convert their children. The hideous Indian *chureyl* or *dayan* with her twisted feet, her mumbled speech and her predilection for the hearts and livers of children, is a creature from rustic folk memory, unable to die until she has passed on her secret formula, an inverse religious *mantra*, to a worthy neophyte. The perversion of religious formulae is also alleged to occur among the witches of Christian nations, believed to have promised their souls to the Devil for personal gain. Folklore illustrates that mortal witches are tough adversaries, vanquished only by those possessing skill, might and steely determination.

Too easily overlooked are the wise women. The incidental helpers, the exacting employers, the canny guides, the riddlers, the healers and the givers of gifts. We see them weave in and out of the rich fabric of fairytales without really pausing to consider their identity or intent. They represent the essence of the feminine mind, teaching us their ancient wisdom, their wiles and their guiles and the truth that every woman must learn about her own magic. All witches possess formidable magic and this, from the beginning, has caused them to be driven out of society, cloaking them in the inalienable garb of Otherness.

Often feared and revered in primal societies, witches were shunned by monotheists, notably Christians. The western world saw them as the antithesis of the established ideals of womanhood. According to various descriptions authorised by the church, women were in any case highly susceptible to evil and weakness. The ideal woman, however, was mindful of socio-religious norms – industrious, meek, obedient, modest, and forgiving. A free spirit, laziness, vulgarity, active sexuality, independence (financial or other), and a vengeful temperament marked her out as a witch. Luckily, fairytales safeguard all kinds of women, both in their defiant or independent positions and as models of industry or piousness. Less often there is a tale in the category of 'The Old Witch' (Grimm) where a girl is burned for defying social mores or 'The Red Shoes' (Hans Christian Andersen) where she has her feet amputated because of childish narcissism.

In medieval Europe and North America many such a girl or woman burned at the stake or was drowned with a boulder tied to her body because a muttered curse (*damnum minatum*) was alleged to have worked (*malum secutum*) or because she celebrated her menstrual periods with joy and failed to suffer in childbirth. Since this established lack of shame and contrition for the original sin, it indicated a link with the Devil. Furthermore, medieval witches were believed to conjure up storms, poison the air, damage crops and landscapes with the merest glance and generally relish the thought of stirring up trouble. The Dominican friar Johannes Nider, writing in 1435, categorized the effects of witchcraft into six main areas. The ability to make people love or hate, to make men impotent, to damage livestock and property, spread disease and cause madness or death. Witches attended revels with the Devil, where they denounced God and Catholicism, kissed the Devil's backside in homage and sacrificed and ate children who had not been baptized. They also had carnal intercourse with incubi and succubi. Their sexual activities with animals and devils are well-documented as in this verse by the poet-clergyman Robert Herrick (1591–1674).

> *The Staffe is now greas'd*
> *And very well pleas'd,*
> *She cocks out her arse at the parting,*
> *To an Old Ram Goat,*
> *That rattles i'th'throat,*
> *Half choakt with the stink of her farting*
>
> The Hagg

Old Goat-legs, the Devil, is of course very like the Pan-type nature god worshipped along with the goddess by witch cults.

So the Devil became the sexually omnipotent master and witches came to be associated with filthy practices, dirt and decay. A typical witch image was probably of an unwashed and unkempt woman with long, dirty fingernails, mucoid eyes and decaying teeth. She had hair in unattractive places – sprouting out of her nose, ears or chin. Her voice was shrill, squeaky or cracked. Her skin was blemished with moles and sores believed to be inflicted by the suckling of imps and devils, sometimes in the form of animal familiars of the kind supposed to be 'born of putrefaction'. She was surrounded by bats, toads, rats, crows and malevolent cats. Even more obscene was the fact that she was still sexually active. Young men were in constant danger of the witch's lust which, sharpened by the expert sex-play of Old Nick and his virile imps, threatened to strip them of their vitality – or make them redundant. For

> the witches themselves have often been seen lying on their backs in the fields or in the woods, naked up to the very navel, and it has been apparent from the dispositions of their limbs and members which pertain to the venereal act and orgasm, as also from the agitation of their thighs that, all invisibly to the bystanders, they have been copulating with the devil (*Malleus Maleficarum*, 1486, translated by Montague Summers, John Rodker, 1928, *Part II, Chapter IV*, p.114).

The two Dominican friars, Jakob Sprenger and Heinrich Kramer, responsible for the authorship of the infamous *Malleus Maleficarum (Hammer of the Witches)*, the witch hunter's bible, spared a few words to console ordinary men anxious about their sexual inadequacy:

> the pleasures should naturally be greater when like disports with like, yet that cunning Enemy can so bring together the active and positive elements, not indeed naturally but in such qualities of warmth and temperament, that he seems to excite no less degree of concupiscence (*Part II, Section V*, p. 114).

Of course none of these beliefs are unique to Christianity, though no other religion or culture was at any time so obsessed with purging itself of them. It is all the more grotesque, therefore, that this prejudiced piece of cant should have endorsed the murders of thousands of people beginning (before the treatise) around 1330 in France and enforced throughout the Christian world between the fifteenth and seventeenth centuries. Most of the victims were women, their pact with the Devil established by little more than eccentricity, poverty or a preference for living alone with a large, black cat. Others were burned at the stake for allegedly glancing at a field that had withered or a cow that had stopped giving milk. A number of women spinners, midwives and herbalists were also convicted of witchcraft and a correlation appears possible with the concurrent efforts of men setting up Worshipful Societies to monopolise these professions for themselves. Ireland was barely touched by the persecutions – possibly because the Irish never entirely disavowed their Druid culture and the immanent presence of the Mother goddess as warrior queen loomed large in epic cycles and oral tales.

The Jungian analyst Marie-Louise von Franz suggests that the lack of a transcendent mother with both sides – negative and positive – may be a cause of the persecutions.

In fairytales which, in the main, are under the influence of Christian civilization, the archetype of the Great Mother, like all others, is split into two aspects. The Virgin Mary for example is split off from her shadow and represents only the light side of the mother image; consequently, as Jung points out, the moment when the figure of the Virgin Mary became more important was also the time of the witch persecutions. Since the symbol of the Great Mother was too one-sided, the dark side got projected onto women, which gives rise to the persecution of witches . . . the figure of the mother became split into the positive mother and the destructive witch (*Shadow and Evil in Fairytales*, 1987, Marie-Louise von Franz, p. 105).

Many mysteries remain unsolved. The Bible itself contains accounts of benign and useful witches such as the witch of Endor. The Quran refers to the universal witch's practice of tying knots to cause obstructions in the lives of people but goes no further than praying for God's protection against them. It may be that for Europeans the relatively recent and superficial layer of Christianity, an imported (Middle Eastern) religion, was simply not yet deep-seated enough to keep at bay their past pagan culture. As a result the resurgence of a Mother Goddess in the guise of the Maleficae presented a more focused threat. It certainly led to the dedicated bowdlerization of the indigenous myth of Britain – preserved today primarily as the Legends of Arthur. The heavy overlay of Christianity in the literary versions of Geoffrey of Monmouth (*Vitae Merlini*, c. 1150) and Thomas Malory (*Morte d'Arthur*, c. 1469) leave no room for Morgan le Fey, the lost British goddess, Sovereignty, whose names mean Mother (Morgan) and Fate/Fairy (Le Fey) and who was guardian of King and Country. Both texts, though rich in many ways, are unsatisfying in their depiction of Morgan. Devaluing her to a mere sorceress, Monmouth presents her seeking her skills from a man – Merlin – whom she repays with gross treachery, while Malory spares only a few incoherent lines to her in his text. Both poets fail patently to provide any clue to her jealousy and malice against Arthur and his supporters. Deprived of the function of Sovereignty, Morgan is the incomplete and confusing quintessence of evil.

Like many other witch figures still thankfully at large in the folklore of most cultures, Morgan is descended from the Mother Goddess who represents three facets of existence – virginity, reproduction and death. Here evolve the personae of the triple goddess seen in virtually every culture: Juventa-Juno-Minerva (the Capitoline triad of Rome), Hebe-Hera-Hecate (Greek), Lat-Manat-Al'Uzza (Arab) and Parvati-Durga-Kali (Indian) represent just a few female trinities. The trinity symbolizes the phases of the moon, making the witch a creature of the night, closely linked with menstruation, tides, seasonal cycles and darkness. Diana is often referred to as the Queen of Witches.

Each of the goddesses' three aspects wields its own particular terror over men. The Virgin (crescent moon), wilful and vital, threatens an enchantment so piercing that young men waste away. The Mother (full moon), full and fecund, is depicted in ancient cultures with a glowing red vulva inviting entry, or a massive pudendum and breasts so long and large that she flings them over her shoulder as she pursues her quarry – a man, of course – fearful that she will use him so ruthlessly to her own ends that he will be left impotent and robbed of semen. In many Middle-Eastern tales the hero is advised to approach her from behind and kiss one of her breasts, impelling her to acknowledge him as her son and aid his quest. Last is the Crone (the waning moon), perhaps the most dread-inspiring form – intimate with death and guarding its mysteries, still sexually demanding and able to infiltrate his mind and his body. Refusal to obey her brings destruction, for the goddess is ruthless and vengeful. Her commitment to justice, however, is perceived by the patriarchal world as revenge, whereas its own is termed punishment. The former implies at best equality, the latter superiority, the dispensing of a code of ethics from above. In addition, the notion of revenge has acquired over the years connotations of baseness, impulsiveness, subjectivity and personal satisfaction, whereas punishment remains hallowed – noble, considered, detached and for the common good. Each achieves the same end – Goddess in the more chthonic and passionate style that underlies her female principle, God in an ethereal and aloof manner. And it is the very female quality of her interaction with them that appears to drench men in fear of enslavement and impotence – a metaphorical unmanning, resulting in loss of honour. Men are happiest with a witch when they have some form of witch-control as practised among shamans and she, for a change, serves them.

Japanese witch masters often obtained the services of vixens, dogs or serpents by feeding their young or providing some other protective service. The homes of such families were said in the middle ages to be prosperous and their roofs and driveways lined with foxes and dogs while snakes lay coiled in various pots. But it is as well to remember that it is only through gratitude and her own personal commitment to contract that the witch remains obedient.

Over the years the goddess was ousted first by patriarchal pantheons, then by the One God. Men gradually took over her fertility rituals. Monotheists, in their desperate attempts to rationalize the synthesis of the fairy-woman's beauty with her evil, developed the theory that fairies are fallen angels. They are those who in the dispute between God and Satan refused to commit to either side and so were condemned to live below ground in streams, caves and tunnels or above ground in the clouds and air.

Whatever her provenance, the witch takes on fearsome qualities because the 'ruling collective unconscious outlaws the Great Mother archetype so she strikes back at it' (M-L. von Franz). Frequently in fairytales it is the male who is under direct threat from a witch and the female who redeems him (Gretel saves Hansel), though she in her turn may be the witch's quarry. Snow-White and Sleeping Beauty are two famous examples of the latter. The Bad Fairy of the Sleeping Beauty stands as a case in point – her undermined dignity demands revenge much as does the injured ego of a god who constantly requires adulation and acknowledgement and imposes eternal hell-fire and damnation upon those who ignore him. The one – like Morgan and Lilith and others since the beginning of time – is demonized and the other not.

Violent witches are begotten of insult and alienation. The common witch-tale motifs of malicious testing, power-lust and child-killing illustrate the witch's ways of administering justice, attempting to reclaim lost powers and replenish drained vitality. Understandably, such strange and menacing creatures are forced outside civilization and into uncharted wildernesses. And just as they are alienated and isolated from society, so their qualities are disowned by individuals and driven underground into the unexplored subconscious deep within ourselves, creating something fearful and ever-present. It is this creation of an incomplete creature of pure evil within us that makes us susceptible to the fear witches generate. We are aware of this vulnerability, conscious that a longing for love and nurturing could flood its banks and turn us into demanding, devouring beings. We create the nourishing-devouring witch of Hansel and Gretel who feeds us first, then expects to be fed. This is when Gretel has to conjure up all her natural resources, the witch within, who tells her instinctively what her menacing adversary will respond to. And again it is the witch's sense of ruthless justice and fairplay in the child that sustains her determination to punish the witch and save herself. Standing up to and destroying or disempowering the witch in fairytales represents a vital stage of growing up and learning to respond resourcefully to the crisis at hand. However, this can only occur when we begin to acknowledge the witch in ourselves. Like her ancestresses in ancient societies, she can be propitiated through nourishment and acceptance and integrated into our psychic worlds to our advantage.

But it is easy to become over-serious and injured about the treatment of the witch by history and literature, to forget that she is essentially a mischievous character, a survivor. Centuries of calumny have failed to expel her from our minds or to reduce her power over us. She remains a vivid, magnetic and mystifying being, sometimes human, at others supernatural, riding through the imagination of child and adult alike, black-clad, on broom-stick or tree, returning from some waggish encounter to her sinister abode to indulge in her wicked pursuits. It is perhaps this commonplace image of the witch that best and most enjoyably conveys her sense of anarchy and her continual challenge to authority while often upholding a mysterious set of her own personal rules.

In making this selection I have not attempted to smash the fearsome stereotypes of the witch. Nor is my choice intended to present her in a favourable light. I have simply chosen stories which thrilled me, scared me or made me laugh. And I have not been able to answer the question I was most asked during the pleasurable months spent compiling this anthology: 'How do you define a witch?' I hope this selection will demonstrate that the witch constantly challenges definition, remaining baffling and enigmatic to the end.

Shahrukh Husain
London, April 1993

PART ONE

Alluring Women and Ailing Knights

Indravati and the Seven Sisters

(Indian)

There was a king and he and his wife had a daughter, a princess more beautiful than the sun, the moon and the flowers. Since she was even more beautiful than the dancing apsaras in the celestial court of Indra, the queen decided to call her Indravati. She thought if she called her Indra's daughter, which is what the name means – Indra's daughter – then the girl would be safe from the god when she needed his help. The queen was a clever woman and she knew that a girl so beautiful would some time in her life surely need to be saved from the vices and designs of men. When such a time came, she could call upon Indra without fear of falling out of the sky only to be tangled in the interminable locks of Shiva like the Ganges so long ago, you remember. Because Indra was a ribald and lustful god – which in its place is fine but the queen didn't want her daughter to become his prey if she needed to ask for help. So that's why she chose the name.

Indravati grew up. Her marriage was arranged to a very hand-some son of another king. He was handsome enough for her and so he was naturally beautiful enough for the fairies. A moon-like face, eyes like stars, a soft supple skin not only on his face but his body too – and just ever so slightly downy like a peach. (He was very young and his manly hair was only just beginning to sprout, you understand. Oh! In such places, he had a surprise every time he looked.) The princess would surely shudder with desire in the wed-ding chamber and would be in danger of betraying her virginal appetite without a long enough pretence of maidenly restraint and shyness. But he was a prince whose limbs were desirable enough to make any woman lose shame without shame.

3

The thing was that seven sisters who lived in a pipal tree had seen the prince on his way to his wedding celebrations. They were women with their feet twisted back to front, so that their heels protruded in the front, not very different to a club or like the base of a rich man's walking stick. The type with a small brass ball at the bottom, you know? And their toes, splayed like an eagle's talons, stuck out at the back. But they kept these covered with their long, flowing skirts. And who would look at their feet when their faces were so enticing? They made eyes at men, then pulled the corners of their mantillas between their teeth, blinking huge, hooded eyes and looking down to show fan-like lashes. In such a way too, that any man following their dropped gaze – God forgive us – would find his eyes fixed on their burgeoning breasts. They fell in love with him and wanted him for themselves – these, you know, witches – God protect us – we shouldn't say that word. They may hear us and come. Anyway, they followed the prince to his bride's palace. They were angry at first to see he was to be married but then they were calm. Why should a witch find such things daunting? They know magic and are ignorant of morals. They followed him and they waited, biding their time.

The prince and princess married with much pomp and ceremony and the musicians played for a month until their fingers were lacerated and their bones were stiff. The cooks cooked until the heat of the kitchens warmed the entire kingdom and the stomachs of every last person and even the scavengers on the rubbish piles were full to bursting. In fact beggars from other kingdoms paid visits to the piles of leftovers from the feasts and loaded up their barrows to take home to their families because the rubbish itself was worthy to be called a feast in its own right. The sisters watched him and they waited, biding their time. Well, finally the feasting and celebrating was over and Indravati and her prince got into their chariot and were on their way to his kingdom where at last they would pleasure their bodies in privacy.

They travelled most of the morning but as afternoon came it grew hot and they decided they would stop for a rest. That was under the same tree where the seven sisters had first seen the prince. Maybe they put the idea in his head. We can't tell. But, impatient to explore each other, the couple dismissed their attendants.

'Solitude,' the prince commanded and the courtiers and servants understood and left, making private jokes about what the prince and princess would do in their solitude.

But as they turned to each other, the prince and princess were
overcome by sleep. The family of sisters perched in the branches of
their pipal tree knew their wait was coming to an end. Their time
had nearly come. They decided to act before the prince tasted of his
bride, before his fertile rain could drench her swollen thirsty lotus.
For they had been devouring his limbs and his youth with their eyes
and their minds for a long while, and had been patient so long, they
wanted him innocent.

They devised how to get him for themselves while he was still a
virgin. As the bridal couple became drowsy, the witches swooped
down and carried them up to a tower they had created for the
prince. They threw the princess out of the window to kill her and
she, awakened by their cackling and hissing, regained consciousness
in time to snatch at the branches of a nearby lemon tree and break
her fall. Then she slid down to the foot of the tree and from there
crept to the base of the tower where she hid herself behind a pile of
rocks.

Now the witches left the prince up in the top of the tower and laid
him on a bed so soft it was like a cloud. And he felt all the time as if
he were floating off. They danced for him with their jangling bells
and looked beautiful – very beautiful, terrifyingly beautiful. And

they put a spell on him so that he was always as if slightly intoxicated and so he didn't notice their feet twisted backwards, which is the mark of a witch. Or that their eyes had more lust in them than an ordinary woman; even one of those wonderfully wanton women who pleasure men in the course of their ordained nightly and daily business. For the gleam of desire in their eyes comes from skill, whereas the seven sisters had it by way of their lascivious characters.

Anyway they danced for him, all but revealing secret parts of their bodies. They undulated and let their garments swirl up enough to see the swaying tree trunks but not the flowers nestling at the top, and dropped their bodice straps, but not sufficiently to expose those full, heaving breasts, even more swollen now with the lust that surged inside them, crashing above and below the navel in crazed, maddening waves of frothing desire. They tried that night – oh, how they tried – to make his virgin limbs (so succulent!) and his peachy, golden skin (so seductive!) weave into theirs, to entwine together like a wild and rampant vine; tendrils and creepers entangled inextricably, pods popping to produce catkins, penetrating into apertures and cavities, saturating them. Fluids mingling, from flower and from fruit, until he was drained, empty and temporarily exhausted and they replete.

And so they planned to use him, feeding of the fruit, sucking its juices with body and with tongue, until he wilted and eventually withered away forever. Every day they would bring him foods spiked with potent aphrodisiacs like ground tiger's tooth, herbal remedies and menstrual blood. They would leave it there all night, but the prince never touched the food and each morning before departing, they would throw it away. After all, if the food were to take effect while they were away, then the juices that engorged his loin might be disgorged elsewhere. So they threw the food out of the window.

The food would fall a long way down to where the princess was sitting and she would force a few morsels into her mouth, enough to survive on, no more. And each morning when the seven sisters flew away in their tree, she would climb the lemon tree and enter the prince's tower and tend him and speak with him, stroking his brow and begging him to wake up. But of course he could not. Naturally. And the princess understandably became angrier and angrier until finally she decided she could not just sit and wait. 'I have to do something,' she thought.

And she did.

She waited for the witches to leave her husband's chamber the next day. And when they came to their tree she was standing below, clutching its roots, and she held on fast as the witches cast their spells. They took some strands of hair, they tied knots in it and then they blew on them, muttering and mumbling, their lips moving ferociously as they muttered faster and faster, louder and louder, until suddenly the tree took off and the princess in it. She flew, watching the jungles and deserts, rivers and mountain-lands so high and so deserted that there was no sign of Adam or his progeny. She saw a lot pass beneath her until they came to a semicircle of mountains and there the witches' tree hovered a little before landing. The princess realized she had come to the land called Koh Qaf, the Land of the Fairies, and it was ruled by Indra, the King of Fairies. Her mother and her maids had told her stories about this place and its inhabitants.

The princess leapt off the tree and mingled with the fairy people. They were very beautiful but that was no problem for her because she was even more beautiful, in spite of the fact they were made from fire and air while she was made only of clay and water. But it didn't matter. She was so beautiful, they didn't notice a difference. The princess asked passers-by where the king's court was and made her way to it. When she arrived she saw the seven sisters dancing there, for the king. They danced with such grace and beauty that even the princess was enchanted and could feel her body begin to be roused and allowed herself a moment of doubt about her husband's chastity – wondering whether he still had his virginity. Then she pulled herself to her full and majestic stature.

'Raja Indra!' she said in an imperious tone.

The king looked up, amazed that anyone should have interrupted his pleasure. And in such a daring tone.

'Who are you?' he demanded, his eyes seeking out the sound. Then he saw her and felt the juices already so near the surface with the sensuality of the sisters' dance, and contained only because of the expanded space created in his distended organ, spill over into his splendid brocaded garments. He silently reproached himself for losing the fluid to his clothes and not to one of the hundreds of divine, blooming flowers that waited for him.

The woman who had spoken was indeed ravishing and as she saw his eyes fill up with lust and design, she said loudly, 'I am Indravati.'

The king sank back into his throne reduced, limp. Her name meant daughter of Indra; he could not even woo or court her, much less mate with her – his daughter.

'What do you want?' he asked, and his voice had lost its thundering quality.

'These women who dance for you, Lord,' said Indravati. 'They have enchanted my bridegroom and imprisoned him in a tower. I want him back.'

The king hesitated.

'They are exquisite women,' he ventured, unwilling to deprive the beautiful dancers of their sexual prey. 'If they are skilled enough to enchant him then . . .'

'They are *chureyls*, Lord!' Indravati announced.

The sisters stopped dancing now and clustered together, crouching in an odd manner, their eyeballs rolling and sliding, their tongues flickering, their breath hissing strangely.

'Lift your skirts!' demanded the king.

'No! Not that Lord!' shrieked the sisters. 'Not that!'

But the king insisted, and when the sisters raised their hems to their ankles, they revealed their sinister feet, you know, like a rich person's walking stick with a ball below the stub, and splayed talon-like toes poking out at the back.

Indra banished the sisters from his kingdom to their tree and the spell broke. Indravati saw her husband standing before her beneath the tree with his attendants and they made their way back to his kingdom where everyone had become very anxious. They had waited so long. It must have been at least a month or two.

At last the bridal couple enjoyed the pleasures of the bridal chamber and the princess could behave in an abandoned way and enjoy the sensual pleasures the prince offered because it was she who had saved his life and his chastity and had no need of modesty or innocence to prove her love and loyalty.

The sisters are still there, in the pipal tree. They look like crows, mostly. And sometimes they move to other pipal trees. But they cannot die until they find an initiate to whom they can hand down the profane secret formula of words through which the *chureyl* passes on her powers.

Finn's Madness

(Irish)

One time Finn and the Fianna were come to a ford of the Slaine, and they sat down for a while. And as they were sitting there they saw on the round rock up over the ford a young woman, having a dress of silk and a green cloak about her, and a golden brooch in the cloak, and the golden crown that is the sign of a queen on her head. 'Fianna of Ireland,' she said, 'let one of you come now and speak with me.'

Then Sciathbreac, of the Speckled Shield, went towards her. 'Who is it you are wanting?' he said. 'Finn, son of Cumhal,' said she. Finn went over then to talk with her. 'Who are you?' he said, 'and what is it you are wanting?' 'I am Daireann, daughter of Bodb Dearg, son of the Dagda,' she said; 'and I am come to be your wife if you will give me the bride-gift I ask.' 'What bride-gift is that?' said Finn. 'It is your promise,' said she, 'I to be your only wife through the length of a year, and to have the half of your time after that.' 'I will not give that promise,' said Finn, 'to any woman of the world, and I will not give it to you,' he said.

On that the young woman took up a cup of silver from under a covering, and filled it with strong drink, and she gave it to Finn. 'What is this?' said Finn. 'It is very strong mead,' said she. Now there were bonds on Finn not to refuse anything belonging to a feast, so he took the cup and drank what was in it, and on the moment he was like one gone mad. And he turned his face towards the Fianna, and every harm and every fault and every misfortune in battle that he knew against any one of them, he sprang it on them, through the mad drunkenness the young woman had put on him.

Then the chief men of the Fianna of Ireland rose up and left the

9

place to him, every one of them setting out for his own country, till there was no one left upon the hill but Finn and Caoilte. And Caoilte rose up and followed after them, and he said: 'Fianna of Ireland,' he said, 'do not leave your lord and your leader through the arts and tricks of a woman of the Sidhe.' Thirteen times he went after them, bringing them back to the hill in that way. And with the end of the day and the fall of night the bitterness went from Finn's tongue; and by the time Caoilte had brought back the whole of the Fianna, his sense and his memory were come back to him, and he never would sooner have fallen on his sword and got his death, than have stayed living.

And that was the hardest day's work Caoilte ever did.

The Nixy

(Hungarian)

There was once upon a time a miller who was very well off, and had as much money and as many goods as he knew what to do with. But sorrow comes in the night, and the miller all of a sudden became so poor that at last he could hardly call the mill in which he sat his own. He wandered about all day full of despair and misery, and when he lay down at night he could get no rest, but lay awake all night sunk in sorrowful thoughts.

One morning he rose up before dawn and went outside, for he thought his heart would be lighter in the open air. As he wandered up and down on the banks of the mill-pond he heard a rustling in the water, and when he looked near he saw a white woman rising up from the waves.

He realized at once that this could be none other than the nixy of the mill-pond, and in his terror he didn't know if he should fly away or remain where he was. While he hesitated the nixy spoke, called him by his name, and asked him why he was so sad.

When the miller heard how friendly her tone was, he plucked up heart and told her how rich and prosperous he had been all his life up till now, when he didn't know what he was to do for want and misery.

Then the nixy spoke comforting words to him, and promised that she would make him richer and more prosperous than he had ever been in his life before, if he would give her in return the youngest thing in his house.

The miller thought she must mean one of his puppies or kittens, so promised the nixy at once what she asked, and returned to his mill full of hope. On the threshold he was greeted by a servant with the news that his wife had just given birth to a boy.

The poor miller was much horrified by these tidings, and went to his wife with a heavy heart to tell her and his relations of the fatal bargain he had just struck with the nixy. 'I would give up all the good fortune she promised me,' he said, 'if I could only save my child.' But no one could think of any advice to give him, beyond taking care that the child never went near the mill-pond.

So the boy throve and grew big, and in the meantime all prospered with the miller, and in a few years he was richer than he had ever been before. But all the same he did not enjoy his good fortune, for he could not forget his compact with the nixy, and he knew that sooner or later she would demand his fulfilment of it. But year after year went by, and the boy grew up and became a great hunter, and the lord of the land took him into his service, for he was as smart and bold a hunter as you could wish to see. In a short time he married a pretty young wife, and lived with her in great peace and happiness.

One day when he was out hunting a hare sprung up at his feet, and ran for some way in front of him in the open field. The hunter pursued it hotly for some time, and at last shot it dead. Then he proceeded to skin it, never noticing that he was close to the mill-pond, which from childhood up he had been taught to avoid. He soon finished the skinning, and went to the water to wash the blood off his hands. He had hardly dipped them in the pond when the nixy rose up in the water, and seizing him in her wet arms she dragged him down with her under the waves.

When the hunter did not come home in the evening his wife grew very anxious, and when his game bag was found close to the mill-pond she guessed at once what had befallen him. She was nearly beside herself with grief, and roamed round and round the pond calling on her husband without ceasing. At last, worn out with sorrow and fatigue, she fell asleep and dreamt that she was wandering along a flowery meadow, when she came to a hut where she found an old witch, who promised to restore her husband to her.

When she awoke next morning she determined to set out and find the witch; so she wandered on for many a day, and at last she reached the flowery meadow and found the hut where the old witch lived. The poor wife told her all that had happened and how she had been told in a dream of the witch's power to help her.

The witch counselled her to go to the pond the first time there was a full moon, and to comb her black hair with a golden comb, and then to place the comb on the bank. The hunter's wife gave the witch a handsome present, thanked her heartily, and returned home.

Time dragged heavily till the time of the full moon, but it passed at last, and as soon as it rose the young wife went to the pond, combed her black hair with a golden comb, and when she had finished, placed the comb on the bank; then she watched the water impatiently. Soon she heard a rushing sound, and a big wave rose suddenly and swept the comb off the bank, and a minute after the head of her husband rose from the pond and gazed sadly at her. But immediately another wave came, and the head sank back into the water without having said a word. The pond lay still and motionless, glittering in the moonshine, and the hunter's wife was not a bit better off than she had been before.

In despair she wandered about for days and nights, and at last, worn out by fatigue, she sank once more into a deep sleep, and dreamt exactly the same dream about the old witch. So next morning she went again to the flowery meadow and sought the witch in her hut, and told her of her grief. The woman counselled her to go to the mill-pond the next full moon and play upon a golden flute, and then to lay the flute on the bank.

As soon as the next moon was full the hunter's wife went to the mill-pond, played on the golden flute, and when she had finished, placed it on the bank. Then a rushing sound was heard, and a wave swept the flute off the bank, and soon the head of the hunter appeared and rose up higher and higher till he was half out of the water. Then he gazed sadly at his wife and stretched out his arms towards her. But another rushing wave arose and dragged him under once more. The hunter's wife, who had stood on the bank full of joy and hope, sank into despair when she saw her husband snatched away again before her eyes.

But for her comfort she dreamt the same dream a third time, and betook herself once more to the old witch's hut in the flowery meadow. This time the old woman told her to go the next full moon to the mill-pond, and to spin there with a gold spinning-wheel, and then to leave the spinning-wheel on the bank.

The hunter's wife did as she was advised, and the first night the moon was full she sat and spun with a golden spinning-wheel, and then left the wheel on the bank. In a few minutes a rushing sound was heard in the waters, and a wave swept the spinning-wheel from the bank. Immediately the head of the hunter rose up from the pond, getting higher and higher each moment, till at length he stepped on to the bank and fell on his wife's neck.

But the waters of the pond rose up suddenly, overflowed the bank where the couple stood, and dragged them under the flood. In her despair the young wife called on the old witch to help her, and in a moment the hunter was turned into a frog and his wife into a toad. But they were not able to remain together, for the water tore them apart, and when the flood was over they both resumed their own shapes again, but the hunter and the hunter's wife found themselves in a strange country, and neither knew what had become of the other.

The hunter determined to become a shepherd, and his wife too became a shepherdess. So they herded their sheep for many years in solitude and sadness.

Now it happened once that the shepherd came to the country where the shepherdess lived. The neighbourhood pleased him, and he saw that the pasture was rich and suitable for his flocks. So he brought his sheep there, and herded them as before. The shepherd and shepherdess became great friends, but they did not recognize each other in the least.

But one evening when the moon was full they sat together watching their flocks, and the shepherd played upon his flute. Then the shepherdess thought of that evening when she had sat at the full moon by the mill-pond and had played on the golden flute; the recollection was too much for her, and she burst into tears. The shepherd asked her why she was crying, and left her no peace till she told him her story. Then the scales fell from the shepherd's eyes, and he recognized his wife, and she him. So they returned joyfully to their own home, and lived in peace and happiness ever after.

The Maiden on the Loreley

(Rhineland)

Downstream from Caub on the Rhine, at the foot of the towering Loreley rock, the water-nymphs in olden times had their kingdom. In the rushing waters stood glittering palaces, surrounded by green meadows and stately forests.

As more and more people came to live on the river bank and the river became full of barges and big ships, the water-nymphs sadly withdrew from their home. Only one of them stayed behind, for she could not bear to part from her beloved river. She often used to sit on the top of the rock, combing her golden hair in the moonlight, and in her enchanting voice she sang wonderful melodies, which bewitched everyone who heard them. Many a boatman who listened to her sweet singing could not resist looking up at the maiden, and was so enthralled by her beauty that he did not notice the dangers threatening his boat. Thus it often happened that boat and boatman were seized by the treacherous whirlpool and swallowed up in its depths.

During the Middle Ages, when the proud castles along the Rhine echoed with the clash of arms, with singing and happy laughter, a young knight – the son of the Count Palatine – decided to climb the steep rock and see the beautiful nymph at close quarters. He went down the Rhine in a small boat, accompanied only by his esquire. As he came close to the foot of the rock, he saw the maiden sitting on the top of it, in the last rays of the evening sun. The sound of her voice bewitched him so completely that he forgot everything, and the mighty river dashed his light craft against the sharp rocks, where it sank, taking the knight down with it. The esquire, who managed to save himself, brought the sad news to the count.

15

Full of sorrow and anger, the Count Palatine ordered his servants to seize the maiden and to cast her from her high rock into the river. As the men approached her she loosed a necklace of pearls from her throat and threw them into the Rhine, saying:

Father, in your watery glen,
Save me from the powers of men!
Send the white horses from their cave,
That I may ride on wind and wave!

At once two waves rose up and out of the river, like great, shining horses. They climbed to the very summit of the rock and carried the nymph down into the flood, where she vanished for ever.

Coonlagh and the Fairy Maiden

(Irish – as told by Pat Ryan)

Long ago when Cahoun of the Hundred Fights was High King of all
Ireland it came time for the feast of Beltaine and on the evening
before the first of May, Cahoun and his son Coonlagh Ruadh did go
to the Hill of Usnach to light the fires and set off the festivities in
honour of the beginning of summer.

And as Cahoun walked along the hill with his son Coonlagh every
eye gazed upon them for no warriors were greater than they. And
Coonlagh Ruadh – Coonlagh of the Red Hair – won the heart of all
the women in that place. For his hair was as red as the sun when it
sets in the evening. And his skin was as white as milk. His eyes were
as blue as the skies and his cheeks as red as the blood of a newly
slaughtered calf. And so they went about, king and heir, beloved
son, dearest one to Cahoun of the Hundred Fights. And they did
talk of all manner of things; of song; of bird; of beauty of women;
and as they walked there came a wind, a breeze sent from beyond
the lands of mist and rain far to the west. And with that breeze came
a voice, sweeter than the lark as she rises in the morning. And the
voice called out, 'Coonlagh, Coonlagh Ruadh, come and be dear to
me. For I am for you and you for me. Come and be my love.'

Now all stood and wondered, listened to this voice on the wind.
Then Coonlagh Ruadh himself looked about and his cheeks grew
pale as he stared into the sky.

'What is it my son?' said the High King Cahoun of the Hundred
Fights. 'What is it that you see?'

And Coonlagh Ruadh spoke: 'I see a fairy maiden more beautiful
than any woman I have seen before. And her hair is as bright as the
sun when it rises and her eyes are as green as the hills. Her skin is as

soft and white as the foam of the sea. And her cheeks red as the rose, her lips pink as coral. And she says that she loves none but me.'

And once again they heard the voice of the fairy maid cry out on the wind, 'Coonlagh Ruadh come to me and be my love. Let our limbs entwine like the limbs of the trees and let our bodies mould together as one, for I am nought but for you and you for me. I shall take you to Tir Na n'Og, Land of the Ever Young, beyond mist, beyond rain and there you shall be my husband.'

Cahoun of the Hundred Fights, great warrior that he was, shook that day. He feared that his son would go with this maiden and he called forth all the warriors and wizards and wise men and wise women and he commanded them to build their fires and to sing their songs and to chant their rhymes and spells against this fairy magic to save his son and heir. And so those magicians, the druids of Ireland, cast up the fires and built them higher than the highest tree and with their spells they brought a change in the wind and the fairy maiden was carried away like a cloud. But before she went she withdrew from her bosom an apple of the goldest hue and this golden apple she threw down to the feet of Coonlagh Ruadh. Coonlagh picked up this apple and placed it by his breast.

For a year and a day he did not speak nor lift his head, nor smile or laugh. Nor did he take any food for nourishment, nor drink to quench his thirst. For a year and a day he kept the apple by his heart and whenever he felt need to take sustenance he would only lift the apple to his lips, take one bite and his taste was satisfied. And no sooner had he put the apple next to his heart once again than it was made whole.

So all this was for a year and a day, until once again it was the first of May. The feast of Beltaine came upon the land and the fires were built up in honour of the summer season. Once again Cahoun of the Hundred Fights, High King of all Ireland, did walk the Hill of Usnach with his son and heir, his beloved and dearest Coonlagh Ruadh. But Coonlagh's head was not lifted and they did not talk that day the talk of kings; of women and song and story and wisdom. And as they came to the top of the hill the wind shifted and from beyond the mist and rain came a breeze and with it a voice as sweet as the songbirds of the air and the voice cried out, 'Coonlagh! Coonlagh Ruadh! Come and be dear to me.'

And Cahoun of the Hundred Fights knew the voice as the same voice he had heard that day and year before. He called out to his wizards, commanded them to say their spells. But their words were in vain and the fairy maiden could not be silenced.

'Coonlagh Ruadh, come with me and be my love. O greatest of warriors! Bonniest of men! Ye shall come with me in my coracle of crystal, beyond mist, beyond rain, to Tier Na n'Og, Land of Ever Young, and there I shall give you the greatest of joys. Every pleasure shall be yours. We shall entwine as the vines and the trees entwine in the wood and I shall take you to the island of fair maids and women and there every joy shall be shown and given to you and you will be my husband.'

So great was the love of Coonlagh Ruadh for the fairy maiden that he forgot his father the king, he forgot his people, he forgot the priests and wizards on the Hill of Usnach and the celebrations for the summer on the feast of Beltaine. In one leap he went from the top of that hill to the earth below. In seven leaps he had crossed from the navel of Ireland to the western shore. From the shore he plunged into the ocean and in seven strokes reached the seventh wave of the sea and climbed into a canoe of glass – the coracle of the fairy maid – and there she sat awaiting him. Their arms entwined and they kissed sweetly with joy. Cahoun of the Hundred Fights and all of his warriors and wizards and people ran to see their son and heir sail away beyond the mist, beyond the rain.

Never again was Coonlagh Ruadh seen in that land. Cahoun of a Hundred Fights did have to beget another son to be his king after. And many years did pass and many tales were told of the fairy maiden. But one day, there came to the western part of Ireland a group of children – and their hair was as red as the sun when it sets in the evening and as bright as the sun when it rises in the morn – and they said they were the children of Coonlagh Ruadh and the fairy maiden and they had come from the land of Tir Na n'Og, hidden by the mist and rain, to the children of the Middle Earth for to tell them the sweet stories they had learned in that land and to sing the songs sweeter than the song of the lark as she rises in the morn. And so it was that the tales of Tir Na n'Og come to us today.

The Marriage of Sir Gawain

(English)

I expect, boy, you think you'll make your life: hammer it to the shape you want as a blacksmith hammers metal. But life makes us, not the other way round. I can see that clearly now, as I tell you, as I tell myself the stories that have brought me to this tent. Why, even the king has had to live on the terms life offered to him; he hasn't made his own.

I'll tell you a story, to show you how life takes us, and shakes us, and makes us do its bidding.

The king was travelling one time in the north of his realm, when his path was blocked by a huge hairy man holding a wooden club. 'Out of my way and let me pass,' said the king.

'Pass if you can,' said the huge hairy man.

'I'll teach this lout a lesson,' thought the king. Up went his sword; down came the club. And somehow the king of England was lying in the dirt, learning a lesson himself. The huge hairy man beat King Arthur black and blue, and then tied the king's hands and feet beneath the belly of his horse and led him away.

Next morning, King Arthur woke where he had been thrown down, in a corner of the great hall in his captor's house. The huge hairy man was poking him with a stick. 'Still alive, eh?' said the man. He drew a wicked greasy knife from his belt and cut the king's bonds. Arthur tried to stretch. He was as stiff as an old horse.

'You're my boot boy now,' said the huge hairy man. 'You do what I say.'

So for weeks the king was a drudge, fetching and carrying for this surly, bullying master. At last he could bear his life no longer. There was no escape. So he humbled himself and knelt, though a king kneels to no man, and begged for release from his hard service. 'If you will not accept a ransom,' he said, 'tell me what it is you do want of me. If it is in my power, you shall have it. But let me go.'

The huge hairy man laughed his slow rumbling laugh, a laugh that was more than half a snarl, and said, 'I will let you go, *king*, on one condition. Within a year and a day you will bring me the answer to a riddle I shall ask you. If you bring no answer, you must answer with your life.'

King Arthur did not know what riddle he would be asked, but he was good at riddling. Such games were popular at court. So he eagerly accepted the terms. 'Now tell me,' he said. 'What is the riddle I must answer?'

'Simply this,' replied the huge hairy man. 'You must tell me what it is that women most desire.'

'In a year and a day, then,' said the king.

Riding back to court, King Arthur asked everyone he met what it was that women most desired. Some said 'a good husband', and some 'a rich one'; some said 'handsome sons', and some 'beautiful daughters'; some said 'clothes' or 'jewels'; some 'flattery', or 'attention'; many a husband said 'a life of idleness'. But never did the king get an answer that he thought would satisfy the huge hairy man.

No one at court could tell him the answer either. He asked me for my help, and he rode east and I rode west, asking, questioning. At last we had both filled a whole book with answers, but never a one with which all agreed.

When King Arthur set out to fulfil his promise, he took the two books of answers with him, but he was too discouraged now to ask any more people the question that had seemed so easy a year ago. He rode silent and alone through the dark and gloomy woods.

On one narrow winding path his horse stumbled. Looking up, King Arthur saw a clearing filled with light, and four and twenty of the folk it is better not to name dancing there. He urged his horse forward; the dancers disappeared. Now there was only a dark loathly womanish figure, draped in black, sitting on a rock in the middle of the clearing. So ugly, so old and so evil it looked that Arthur shuddered, and turned his horse aside.

A cry that was more like a croak stopped him. The figure rose, and spoke. Arthur could see that it was indeed a hag-like old woman. He rode towards her to hear what she had to say to him. As he approached, mist coiled and wreathed round the legs of his horse.

'King Arthur is your name,' the woman said, 'and you ride to your doom if you do not answer the hardest question ever asked. Speak, if this is true.'

'It is true, though how you know it I cannot guess.'

'What is it, then, King Arthur, that women most desire?' the hag demanded.

Arthur racked his brains once again, searching for an answer that was true for every woman, and once again he failed. 'I cannot tell you,' he said.

'But I can tell you,' replied the withered woman, 'if you will grant my wish.'

'It is granted,' said Arthur without thought. 'Now, tell me the answer to the riddle.' The crone whispered her answer in his ear, and Arthur, seeing at once that it was the true one, breathed a sigh of relief from the depths of his heart. 'And now, good lady,' he said, 'what is your wish of me? Gold, jewels, titles, lands – all these are yours for the asking.'

'I want no gold, or jewels, or titles, or lands,' she answered, 'but simply this: that in one month's time when I come to your court you will marry me to one of your knights.'

King Arthur's reply died in his throat. None of his knights would wish to marry such a bride. Before he could speak, she had faded into the mist and he was alone.

When King Arthur arrived at the house where he had been a servant and knelt to a master, he did not know what to do. He tried every answer that he and I had collected, but each time the huge hairy man just laughed and shook his head. At last, Arthur ran out of answers and fell silent. He would rather die than give the old woman's solution and condemn one of his knights to marriage with such a creature.

'So you have not been able to find the answer. In that case, I shall have your head.' The giant roared with laughter. 'Your famous knights are obviously as puny in the brain as they are in the arm.'

King Arthur couldn't help himself. He fixed his taunter with his eyes, and slowly, deliberately he recited,

Since Eve first walked, her one desire is still
In all her dealings, just to have her will.

He turned and rode away, and the huge hairy man made no attempt to stop him.

When King Arthur arrived home and told his story, in all the court there was no woman – girl, wife or widow – who would gainsay the old hag's answer. We all rejoiced that the king was safe. Only Arthur did not smile. He told us that to get the answer he had promised the old woman the hand of one of his knights in marriage. 'And,' he said, 'she is the foulest-looking woman I ever saw.'

I had been ensnared by beauty in Sir Bertilak's castle; I knew that the pleasure we take in another's face is mostly the reflection of our own vanity. This woman sounded like a fit companion for my days and nights of shame. I told the king I would gladly wed her and wed her again, though she were a fiend and foul as Beelzebub. So the wedding date was set, and preparations for the feast set in hand.

At last the day came, and all the court lined the streets to welcome the old woman who had saved the king. My bride-to-be rode into Camelot on a moth-eaten, broken-down old donkey, and the crowd recoiled in horror from her. From her filthy tangled hair, bald in patches so her scaly scalp showed through, to her claw-like feet, there was no limb or feature that was not deformed and ugly. Her shapeless scrawny body was bad enough, but it was her face that made the onlookers shudder: her skin was coarse and wrinkled, her eyes bleared, her nose dribbling and warty, her mouth a simple gash, with shrunken lips drawn back over yellow, decaying teeth. Dressed in a white lace gown, she seemed a horrid mockery of a bride.

It was, in truth, a dismal ceremony. And at the wedding feast, while all around her toyed with their food, my bride ignored both plates and cutlery. With her ragged nails she tore into the bread and meat, cramming food into her mouth till the gravy ran down her chin. She ate enough for six, and drank enough for nine.

When we were left alone in the bridal chamber, I could not control the trembling of my hands. The blood had drained from my face. The hideous woman plucked at my arm. 'What's the matter, chuck?' she asked. 'Come on, give us a kiss.'

My gorge rose. But I swear, as I turned to kiss her, I was overtaken with such a loving pity for her, that people should spurn her like some vile animal, that her touch no longer revolted me, ugly as she was. I closed my eyes and kissed her on her watery old mouth.

Then she embraced me, and said, 'Come, look at me, husband, for we two now are one.' And I opened my eyes.

There she stood, an unscarred graceful girl of no more than eighteen winters, such a beauty trembling in her I fell to my knees before it. The chamber was full of light.

'I am your bride,' she said. 'I was enchanted into that foul shape by my evil father, the huge hairy man who overcame King Arthur. Your kiss has freed me, but not completely. Now you have the choice of two things: you may have me in this shape either by day or by night, but not both. For twelve hours out of each twenty-four I must still appear as loathsome as I did when you married me. Think hard, Sir Gawain, before you choose. Imagine how I will feel as I walk among the ladies of the court in that witch-like shape by day; how you will feel if I greet you in that shape each night. Consider well, and choose the lesser of the two evils.'

I was so overcome with her loveliness I scarcely needed to think. 'It is you, my bride,' I said, 'on whom the main burden of this dreadful enchantment falls. You choose for both of us and I will be content. Whatever is your wish is my wish also.'

She smiled, and said, 'Your love has solved my father's riddle. You have given me what women most desire, my own will, and the enchantment is now completely dissolved. This will be my shape forever now, and I will be beautiful both night and day.'

Yes, boy, we think we take our own decisions, but in the end they're taken for us. At least that's so for men in this world, poor creatures that we are. Even for the king. Even, though I curse him with every painful breath I draw, even for Sir Lancelot.

PART TWO
Wise Old Women

I Love You More Than Salt

(Scottish)

Many years ago there once lived a king and his queen and they had three beautiful daughters. The king and queen loved these daughters from their heart, but lo and behold the queen took sick, very very sick. She pined away and she died. The king was so upset to lose his beautiful queen, and his daughters were very sad to lose their mother.

But the king drew his daughters together; he told them, 'Look, children, your mother has gone to another world and some day I hope we'll meet her again. But the main thing is you must be happy an take it for grantit ye have me to take care of you. And some day when I'm gone one of youse will be queen of all this country.'

So years passed by and the three little princesses grew up. The king enjoyed his hunting and his shooting, he enjoyed everything; he was a good king, his people, subjects of the country, loved him. But one particular night the king thought to himself, 'I'm gettin older as the years pass by an I don't have a son to come after me to be king. One o' my daughters will surely make a good queen. But who? Which one would be the best? I know they are caring and they're loving, they're very nice. But I'll have to put them to the test – see which one is fit to be queen tae rule after me.'

So the king being a busy king attending to all his subjects and things in his country, he didn't have a lot of time to spend with his princesses. He saw them from day to day and dined with them and talked to them, but he never had a serious discussion with them. So one evening he told his courtiers and all the people in the palace he wanted to be left alone, because he was going to spend this evening with his daughters. After their meal he called the three princesses together, and they came and sat round beside him.

'Now,' he said, 'young ladies, I want tae talk to youse. You know that it's been a long while since your mother died. And I've tried my best, everyone around the palace has tried their best, to bring you up an teach you, make you what we want you to be – young princesses of this kingdom. I've not really had a serious talk to youse before, but tonight I want to find out which of youse will be queen after I'm gone!'

And the princesses were upset! They said, 'Daddy, we don't want tae be queen, we would just want you to be here forever!'

And he said, 'No way can I be here forever, children. Some day I will have to be gone from this world. I'll join your mother in a far-away place and youse'll be left alone by yourselves. I don't want any arguin, disputin an fallin out among the three of youse – if there was only one it'd be different! So,' he said, 'to love me is to love my people. I'm gaunna put youse a task this evening: I want youse to tell me how much youse really love me.' So he spoke to the oldest daughter first.

And she says, 'Father, I love you more than diamonds an pearls an all the jewels in this world.'

'Very well,' he says, 'that's nice.' So he spoke to the second daughter. 'How much do you really love me?'

She says, 'I love you more than all the gold in the earth, I love you more than all the money in this land.'

He says, 'That is very nice, that is very good.' So to the youngest daughter of all, who was lovely and beautiful and only fifteen at that time. 'Now,' he says, 'little one, how much do you love me?'

'Well, Daddy,' she says, 'I love you more than salt.'

'You love me more than salt?' he says.

'Yes, Daddy,' she says, 'I love you more than salt.'

And the king was upset, very upset! He said, 'Your sister loves me more than diamonds an jewels, and your other sister loves me more than gold, all the gold in this world. And you – you love me more than salt! Well, if that's the way you feel, I don't love you! And tomorrow morning you shall go on your way, you are banned from me. I never want tae see you again! You have disgraced me – the lowest thing on earth is salt!'

The king ordered her the next morning to be on her way, find her own way in the world and never show her face again back at the palace. He was so upset. So the poor little princess felt sad and broken-hearted. She gathered a few possessions together . . .

and her sisters laughed and giggled. She was sent on her way for disgracing her father.

The princess wandered, she travelled on, she had nowhere to go. She travelled on and on. But she came to a great forest and she found a wee path. She followed the path and said, 'Pro'bly it'll lead to a little village or a little hamlet where I can find some place to shelter.'

But the path led right into the middle of the forest, many many miles from the palace. There, lo and behold, she came to a little cottage. And the princess thought to herself, 'Pro'bly I'll find shelter here.'

She came up to the cottage and knocked on the door. And as the door opened, out came an old woman with long grey hair and a ragged dress on her.

She said, 'What are you doing here, dearie?'

And the princess said, 'Well, it's a long story. I'm seekin' shelter fir the night.'

'But where in the world are you bound for?' said the old woman.

And the princess said, 'I'm bound fir nowhere, I'm on my way . . . I've been ordered away from my father.'

'Your father?' said the old woman.

'Yes,' she said, 'my father the king!'

'Your father the king,' she says, 'has ordered you on your way? You'd better come in an tell me the story.'

So the old woman brought the young princess into the little cottage in the forest and gave her something to eat. She sat her down by the fire. There sitting by the fire was a large black cat. And the big black cat came over, and put its head on the top of the lassie's knee. She petted it. It purred as if it was a kitten. And the old woman when she saw this was amazed, said, 'You know, there's never been anyone, though my visitors are few and far between, has ever come here and been friendly with my cat. Because it knows good from bad . . . you are good! Tell me your story.'

So the princess told her story about her mother dying; she was reared up with her father and she spent all her life in the palace, then her daddy had called her before them. She told the whole story I've told you before.

And the old woman said, 'Such a sad event. Your daddy is needing tae be taught a lesson.'

'But,' she said, 'I can't go back. I am banned from the palace, my daddy never wants to see my face again.'

And the old woman said, 'Well, mebbe some day he will be glad tae see ye!'

Now back in the palace the king lived with his two daughters; the third little daughter was gone. And naturally the king used to get all his meals brought into him. They brought him beef and roast and mutton, and the king loved his meat with salt. But lo and behold when one meal was placed before the king one day, and he tasted it, 'Bring me some salt!' he told the chef and the cook. 'Bring me salt!'

And they came in shaking in fright, 'Master, we have no salt.' they said.

Said the king, 'I need salt for my food!'

'Master,' the cook said, 'we've searched the town, we've searched all around and there's not one single grain of salt to be found anywhere!'

The king said, 'Take it away, I can't eat it without salt! Bring me something else!'

So they brought him sweetmeats to eat. And they brought him sweetmeats the next day, and the next and the next. But by this time the king was getting sick of all this. He said, 'Bring me some beef, bring me some roast, some pork, something I can eat! Bring me food, some sensible food!'

The cooks and the chefs brought him sensible food, but there was no salt. The king sent couriers, he sent soldiers, he sent everybody around the country . . . It was all right for the princesses, they could eat sweetmeats which they loved. But their father the king couldn't get one grain of salt in the whole kingdom.

In the little cottage in the forest the princess stayed with the old woman and they became the greatest of friends. She cooked and she cleaned for the old woman, and the cat was her dearest friend. The old woman loved the young princess like she never loved anything in this life. But one day the old woman came back from the forest with a basket of herbs – which she spent most of her time in the forest gathering.

She said to the princess, 'Ye know, I'm gaunna be sad tomorrow.'

And the princess said, 'Why, grandmother, are you sad tomorrow?'

'Because you must leave me.'

'But,' she said, 'grandmother, I don't want to leave you. I've nowhere to go.'

She says, 'You must go back to your father!'

Princess says, 'I can't make my way back tae the palace, because my father has banned me.'

'Not this time,' she said. 'Luik, give me yir dress!' And the young princess took her dress off.

The old woman went into the back room, she was gone for minutes. But when she came back the dress was full of patches and tatters, in rags. 'Now,' she said to the princess, 'take off your shoes.' The princess took off her shoes. And then the old woman took a pair of scissors and she cut the princess's hair. Next she went to the fire and gathered a handful of soot. She rubbed it on the princess's face, 'Now,' she said, 'you make yir way back to your father!'

'I'm banned, I'm not – I can't go back to the palace!'

'You must,' said the old woman, 'because *you* are going to be the next queen!'

'Me,' said the princess, 'the next queen? One of my sisters are gaunna be the next queen: they love my daddy like gold, they love my daddy like diamonds.'

'But,' she says, 'you love your daddy more than salt!' And she goes into the kitchen, takes a wee canvas bag and fills it full of salt. 'Now,' she says, 'you take this and make yir way back to the palace – I'm sure you'll be welcome.'

So, the princess knew the old woman was telling the truth, she knew the old woman had been good to her. She says, 'Remember, I'll be back!'

'Come back,' says the old woman, 'when you're queen! Make yir way back tae your father's palace the way you came!'

So she bade the old woman 'goodbye'.

Now unknown to the princess this old woman was a witch. And she had destroyed every particle of salt in the country because the princess had told her the story . . . And even if somebody had brought some within a certain distance of the palace, the salt just disappeared, because the old witch had put a spell on the palace – no salt would ever be near it.

And by this time the king is going out of his mind, he can't taste anything – he'd give his kingdom for one particle of salt. Then lo and behold, two days later when he's calling up for salt and says he's going to die for the want of it . . . there comes a bare-footed beggar maid to the palace. And the guard stops her, asks her what she wants.

She says. 'I want to see the king.'

'And why do you want tae see the king?' he said.

'Well,' she said, 'I've brought the king a present.'

'What could a bare-footed beggar maid bring the king?'

She says, 'I have brought him a bag o' salt.'

And when he heard this she was rushed – they couldn't take time to get a hold of her – they just rushed her before the king. And the guard said, 'Yir Majesty, we have brought someone tae see ye.' She was there before the king, hair cut short, face blackened with soot, bare feet, ragged dress. And in her hand she carried a little bag.

The king said, 'Who is this you've brought before me, this ragged beggar maid?'

And the guards, the cooks and everyone were so excited, they said, 'You don't know what this beggar maid has brought . . . she has brought something special!'

'What could she bring tae me?' said the king. 'Nothing in the world I desire: I have gold, I have diamonds, I have everything.' He said, 'If only I had a little salt.'

He said, 'Yir Majesty, the beggar maid has brought you a bag of salt.'

'Oh, oh,' said the king, 'she's brought me – she . . . bring it to me!'

And she walked up and said, 'Here you are . . .'

The king looked in. He put his finger in and he tasted it. 'At last,' he said, 'sal-l-t, the most wonderful thing in this world! It is better to me than diamonds or pearls or gold or anything in my kingdom! At last I can have food, I can have something to eat. And he turned to the beggar maid, he said, 'What would you desire? You have brought me the one thing in this world that I need . . . What do you want? What kind o' reward do you want?'

She turned round and she said, 'Daddy, I want nothing!'

And the king said, 'What?'

She says to him, 'Daddy, I want nothing. Because I love you more than I love salt!'

And then the king knew, this maid was his youngest daughter. He put his arms round her and kissed her, he made her more than welcome. He had found the truth – salt was more important to him than anything in the world. And she was made welcome by everyone in the palace. When the old king died she became queen and reigned over the country for many years, and she never forgot her friend the old woman in the forest. And that's the last of my story.

The Tale of the Merchant, the Crone, and the King

(Arab)

There was once a family of affluence and distinction, in a city of Khorasan, and the townsfolk used to envy them for that which Allah had vouchsafed them. As time went on, their fortune ceased from them and they passed away, till there remained of them but one old woman. When she grew feeble and decrepit, the townsfolk succoured her not with aught, but thrust her forth of the city, saying, 'This old woman shall not neighbour with us, for that we do good to her and she requiteth us with evil.' So she took shelter in a ruined place and strangers used to bestow alms upon her, and in this way she tarried a length of time.

Now the king of that city had aforetime contended for the kingship with his uncle's son, and the people disliked the king; but Allah Almighty decreed that he should overcome his cousin. However, jealousy of him abode in his heart and he acquainted the Wazir, who hid it not and sent him money. Furthermore, he fell to summoning all strangers who came to the town, man after man, and questioning them of their creed and their goods, and whoso answered him not satisfactorily, he took his wealth.

Now a certain wealthy man of the Moslems was wayfaring, without knowing aught of this, and it befell that he arrived at that city by night, and coming to the ruin, gave the old woman money and said to her, 'No harm upon thee.' Whereupon she lifted up her voice and blessed him: so he set down his merchandise by her and abode with her the rest of the night and the next day.

Now highwaymen had followed him that they might rob him of his monies, but succeeded not in aught: wherefore he went up to the old woman and kissed her head and exceeded in bounty to her.

Then she warned him of that which awaited strangers entering the town and said to him, 'I like not this for thee and I fear mischief for thee from these questions that the Wazir hath appointed for addressing the ignorant.' And she expounded to him the case · according to its conditions: then said she to him, 'But have thou no concern: only carry me with thee to thy lodging, and if he question thee of aught enigmatical, whilst I am with thee, I will expound the answers to thee.' So he carried the crone with him to the city and lodged her in his lodging and entreated her honourably.

Presently, the Wazir heard of the merchant's coming; so he sent to him and bade bring him to his house and talked with him awhile of his travels and of whatso had befallen him therein, and the merchant answered his queries. Then said the Minister, 'I will put certain critical questions to thee, which and thou answer me, 'twill be well for thee,' and the merchant rose and made him no answer.

Quoth the Wazir, 'What is the weight of the elephant?'

The merchant was perplexed and returned him no reply, giving himself up for lost; however, at last he said, 'Grant me three days of delay.'

The Minister granted him the time he sought and he returned to his lodging and related what had passed to the old woman, who said, 'When the morrow cometh, go to the Wazir and say to him, "Make a ship and launch it on the sea and put in it an elephant, and when it sinketh in the water, mark the place whereunto the water riseth. Then take out the elephant and cast in stones in its place, till the ship sink to that same mark; whereupon do thou take out the stones and weigh them and thou wilt presently know the weight of the elephant."'

Accordingly, when he arose in the morning, he went to the Wazir and repeated to him that which the old woman had taught him; whereat the Minister marvelled and said to him, 'What sayest thou of a man, who seeth in his house four holes, and in each hole a viper offering to sally out upon him and slay him, and in his house are four sticks and each hole may not be stopped but with the ends of two sticks? How, then, shall he stop all the holes and deliver himself from the vipers?'

When the merchant heard this, there befell him such concern that it garred him forget the first and he said to the Wazir, 'Grant me delay, so I may reflect on the reply'; and the Minister cried, 'Go out, and bring me the answer, or I will seize thy monies.'

The merchant fared forth and returned to the old woman who,

seeing him changed of complexion, said to him, 'What did his hoariness ask thee?' So he acquainted her with the case and she cried, 'Fear not, I will bring thee forth of this strait.'

Quoth he, 'Allah requite thee with weal!'

Then quoth she, 'Tomorrow go to him with a stout heart and say: "The answer to that whereof thou asketh me is this. Put the heads of two sticks into one of the holes; then take the other two sticks and lay them across the middle of the first two and stop with their two heads the second hole and with their ferrules the fourth hole. Then take the ferrules of the first two sticks and stop with them the third hole."'

So he repaired to the Wazir and repeated to him the answer; and he marvelled at its justness and said to him, 'Go; by Allah; I will ask thee no more questions, for thou with thy skill marrest my foundation.'

Then he treated him as a friend and the merchant acquainted him with the affair of the old woman; whereupon quoth the Wazir, 'Needs must the intelligent company with the intelligent.' Thus did this weak woman restore to that man his life and his monies on the easiest wise.

The Four Gifts

(Breton)

In the old land of Brittany, once called Cornwall, there lived a woman named Barbaïk Bourhis, who spent all her days looking after her farm with the help of her niece Téphany. Early and late the two might be seen in the fields or in the dairy, milking cows, making butter, feeding fowls; working hard themselves and taking care that others worked too. Perhaps it might have been better for Barbaïk if she had left herself a little time to rest and to think about other things, for soon she grew to love money for its own sake, and only gave herself and Téphany the food and clothes they absolutely needed. And as for poor people she positively hated them, and declared that such lazy creatures had no business in the world.

Well, this being the sort of person Barbaïk was, it is easy to guess at her anger when one day she found Téphany talking outside the cow-house to young Denis, who was nothing more than a day labourer from the village of Plover. Seizing her niece by the arm, she pulled her sharply away, exclaiming: 'Are you not ashamed, girl, to waste your time over a man who is as poor as a rat, when there are a dozen more who would be only too happy to buy you rings of silver, if you would let them?'

'Denis is a good workman, as you know very well,' answered Téphany, red with anger, 'and he puts by money too, and soon will be able to take a farm for himself.'

'Nonsense,' cried Barbaïk, 'he will never save enough for a farm till he is a hundred. I would sooner see you in your grave than the wife of a man who carries his whole fortune on his back.'

'What does fortune matter when one is young and strong?' asked

36

Téphany, but her aunt, amazed at such words, would hardly let her finish.

'What does fortune matter?' repeated Barbaïk, in a shocked voice. 'Is it possible that you are really so foolish as to despise money? If this is what you learn from Denis, I forbid you to speak to him, and I will have him turned out of the farm if he dares to show his face here again. Now go and wash the clothes and spread them out to dry.'

Téphany did not dare to disobey, but with a heavy heart went down the path to the river.

'She is harder than these rocks,' said the girl to herself, 'yes, a thousand times harder. For the rain at least can at last wear away the stone, but you might cry for ever, and she would never care. Talking to Denis is the only pleasure I have, and if I am not to see him I may as well enter a convent.'

Thinking these thoughts she reached the bank, and began to unfold the large packet of linen that had to be washed. The tap of a stick made her look up, and standing before her she saw a little old woman, whose face was strange to her.

'You would like to sit down and rest, Granny?' asked Téphany, pushing aside her bundle.

'When the sky is all the roof you have, you rest where you will,' replied the old woman in trembling tones.

'Are you so lonely, then?' inquired Téphany, full of pity. 'Have you no friends who would welcome you into their houses?'

The old woman shook her head.

'They all died long, long ago,' she answered, 'and the only friends I have are strangers with kind hearts.'

The girl did not speak for a moment, then held out the small loaf and some bacon intended for her dinner.

'Take this,' she said; 'today at any rate you shall dine well,' and the old woman took it, gazing at Téphany the while.

'Those who help others deserve to be helped,' she answered; 'your eyes are still red because that miser Barbaïk has forbidden you to speak to the young man from Plover. But cheer up, you are a good girl, and I will give you something that will enable you to see him once every day.'

'You?' cried Téphany, stupefied at discovering that the beggar knew all about her affairs, but the old woman did not hear her.

'Take this long copper pin,' she went on, 'and every time you stick it in your dress Mother Bourhis will be obliged to leave the house in order to go and count her cabbages. As long as the pin is in your dress you will be free, and your aunt will not come back until you have put it in the case again.' Then, rising, she nodded to Téphany and vanished.

The girl stood where she was, as still as a stone. If it had not been for the pin in her hands she would have thought she was dreaming. But by that token she knew it was no common old woman who had given it to her, but a fairy, wise in telling what would happen in the days to come. Then suddenly Téphany's eyes fell on the clothes, and to make up for lost time she began to wash them with great vigour.

Next evening, at the moment when Denis was accustomed to wait for her in the shadow of the cowhouse, Téphany stuck the pin in her dress, and at the very same instant Barbaïk took up her sabots and went through the orchard and past to the fields, to the plot where the cabbages grew. With a heart as light as her footsteps, the girl ran from the house, and spent her evening happily with Denis. And so it was for many days after that. Then, at last, Téphany began to notice something, and the something made her very sad.

At first Denis seemed to find the hours that they were together fly as quickly as she did, but when he had taught her all the songs he knew, and told her all the plans he had made for growing rich and a great man, he had nothing more to say to her, for he, like a great many other people, was fond of talking himself but not of listening to anyone else. Sometimes, indeed, he never came at all, and the next evening he would tell Téphany that he had been forced to go into town on business, but though she never reproached him she was not deceived and saw plainly that he no longer cared for her as he used to do.

Day by day her heart grew heavier and her cheeks paler, and one evening, when she had waited for him in vain, she put her water pot on her shoulder and went slowly down to the spring. On the path in front of her stood the fairy who had given her the pin, and as she glanced at Téphany she gave a little mischievous laugh and said: 'Why, my pretty maiden hardly looks happier than she did before, in spite of meeting her lover whenever she pleases.'

'He has grown tired of me,' answered Téphany in a trembling voice, 'and he makes excuses to stay away. Ah! Granny dear, it is not enough to be able to see him, I must be able to amuse him and to keep him with me. He is so clever, you know. Help *me* to be clever too.'

'Is that what you want?' cried the old woman. 'Well, take this feather and stick it in your hair, and you will be as wise as Solomon himself.'

Blushing with pleasure, Téphany went home and stuck the feather into the blue ribbon which girls always wear in that part of the country. In a moment she heard Denis whistling gaily, and as her aunt was safely counting her cabbages, she hurried out to meet him. The young man was struck dumb by her talk. There was nothing that she did not seem to know, and as for songs she not only could sing those from every part of Brittany, but could compose them herself. Was this *really* the quiet girl who had been so anxious to learn all he could teach her, or was it somebody else? Perhaps she had gone suddenly mad, and there was an evil spirit inside her. But in any case, night after night he came back, only to find her growing wiser and wiser.

Soon the neighbours whispered their surprise among themselves, for Téphany had not been able to resist the pleasure of putting the feather in her hair for some of the people who despised her for her poor clothes, and many were the jokes she made about them. Of course they heard of her jests, and shook their heads saying: 'She is an ill-natured little cat, and the man that marries her will find that it is she who will hold the reins and drive the horse.'

It was not long before Denis began to agree with them, and as he always liked to be master wherever he went, he became afraid of Téphany's sharp tongue, and instead of laughing as before when she made fun of other people he grew red and uncomfortable, thinking that his turn would come next.

So matters went on till one evening Denis told Téphany that he really could not stay a moment, as he had promised to go to a dance that was to be held in the next village.

Téphany's face fell; she had worked hard all day, and had been counting on a quiet hour with Denis. She did her best to persuade

him to remain with her, but he would not listen, and at last she grew angry.

'Oh, I know why you are so anxious not to miss the dance,' she said; 'it is because Azilicz of Penenru will be there.'

Now Azilicz was the loveliest girl for miles round, and she and Denis had known each other from childhood.

'Oh yes, Azilicz will be there,' answered Denis, who was quite pleased to see her jealous, 'and naturally one would go a long way to watch her dance.'

'Go then!' cried Téphany, and entering the house she slammed the door behind her.

Lonely and miserable she sat down by the fire and stared into the red embers. Then, flinging the feather from her hair, she put her head on her hands, and sobbed passionately.

'What is the use of being clever when it is beauty that men want? That is what I ought to have asked for. But it is too late, Denis will never come back.'

'Since you wish it so much you shall have beauty,' said a voice at her side, and looking round she beheld the old woman leaning on her stick.

'Fasten this necklace round your neck, and as long as you wear it you will be the most beautiful woman in the world,' continued the fairy. With a little shriek of joy Téphany took the necklace, and snapping the clasp ran to the mirror which hung in the corner. Ah, *this* time she was not afraid of Azilicz or of any other girl, for surely none could be as fair and white as she. And with the sight of her face a thought came to her, and putting on hastily her best dress and her buckled shoes she hurried off to the dance.

On the way she met a beautiful carriage with a young man seated in it.

'What a lovely maiden!' he exclaimed, as Téphany approached. 'Why, there is not a girl in my own country that can be compared to her. She, and no other, shall be my bride.'

The carriage was large and barred the narrow road, so Téphany was forced, much against her will, to remain where she was. But she looked the young man full in the face as she answered: 'Go your way, noble lord, and let me go mine. I am only a poor peasant girl, accustomed to milk, and make hay and spin.'

'Peasant you may be, but I will make you a great lady,' said he, taking her hand and trying to lead her to the carriage.

'I don't want to be a great lady, I only want to be the wife of

Denis,' she replied, throwing off his hand and running to the ditch which divided the road from the cornfield, where she hoped to hide. Unluckily the young man guessed what she was doing, and signed to his attendants, who seized her and put her in the coach. The door was banged, and the horses whipped up into a gallop.

At the end of an hour they arrived at a splendid castle, and Téphany, who would not move, was lifted out and carried into the hall, while a priest was sent for to perform the marriage ceremony. The young man tried to win a smile from her by telling of all the beautiful things she would have as his wife, but Téphany did not listen to him, and looked about to see if there was any means by which she could escape. It did not seem easy. The three great doors were closely barred, and the one through which she had entered shut with a spring, but her feather was still in her hair, and by its aid she detected a crack in the wooden panelling, through which a streak of light could be dimly seen. Touching the copper pin which fastened her dress, the girl sent everyone in the hall to count the cabbages, while she herself passed through the little door, not knowing whither she was going.

By this time night had fallen, and Téphany was very tired. Thankfully she found herself at the gate of a convent, and asked if she might stay there till morning. But the portress answered roughly that it was no place for beggars, and bade her begone, so the poor girl dragged herself slowly along the road, till a light and the bark of a dog told her that she was near a farm.

In front of the house was a group of people; two or three women and the sons of the farmer. When their mother heard Téphany's request to be given a bed the good wife's heart softened, and she was just going to invite her inside, when the young men, whose heads were turned by the girl's beauty, began to quarrel as to which should do most for her. From words they came to blows, and the women, frightened at the disturbance, pelted Téphany with insulting names. She quickly ran down the nearest path, hoping to escape them in the darkness of the trees, but in an instant she heard their footsteps behind her. Wild with fear her legs trembled under her, when suddenly she bethought herself of her necklace. With a violent effort she burst the clasp and flung it round the neck of a pig which was grunting in a ditch, and as she did so she heard the footsteps cease from pursuing her and run after the pig, for her charm had vanished.

On she went, scarcely knowing where she was going, till she

found herself, to her surprise and joy, close to her aunt's house. For several days she felt so tired and unhappy that she could hardly get through her work, and to make matters worse Denis scarcely ever came near her. He was too busy, he said, and really it was only rich people who could afford to waste time in talking.

As the days went on Téphany grew paler and paler, till everybody noticed it except her aunt. The water pot was almost too heavy for her now, but morning and evening she carried it to the spring, though the effort to lift it to her shoulder was often too much for her.

'How could I have been so foolish,' she whispered to herself, when she went down as usual at sunset. 'It was not freedom to see Denis that I should have asked for, for he was soon weary of me, nor a quick tongue, for he was afraid of it, nor beauty, for that brought me nothing but trouble, but riches which make life easy both for oneself and others. Ah! if I only dared to beg this gift from the fairy, I should be wiser than before and know how to choose better.'

'Be satisfied,' said the voice of the old woman, who seemed to be standing unseen at Téphany's elbow. 'If you look in your right-hand pocket when you go home you will find a small box. Rub your eyes with the ointment it contains, and you will see that you yourself contain a priceless treasure.'

Téphany did not in the least understand what she meant, but ran back to the farm as fast as she could, and began to fumble joyfully in her right-hand pocket. Sure enough, there was the little box with the precious ointment. She was in the act of rubbing her eyes with it when Barbaïk Bourhis entered the room. Ever since she had been obliged to leave her work and pass her time, she did not know why, in counting cabbages, everything had gone wrong, and she could not get a labourer to stay with her because of her bad temper. When, therefore, she saw her niece standing quietly before her mirror, Barbaïk broke out: 'So this is what you do when I am out in the fields! Ah! it is no wonder if the farm is ruined. Are you not ashamed girl, to behave so?'

Téphany tried to stammer some excuse, but her aunt was half mad with rage, and a box on the ears was her only answer. At this Téphany, hurt, bewildered and excited, could control herself no longer, and turning away burst into tears. But what was her surprise when she saw that each teardrop was a round and shining pearl. Barbaïk, who also beheld this marvel, uttered a cry of astonishment, and threw herself on her knees to pick them up from the floor.

She was still gathering them when the door opened and in came Denis. 'Pearls! Are they really pearls?' he asked, falling on his knees also, and looking up at Téphany he perceived others still more beautiful rolling down the girl's cheeks.

'Take care not to let any of the neighbours hear of it, Denis,' said Barbaïk. 'Of course you shall have your share, but nobody else shall get a single one. Cry on, my dear, cry on,' she continued to Téphany. 'It is for your good as well as ours,' and she held out her apron to catch them, and Denis his hat.

But Téphany could hardly bear any more. She felt half choked at the sight of their greediness, and wanted to rush from the hall, and though Barbaïk caught her arm to prevent this, and said all sorts of tender words which she thought would make the girl weep more, Téphany with a violent effort forced back her tears, and wiped her eyes.

'Is she finished already?' cried Barbaïk, in a tone of disappointment. 'Oh, try again, my dear. Do you think it would do any good to beat her a little?' she added to Denis, who shook his head.

'That is enough for the first time. I will go into the town and find out the value of each pearl.'

'Then I will go with you,' said Barbaïk, who never trusted anyone and was afraid of being cheated. So the two went out, leaving Téphany behind them.

She sat quite still on the chair, her hands clasped tightly together, as if she was forcing something back. At last she raised her eyes, which had been fixed on the ground, and beheld the fairy standing in a dark corner by the hearth, observing her with a mocking look. The girl trembled and jumped up, then taking the feather, the pin, and the box, she held them out to the old woman.

'Here they are, all of them,' she cried; 'they belong to you. Let me never see them again, but I have learned the lesson that they taught me. Others may have riches, beauty and wit, but as for me I desire nothing but to be the poor peasant girl I always was, working hard for those she loves.'

'Yes, you have learned your lesson,' answered the fairy, 'and now you shall lead a peaceful life and marry the man you love. For after all it was not yourself you thought of but him.'

Never again did Téphany see the old woman, but she forgave Denis for selling her tears, and in time he grew to be a good husband, who did his own share of work.

Habetrot

(Anglo-Scottish)

There was once a merry, idle lassie in Selkirkshire who liked roaming over the country gathering flowers much better than blistering her fingers with spinning. The goodwife, her mother, was a great spinster, but lessons did nothing, and at last she lost her temper and drove the lassie up to her bedroom, carried up a spinning-wheel and seven heads of lint and said to the lassie, 'Noo ma lass ye'll spin me seven skeins oot o' yon lint in three days or 'twill be the worse for you.' And she left her there, crying her eyes out.

The lassie knew well that her minnie was in earnest, so for a long day she worked away at the wheel, but she only got sore fingers from twisting the thread and sore lips pulling it out and about three feet of lumpy, uneven thread that no one in her senses would try to knit or weave. So the poor lassie cried herself to sleep. In the morning she woke up very early, and the sun was shining and the birds were singing, and she looked at the poor bit of thread she had spun and she thought to herself: 'I can do no good here; I'll out into the cool air.' So she crept down the ladder and past the curtains of her mother's box-bed, unbolted the kitchen door, and ran down to the burnside. She wandered here and there, plucking wild primroses and listening to the birds singing, until she suddenly thought that however long she loitered she would have to go back home at last, and how angry her mother would be. There was a little mound in front of her and she sat down on a smooth, self-bored stone by the burnside and burst into tears. A self-bored stone is one where the water has made a deep, narrow hole in the rock. People used to say that you can see fairies through a self-bored stone. However that

44

may be the lassie began to hear sounds coming from it, and a kind of whirring, and shrill little voices singing a strange tune. She looked up and there was a strange little woman working busily at her spindle and pulling out the thread with a long lip that looked as if it was made for spinning. 'A fair gude day to ye, gudewife,' said the lassie, who was always friendly and well-spoken. 'And to you too, my dawtie,' said the little woman, well pleased with her. 'What for are ye sae lang-lippit?' said the lassie, like the bairn that she was. 'Wi' pulling oot the thread, my hinnie,' said the old wifie. 'That's what I sud be doing,' said the lassie, 'but it's nae gude, I can mak' naething of it.' And she told the whole story.

'Never heed, my hinnie,' said the kind old wife. 'Fetch me yir lint, and I'll hae it a' spun up in good time for yir mither.' So the lassie ran up and slipped into the cottage, and back with the lint in a flash. 'What will I call ye, gudewife?' she said. 'And whaur will I come for the skeins?' But the old wife took the lint and was gone. The lassie was quite dazed and she sat down on the stone to wait. The sun was hot on her head, and after a while she fell fast asleep and never stirred till the sun went down in the sky and the air began to grow chill. She waked to hear the whirring and singing louder than before, and a ray of light was coming out of the self-bored stone. So she knelt up and put an eye to it and saw a strange sight through the peephole. She was looking down into a great cavern, and a number of queer figures were sitting at their spinning-wheels, spin-spinning away like mad. They all had long, long lips and flat thumbs and hunched backs, and her friend was walking about among them. There was one that was sitting a little apart from the rest and uglier than anyone, and her name was Scantlie Mab, for that's what the head fairy called her. 'They're nearly finished, Scantlie Mab,' she said and then she laughed and cried out, 'Little kens the wee lassie on the brae-head that Habetrot is my name! Bundle up the yarn and give it to me, for I must take it up to the wee lassie at her minnie's door.'

Then the lassie knew where they were to meet, and she ran up to her cottage, and she'd hardly been there a moment before Habetrot appeared and gave her seven beautiful hanks of yarn. 'Oh what can I do for you in return?' said the lassie. 'Dinna tell yir mither wha spun the skeins,' said Habetrot, 'and cry on me whiles if ye need me.' And she was gone into the darkness.

Her mother had gone to bed early, for she had been working hard all day making black puddings – 'black sausters' they called them in that part of the world – and seven beautiful black puddings were hanging up to dry from the rafters. The girl was as hungry as a hunter, for she had had nothing since breakfast the day before. She spread out the beautiful skeins where her mother would see them first thing when she woke, then she blew up the fire and took down the frying pan and cooked the first sauster and ate it, and she was hungrier than ever. Then she cooked the next, and the next, and suddenly she discovered that she had eaten them all. So she tiptoed up the ladder to bed and fell asleep as soon as her head had touched the pillow.

The mother woke up next morning, and when she drew back the curtains of her bed she saw the seven beautiful skeins, better than any spinster in the country could spin them, and she cast up her eyes in amazement – and where were the fine black puddings that were hanging up there last night? Not one was to be seen, only a black frying pan standing at the side of the fire.

She ran out into the road in her bed-gown like one demented, and cried out:

Ma dawtie ha' spun se'en, se'en, se'en!
Ma dawtie ha' ate se'en, se'en, se'en
An a' afore daylicht.

She sang out so loud that it woke her daughter, who got up and began to dress as quick as she could.

And who should come riding along the road but the young laird himself. 'What's that you're crying, goodwife?' he said; and she sang out again:

Ma dawtie's spun se'en, se'en, se'en
Ma dawtie's eaten se'en, se'en!

'An' if ye don't believe me, laird, come and see for yersel!'

So the laird followed her into the cottage and when he saw the beautiful skeins he asked to see the spinner, and when he saw the spinner he asked her to marry him.

The laird was braw and brave and kind, and the lass was glad to say yes; but there was one thing that troubled her, the laird kept talking of all the fine yarn she would be spinning after the wedding. So one day the lassie went down to the self-bored stone and called for Habetrot. Habetrot knew what her trouble would be, but she said, 'Never need, hinnie; bring your jo here and we'll sort it for ye.'

So next night at sunset the pair of them stood at the self-bored stone and heard Habetrot singing, and at the end of the song she opened a hidden door and let them into the mound. The laird was astonished at all the hideous shapes around him, and said to the lassie, 'Why are their lips all deformed?' Habetrot said aloud, 'Ask them yourself.' And each one said in muttering or whistling tones, 'Wi' spin-spin-spinning.'

'Aye, aye, they were once bonnie enough,' said Habetrot, 'but spinners aye gang that gait. Yir ain lassie'll be the same, bonnie as she is noo, for she's fair mad aboot the spinning.'

'She'll not!' said the laird. 'Not another spindle shall she touch from this day on.'

'Just as ye say, laird,' said the lassie, and from that day she roamed the countryside with the laird, and rode about behind him as blithe as a bird, and every head of lint that grew on that land went to old Habetrot to be spun.

Unfortunate

(Sicilian)

There was the good king of Spain, and there was his good queen, and they had seven beautiful young daughters. They lived happily, none more happily, until one day a neighbouring king came with a great army. The king of Spain and his people fought valiantly, but they were defeated: the king of Spain was carried away captive, and the queen and the seven princesses fled into a distant village, where they lived but poorly in a cottage, and tried to earn a little money by doing embroidery and suchlike. But somehow, though their work was beautiful and faultless, nobody seemed to want it, and very often the queen and the princesses had scarcely enough to eat.

Now one summer evening, when the princesses had gone out into the woods to gather wild strawberries, and the queen was alone in the cottage, cooking broth for their supper, an old gypsy woman came knocking at the door, offering some tawdry pieces of lace in exchange for food or money.

'Well, little old grandmother,' said the queen, 'I can give you a bowl of broth and welcome, but of money today I have none at all. I am that unfortunate queen of Spain whose dear husband was carried away prisoner, and now with my seven daughters I live here in poverty. But come in, rest yourself, and if a bowl of broth will content you, that you shall have.'

So the old gypsy woman went in and sat by the fire. She gobbled up her bowl of broth, and then she sat looking into the fire and muttering to herself.

At last she said, 'Queen, for such as I it is given to look into the past and into the future, and to read the causes of things: of the good fortune and the ill fortune that attend us mortals, and of the

48

bringing of the one, and the curing of the other. In your family you have a daughter who is indeed unfortunate; and it is due to her that all this misery has befallen you. She has an evil Destiny. Send that daughter away, and you will win back your king and your kingdom.'

'What,' cried the queen, 'drive away one of my own daughters?'

'Yes, lady, there is no other remedy.'

'But which daughter?' cried the queen. 'They are all so dear, so good – how can I tell which is the one that brings ill fortune?'

'Easily enough,' said the old gypsy woman. 'Tonight, when your daughters sleep in their beds, take a candle and go from one bed to another. Three of the girls will be sleeping on their right sides, with their hands folded together under their chins. Three will be sleeping on their left sides, with their arms under the coverlet. One will be sleeping on her back with her hands crossed on her breast. That is the one you must send away, for on her lies the curse of an evil Destiny, and misfortune follows her wherever she goes.'

And so having said, the old gypsy woman went away, leaving the queen in great bewilderment.

Well, by and by, the seven princesses came in. 'We didn't find a single strawberry, not a single one!' they cried. 'Somebody had been in the woods before us and picked them all. Oh, why does everything go wrong for us – why, *why?*'

'Never mind,' said the queen, 'perhaps you will have better luck tomorrow.'

But the princesses said they never had any luck at all. They ate their broth in silence, and then they each one curtsied to their mother, like the well-behaved young princesses they were, and all of them went to bed.

The queen sat for a long time looking into the fire, and thinking of the gypsy woman's words. At last she sighed, lit a candle, and went into the room where the seven princesses lay in seven narrow beds, all sleeping soundly. Tiptoeing from bed to bed, the queen looked down at her beautiful sleeping daughters: three lay on their right sides, with their hands folded under their chins, three lay on their left sides, with their arms under the coverlet; but the seventh, and youngest, lay on her back, with her arms crossed on her breast. 'Oh my darling, my darling, must I send you away?' whispered the queen.

And she wept.

The queen's tears fell on the hands of the youngest princess; she stirred in her sleep; she woke; she opened her eyes.

'Dearest little mother, why do you weep?'

'Have we not good cause to weep, little daughter? I a queen, and you, my princesses, living like peasants in a tumbledown cottage?'

'But that cannot be the reason,' said the princess, 'or you would have wept long ago. I think something has happened today whilst we were out – tell me what it is!'

'No, no, no!'

But the princess would not listen to 'no'. She bothered and bothered, until at last the queen had to tell her about the gypsy woman and what she had said.

Then the princess threw her arms about the queen's neck, and kissed her many times. 'Go to bed and sleep, dearest little mother,' she said. 'We will think about it in the morning; for the morning is wiser than the evening.'

So the queen went to bed. And no sooner was the queen sleeping than the little princess got up very, very quietly, dressed herself, packed a small bundle of this and that, and stole out of the cottage.

'Goodbye, dear mother, goodbye, dear sisters,' she whispered. 'Now I, Unfortunate, take my leave, that fortune may come to you again.'

So Unfortunate wandered on her way, and in the morning came to a pleasant house set back in a garden by the side of the road. She peeped in through a window, and saw several ladies at work, some sitting at looms weaving, some spinning, some making lace.

'Perhaps I might find service here,' she thought. And she knocked at the door.

One of the ladies left her loom and opened the door.

'Can I take service here, my lady?' said the princess.

'Oh yes, we need a servant – what is your name?'

'Unfortunate.'

'Well, come in, Unfortunate. If you work well, you will find us easy to please.'

So Unfortunate went in, and the lady set her to work, sweeping, cleaning, cooking. She worked with a will, and for a week all went well. And then one day the lady said, 'Unfortunate, my sisters and I are going on a short journey to visit some friends. We shall not return until tomorrow. You bolt the front door and the back door on the inside, and I will lock them on the outside. We can trust you, can we not, Unfortunate, to see that no one gets in to steal the silk and the lace and the cloth we have made?'

'Oh yes, my lady, you can trust me,' said Unfortunate.

So the ladies went away. They locked the doors on the outside, and Unfortunate bolted them on the inside. She spent the day cleaning and polishing till she had everything shining bright. When night came, she went to bed, well satisfied with all her work, and thinking how pleased the ladies would be when they came back. Almost immediately she fell asleep . . .

But at midnight she woke to hear strange sounds downstairs: muttering and heavy breathing, and the noise of tearing cloth and the snap, snap of rusty scissors. Jumping out of bed and hastily lighting a candle, she ran downstairs. Oh horror, what did she find? A hideous old hag standing beside a heap of torn lace and cut-up cloth – yes, all the fine work of the ladies lay in tattered heaps about the old hag's feet.

'Ha! ha!' laughed the old hag. 'Ha! ha!'

And even as Unfortunate sprang to snatch the scissors from her, the old hag blew out the candle and disappeared. But *how* she went – whether through the locked door, or the barred window – who can tell?

Sobbing bitterly, Unfortunate lit more candles and set about gathering up the tattered cloth and the scraps of cut-up lace. Oh, what would her ladies say when they came back? What *would* they say?

And what *did* they say? 'Ah, you wicked shameless girl, is this our reward for taking you in and being kind to you?' They beat her and drove her from the house: and she wandered on her way, not knowing, or caring, whither she went.

So wandering, she came in the late afternoon to a village; and at the entrance to the village she saw a little shop that sold bread and vegetables and wine. Having eaten nothing all day, she was very hungry. But she had no money. So, as she stood looking longingly at all the good things to eat in the shop window, the shopwoman saw her and came to the door.

'Little one, are you hungry?'

'Oh, I am, I am!'

'Then step in. Things have come to a pretty pass if we can't spare a bite for a poor little soul like you!'

Unfortunate went in, and the shopwoman gave her some bread and cheese and a glass of wine. Then having spoken her thanks most politely, Unfortunate got up to go on her way.

'And where are you going?' asked the shopwoman.

'I . . . I don't know,' said poor Unfortunate.

'But it will soon be dark,' said the shopwoman. 'And the roads are none too safe for young girls. If you care to sleep here at the back of the shop, I can shake down a few sacks for you to lie on.'

So, having again thanked the shopwoman most prettily, Unfortunate lay down on her bed of sacks, and was soon sound asleep, with her hands crossed on her breast.

By and by the shopwoman's husband came in.

'Who is that sleeping on the sacks there?' said he.

'Oh, just a poor little benighted maiden I felt pity for.'

'Well, I hope she may be honest,' said the husband.

And he and his wife went to bed.

All quiet until midnight. Then through the shop window stepped a hideous old hag. The old hag seized up the loaves of bread, tore them into pieces with her claw-like hands, and flung the pieces on the shop floor. Then she knocked over the vegetable baskets, and went striding up and down over the spilled fruit and vegetables until the shop floor was thick with the pulpy mash of everything the baskets had contained. What next? Down into the wine cellar with her, to take the bungs out of all the casks. Now the cellar lay inches thick in a pool of wine and beer. And so, leaving ruin behind her, the old hag stepped out through the window again, and vanished in the darkness.

And all this without a sound.

But when the shopman got up in the morning and saw the wreckage, he snatched up a broom, shook Unfortunate into wakefulness, and beat her. 'You – you – you . . .' He could scarcely speak for rage. 'Get out, before I kick you out! And if ever I see your face again, I'll . . . I'll . . .'

But Unfortunate did not wait to hear what he would do. She ran out of the shop and out of the village, and away and away and away. She ran out of one kingdom and into another kingdom; and still she ran, until, exhausted, she fell by the roadside in a faint.

So the day passed, the sun set, now it was night; and still Unfortunate lay like one dead at the side of the road. When next morning the rising sun shone on her face, she came to herself, opened her eyes and looked about her. Larks were singing overhead, and near at hand she heard the babbling of a brook. Ah, for a drink of water! She got up and climbed over the fence into a meadow, through which a bright little stream was flowing. Stooping over the stream was a woman, washing clothes.

At the sound of Unfortunate's footsteps, the woman raised her head and looked round . . . And who should the woman be – ah, who *should* she be – but the old nurse, Dame Francesca, who had dandled Unfortunate on her knees when Unfortunate was a tiny child!

'Nurse, nurse, nurse!'

'My little princess!'

There they were, hugging and kissing each other.

'But what has come to you, my darling, and what are you doing here all alone, and why so pale, and why so ragged?'

Then Unfortunate told Dame Francesca all that had happened. And the dame, who had brought dinner in a basket, gave Unfortunate to eat and drink.

'I am now laundry woman to the prince of this country,' said Dame Francesca. 'You shall come home with me and live in my cottage until we see better times. For better times will come, my darling, yes, they will come! So now, if you will help me finish my washing, we shall be the quicker done with it, and on our way home. Though to be sure, washing clothes is scarcely work for a princess!'

'I have done every kind of work since I last saw you, dear nurse,' said Unfortunate. And she took up one of the prince's shirts to rinse it in the stream.

Oh me – what happened? The shirt gave a jump and a twist; it jerked itself out of Unfortunate's hands, it floated away down the stream, it caught on the trailing stem of a bramble bush. And when Unfortunate ran to take it off the bush, it had a great tear across the back.

'Yes, I see that you are indeed Unfortunate,' said Dame Francesca. I think you must have an evil Destiny. But never mind, my darling! You shall live with me, and I will wait on you – you shall do no work at all . . . And I have some thoughts about your Destiny, and how we may set all right.'

So Unfortunate went with Dame Francesca to her cottage and lived there. And as long as she put her hand to no work, all went well. But let her try to help Dame Francesca in any way . . . If she tried to wash the crockery, it broke under her hand; if she tried to darn Dame Francesca's stockings, the little holes in them grew bigger and bigger; if she tried to sweep out the kitchen, the dust blew back through the door; until at last Dame Francesca said, 'Leave all, leave all! Out with you into the sunshine!'

But no sooner had Unfortunate gone out into the sunshine than great clouds gathered in the sky, and down came the rain.

'Your Destiny is against us,' said Dame Francesca, 'but we'll beat her yet! Now *my* Destiny is a very different kind of person!'

So one day Dame Francesca baked two sweet cakes. She put the cakes in a basket and said to Unfortunate, 'Take these cakes, go and stand on the sea beach, and call my Destiny. Call loud and clear, call three times: "Ah, Destiny of Dame Francesca, ah, Destiny of Dame Francesca, ah, Destiny of Dame Francesca!" At the third call my Destiny will come to you out of the sea. Give her one of these cakes with my greetings, and ask her – very politely, mind – to tell you where *your* Destiny can be found.'

So Unfortunate took the two cakes and went to stand on the sea beach, and called three times, 'Ah, Destiny of Dame Francesca, ah, Destiny of Dame Francesca, ah, Destiny of Dame Francesca!'

At the third call a beautiful, shining, smiling lady rose out of the sea.

Then Unfortunate took one of the cakes from the basket, and giving the cake to the beautiful shining lady said, 'Dame Francesca sends you this cake with her compliments. And sweet Destiny of Dame Francesca, would your ladyship do me a great kindness, and direct me to the place where I may find my own Destiny?'

The beautiful shining lady smiled and said, 'Take that narrow mule track over the sandhills and through the thicket. In the midst of the thicket you will find an old hag, sitting under a thorn bush by a well. She is your Destiny. Greet her kindly and offer her a cake. She will be very rude to you, and she will refuse the cake; but lay it at her feet and come away.'

So Unfortunate thanked the lovely lady, and went over the sandhills and through the thicket, and came to where the old hag sat under a thorn bush beside the well. Ah, how hideous that old hag was! How dirty, how blear-eyed, how slobbery, how ragged! Unfortunate trembled at the sight of her and almost ran away. But she pulled herself together, curtsied low, and said, 'My little Destiny, I bring you this cake, if you will be pleased to accept it.'

'Away with it! Away with it!' screamed the old hag. 'I want no gifts of *yours!*' And she spat on the ground, and turned her face away.

So then Unfortunate laid the cake at her feet, and went sadly back to tell Dame Francesca all about it.

Dame Francesca was folding up the prince's laundry. She listened to Unfortunate's tale of woe, and laughed. 'Never say die!' she said. 'We'll win that old hag over yet!'

And she packed the neatly folded laundry into a basket, and hurried off with it to the prince's palace.

'Dame Francesca,' said the prince. 'You are a treasure! Your work for me gets better every day! Here is a little present for you.' And he gave Dame Francesca two gold coins.

What did Dame Francesca do with those two gold coins?

She went into the town and bought an elegant dress, fine underclothes, a dainty headscarf, a sponge, a cake of sweet-smelling soap, a hairbrush and comb, and a bottle of scent. And these things she took home and gave to Unfortunate.

'Now, my darling,' said she, 'off with you again to that old hag, your Destiny; and will she or won't she, strip off her rags, wash her from the top of her head to the soles of her feet, brush, comb, and scent her, and dress her in these new clothes. No doubt she will scream and hit out at you, but be firm, be firm, get on with the work and take no notice of her squawkings. She is but a weak old woman, and you are young and strong. And when she is clean from top to toe, sweetly scented, and dressed as a lady should be dressed, give her this cake and say, "My little Destiny, I, Unfortunate, wish you well. Give me, I pray you, a new name!"'

So Unfortunate took all these things and went over the sandhills to the thicket where her Destiny sat under the hazel bush by the well. She pounced on the old hag, stripped off her clothes, dipped the sponge in the well, and began to wash the dirty old thing from the top of her head to the soles of her feet, whilst the old hag screamed and struggled and called Unfortunate every bad name she could think of. But when Unfortunate, having dried her and sprinkled her with scent, began to dress her in all the fine new clothes, the old hag stopped screaming and chuckled, and every moment she became younger and fairer-looking; until, when she was completely dressed, and Unfortunate was combing her hair, that hair turned from dirty grey to shining gold, and there she was laughing and eating her cake.

Then Unfortunate curtsied low and said, 'My little Destiny, I wish you well. Give me, I pray you, a new name.'

'Ah ha!' chuckled the Destiny. 'Ah ha! That's what you're after, is it? Well then, for the good you have done me, I *will* give you a new name, and your name shall be Fortunata. And here, Fortunata, is a christening present for you,' said she, handing Fortunata a little box.

So happily, happily, Fortunata thanked her Destiny, said goodbye to her, took the little box, and went home to Dame Francesca.

'Now let us see what your Destiny has given you, my pretty,' said Dame Francesca.

And they opened the box.

What was in it? Just a piece of gold braid.

'I don't call that much of a present!' said Dame Francesca.

And she tossed the little box into a cupboard, and bustled off to the palace, to see if the prince had any orders for her.

The prince was dressed in his most splendid uniform, with all his medals and decorations glittering on his coat. But he was walking up and down in a state of distraction. 'Dame Francesca,' he said, flinging out his arm, 'this is disgraceful! There is a piece of braid missing from my sleeve, and in all the town there is no such braid to be bought! Now I am due to review my troops, but how can I face them with my coat in this condition?'

'I think they may not notice it, your highness,' said Dame Francesca.

'*Not notice it!*' cried the prince. '*Not notice it!* What do I care whether they notice it or not? *I* notice it! How can I expect my troops to keep themselves in perfect trim, when I, their commander, appear before them in this slovenly condition?'

'There is a remedy for most things,' said Dame Francesca. And she hurried home, picked up the box that Fortunata's Destiny had given her, and brought it to the prince.

The prince opened the box and looked inside. Yes, it was the very same braid as the braid that was missing from his sleeve.

'My good Dame Francesca,' said the prince, 'I will pay you in gold the weight of this little box and its contents.' And he called for a pair of scales. He put the little box on one scale, and a piece of gold on the other scale. But the gold did not weigh down the little box.

The prince put another piece of gold on top of the first one. But neither did the two pieces of gold weigh down the little box. He put a third piece of gold on the scale, he put a fourth piece, a fifth, a sixth piece: and still the scales did not move. He called for a whole bag of gold and laid it on the scale; but that whole bag of gold did not weigh down the little box.

'Dame Francesca,' cried the prince, 'how is this possible? Can you explain this mystery?'

'I will fetch one who can explain it, my prince,' said Dame Francesca.

And off with her again to her cottage.

'Come, my pretty, come,' she said to Fortunata. 'The prince is asking for you!' And holding Fortunata firmly by the hand, she led her to the prince.

Very pretty, very shy the little princess looked in her shabby clothes. She made the prince an elegant curtsey, and stood silent.

'Who are you?' said the prince. 'And what is your name?'

'I am the youngest daughter of the king of Spain, your majesty,' said the princess, 'the king who was taken prisoner, by his enemies. Yesterday I was called Unfortunate; but this morning my Destiny gave me a new name. She said that henceforth I should be called Fortunata.'

'Lovely Fortunata,' said the prince, 'tell me your story.'

So the princess told him everything, and the prince said, 'All this shall now be put right.' He sent for the ladies with whom Fortunata had taken service. And when they stood beside him, he said, 'At what price do you reckon the damage that was done to your work on that unhappy night?'

They told him two hundred pieces of gold, and the prince paid them, and said, 'This poor girl whom you have beaten and driven from your door is the daughter of a king. Think of that, and be ashamed! Now away with you!'

So they went shamefaced away, and the prince sent for the shop-man whose goods were spoiled; and him also he paid and sent away. And then he summoned his army, and marched off to do battle with the enemy of the king of Spain. In the battle he was victorious; he put the enemy to flight, brought the king of Spain out of prison, and restored his kingdom to him. Then the queen, Fortunata's mother, and Fortunata's six sisters left their poor little cottage, and rejoined the king in his palace.

And after that – well, what after that? Of course Fortunata married the prince. Everyone was happy, including Dame Francesca, who went to live at the palace as head nurse, and bustled about and laughed and sang as she tended the princess Fortunata's pretty babies.

Biddy Early's Flying Magic

(Irish)

'There did a man from Flagmount, he went down to the Bridge for pigs – there used to be fairs them times. He went down to buy three slips, an' he bought 'em. But they had no transport in them times, an' a pig, you know, is a very bad walker. He was coming back by Feakle, back by Kilbarron, walking his pigs, an' sure the three of 'em gave up in the road down below Biddy's a small bit. There was a house o' the side o' the road by the name o' Gleeson's an' he went in, to know was there any place he'd put up the pigs for the night. Sure, no one had a cabin them times, unless a small little cabin for a cow an' an ass, so the man told him, "Would you go up there," he said, "to Biddy Early. She's only a few yards up the road there. An' go up an' in. She might do something for you."

'Up goes the man in to Biddy an' –

'"God, my poor man," she said, "your pigs are down" – without he saying anything at all.

'"Indeed they are," he said, "down there below in the road, an' they aren't able to get up."

'"Ah," she says, "sit down an' have a cup o' tea. They'll be all right."

'Sat down, an' she made tea for him an' they talked.

'"I'll do something for you, anyway," she said. "I'll help you out."

'But, after a while, when he had the tea drank, he rose up, an' she gave him three pills, three middling small ones – they could be pieces o' paper but it wouldn't matter. Anything she'd give him would right the thing, whatever it was. Then she gave him another one for himself. She was gone in, in the room while he was drinking the tea, making up this stuff for him.

'"When you go down, now, rise up the pigs' tails," she says; "an' put one each up under their tails. An' maybe," she says, "at the next turn o' the road you might have to let down your pants an' do the same job."

'But when they were going round the turn o' the road, the three pigs started to fly! He hardly got time to let his trousers down to have the operation. An' the four of 'em ran it to Flagmount. Never pulled up until the four of 'em landed above in Flagmount, flying!

'So that was Biddy Early for you, hah!'

PART THREE:

Witches in Love:
Possessive Women and
Devoted Wives

The Morrigu

(Irish)

As Cuchulain lay in his sleep one night a great cry from the North came to him, so that he started up and fell from his bed to the ground like a sack. He went out of his tent, and there he saw Laeg yoking the horses to the chariot. 'Why are you doing that?' he said. 'Because of a great cry I heard from the plain to the north-west,' said Laeg. 'Let us go there then,' said Cuchulain. So they went on till they met with a chariot, and a red horse yoked to it, and a woman sitting in it, with red eyebrows, and a red dress on her, and a long red cloak that fell on to the ground between the two wheels of the chariot, and on her back she had a grey spear. 'What is your name, and what is it you are wanting?' said Cuchulain. 'I am the daughter of King Buan,' she said, 'and what I am come for is to find you and to offer you my love, for I have heard of all the great deeds you have done.' 'It is a bad time you have chosen for coming,' said Cuchulain, 'for I am wasted and worn out with the hardship of the war, and I have no mind to be speaking with women.' 'You will have my help in everything you do,' she said, 'and it is protecting you I was up to this, and I will protect you from this out.' 'It is not trusting to a woman's protection I am in this work I have in my hands,' said Cuchulain. 'Then if you will not take my help,' she said, 'I will turn it against you; and at the time when you will be fighting with some man as good as yourself, I will come against you in all shapes, by water and by land, till you are beaten.' There was anger on Cuchulain then, and he took his sword, and made a leap at the chariot. But on the moment, the chariot and the horse and the woman had disappeared, and all he saw was a black crow, and it sitting on a branch; and by that he knew it was the Morrigu had been talking with him.

After that, Loch, son of Mofebis, was sent for to Maeve, and she asked him would he go out to the next day's fight. 'I will not go,' he said, 'for it would not be fitting for me to go out against a young boy, whose beard is not yet grown; but I have one to meet him,' he said, 'and that is my brother Long, son of Emonis, and you can make an agreement with him.' So then Long was sent for, and Maeve promised him a great reward, suits of armour for twelve men, and a chariot, and Findabair for a wife, and the right of coming to every feast at Cruachan. Then Long went out to the fight, but Cuchulain killed him.

Then Maeve said to her women: 'Go now to Cuchulain, and tell him to put some likeness of a beard on himself, and say to him there is no good warrior in the camp thinks it fitting to go out and fight him, he being young and beardless!'

When Cuchulain heard that, he took blackberries and smeared the juice on his face, the way he would have the appearance of a beard, and then he came out on the hill and showed himself to the men of Ireland. When Loch, son of Mofebis, saw him, he said: 'Is that a beard on Cuchulain?' 'That is certainly what I see,' said Maeve. 'Then I will go out and meet him,' said Loch. So they met beside the ford, where Long had got his death. 'Come to the ford that is higher up,' said Loch, for he would not fight at the ford where his brother died. So they fought at the upper ford, and while they were fighting, the Morrigu came against Cuchulain with the appearance of a white, red-eared heifer, and fifty other heifers along with her, and a chain of white bronze between every two of them, and they made a rush into the ford. But Cuchulain made a cast at her, and wounded one of her eyes. Then she came down the stream in the shape of a black eel, and wound herself about Cuchulain's legs in the water; and while he was getting himself free of her, and bruising her against a green stone of the ford, Loch wounded his body. Then she took the appearance of a grey wolf, and took hold of his right arm, and while he was getting free of her, Loch wounded him again. Then great anger came on him, and he took the spear Aoife had given him, the Gae Bulg, and gave him a deadly wound. 'I ask one thing for the sake of your great name, Cuchulain,' he called out. 'What thing is that?' 'It is not to spare my life I am asking you,' said Loch, 'but let me rise up, the way I may fall on my face, and not backwards towards the men of Ireland, so that none of them can say it was in running away or in going backward I fell.' 'I will surely give that leave,' said Cuchulain, 'for the thing you ask is a right gift for a fighting man.' And after that he went back to his own camping-place.

Now, on that day above any other, a very downhearted feeling came on Cuchulain, he to be fighting alone against the four provinces of Ireland. And he bade Laeg to go to Conchubar and to the men of Ulster, and to say to them that he, the son of Dechtire, was tired with fighting every day, and with the wounds he had got, and not one of his people or his friends coming to help him.

After that Maeve sent out six all together against him, three men and three women that understood enchantments; but he destroyed them all. And now that Maeve had broken her agreement with him, not to send more than one against him at a time, he did not spare her men any longer, but from where he was he used his sling so well that in the whole army there was neither dog, horse, or man that dared turn his face towards Cuchulain.

It was one day at that time that Morrigu came to try and get healing of her wounds from him, for it was only by his own hand the wounds he gave could be healed. She took the appearance of an old woman on her, and she milking a cow with three teats. Cuchulain was passing by, and there was thirst on him, and he asked a drink, and she gave him the milk of one teat. 'May this be to the good of the giver,' he said, and with that her eye that was wounded was healed. Then she gave him milk from another teat, and he said the same words; then she gave him the milk from the third teat. 'The full blessing of the gods, and of the people of the plough, on you,' he said. And with that, all the wounds of the Great Queen were healed.

The Painted Skin

(Chinese)

At T'ai-Yüan there lived a man named Wang. One morning he was out walking when he met a young lady carrying a bundle and hurrying along by herself. As she moved along with some difficulty, Wang quickened his pace and caught her up, and found she was a pretty girl of about sixteen. Much smitten, he inquired whither she was going so early, and no one with her. 'A traveller like you,' replied the girl, 'cannot alleviate my distress; why trouble yourself to ask?' 'What distress is it?' said Wang; 'I'm sure I'll do anything I can for you.' 'My parents,' answered she, 'loved money, and they sold me as concubine into a rich family, where the wife was very jealous, and beat and abused me morning and night. It was more than I could stand, so I have run away.'

Wang asked her where she was going; to which she replied that a runaway had no fixed place of abode. 'My house,' said Wang, 'is at no great distance; what do you say to coming there?' She joyfully acquiesced; and Wang, taking up her bundle, led the way to his house. Finding no one there, she asked Wang where his family were; to which he replied that that was only the library. 'And a very nice place, too,' said she; 'but if you are kind enough to wish to save my life, you mustn't let it be known that I am here.' Wang promised he would not divulge her secret, and so she remained there for some days without anyone knowing anything about it. He then told his wife, and she, fearing the girl might belong to some influential family, advised him to send her away. This, however, he would not consent to do; when one day, going into the town, he met a Taoist priest, who looked at him in astonishment, and asked him what he had met. 'I have met nothing,' replied Wang. 'Why,' said the priest,

'you are bewitched; what do you mean by not having met anything?'
But Wang insisted that it was so, and the priest walked away, saying,
'The fool! Some people don't seem to know when death is at hand.'
This startled Wang, who at first thought of the girl; but then he
reflected that a pretty young thing as she was couldn't well be a
witch, and began to suspect that the priest merely wanted to do
a stroke of business.

When he returned, the library door was shut, and he couldn't get
in, which made him suspect that something was wrong; and so he
climbed over the wall, where he found the door of the inner room
shut too. Softly creeping up, he looked through the window and saw
a hideous devil, with a green face and jagged teeth like a saw,
spreading a human skin upon the bed and painting it with a paint-
brush. The devil then threw aside the brush, and giving the skin a
shake out, just as you would a coat, threw it over his shoulders, when
lo! it was the girl. Terrified at this, Wang hurried away with his head
down in search of the priest, who had gone he knew not whither;
subsequently finding him in the fields, where he threw himself on
his knees and begged the priest to save him. 'As to driving her away,'
said the priest, 'the creature must be in great distress to be seeking
a substitute for herself; besides, I could hardly endure to injure a
living thing.' However, he gave Wang a fly-brush, and bade him
hang it at the door of the bedroom, agreeing to meet again at the
Ch'ing-ti temple.

Wang went home, but did not dare enter the library; so he hung
up the brush at the bedroom door, and before long heard a sound
of footsteps outside. Not daring to move, he made his wife peep out;
and she saw the girl standing looking at the brush, afraid to pass it.
She then ground her teeth and went away; but in a little while came
back, and began cursing, saying, 'You priest, you won't frighten me.
Do you think I am going to give up what is already in my grasp?'
Thereupon she tore the brush to pieces and bursting open the
door, walked straight up to the bed, where she ripped open Wang
and tore out his heart, with which she went away. Wang's wife
screamed out, and the servant came in with a light; but Wang was
already dead and presented a most miserable spectacle. His wife,
who was in an agony of fright, hardly dared cry for fear of making a
noise; and next day she sent Wang's brother to see the priest. The
latter got into a great rage, and cried out, 'Was it for this that I had
compassion on you, devil that you are?' proceeding at once with
Wang's brother to the house, from which the girl had disappeared

without anyone knowing whither she had gone. But the priest, raising his head, looked all round, and said, 'Luckily she's not far off.' He then asked who lived in the apartments on the south side, to which Wang's brother replied that he did; whereupon the priest declared that there she would be found. Wang's brother was horribly frightened and said he did not think so; and then the priest asked him if any stranger had been to the house. To this he answered that he had been out to the Ch'ing-ti temple and couldn't possibly say: but he went off to inquire, and in a little while came back and reported that an old woman had sought service with them as a maid-of-all-work, and had been engaged by his wife. 'That is she,' said the priest, as Wang's brother added she was still there; and they all set out to go to the house together. Then the priest took his wooden sword and standing in the middle of the courtyard, shouted out, 'Base-born fiend, give me back my fly-brush!'

Meanwhile the new maid-of-all-work was in a great state of alarm, and tried to get away by the door; but the priest struck her and down she fell flat, the human skin dropped off, and she became a hideous devil. There she lay grunting like a pig, until the priest grasped his wooden sword and struck off her head. She then became a dense column of smoke curling up from the ground, when the priest took an uncorked gourd and threw it right into the midst of the smoke. A sucking noise was heard, and the whole column was drawn into the gourd; after which the priest corked it up closely and put it in his pouch. The skin, too, which was complete even to the eyebrows, eyes, hands and feet, he also rolled up as if it had been a scroll, and was on the point of leaving with it, when Wang's wife stopped him, and with tears entreated him to bring her husband to life. The priest said he was unable to do that; but Wang's wife flung herself at his feet, and with loud lamentations implored his assistance. For some time he remained immersed in thought, and then replied, 'My power is not equal to what you ask. I myself cannot raise the dead; but I will direct you to someone who can, and if you apply to him properly you will succeed.' Wang's wife asked the priest who it was; to which he replied, 'There is a maniac in the town who passes his time grovelling in the dirt. Go, prostrate yourself before him, and beg him to help you. If he insults you, show no sign of anger.' Wang's brother knew the man to whom he alluded, and accordingly bade the priest adieu and proceeded thither with his sister-in-law.

They found the destitute creature raving away by the roadside, so filthy that it was all they could do to go near him. Wang's wife approached him on her knees; at which the maniac leered at her, and cried out, 'Do you love me, my beauty?' Wang's wife told him what she had come for, but he only laughed and said, 'You can get plenty of other husbands. Why raise the dead one to life?' But Wang's wife entreated him to help her; whereupon he observed, 'It's very strange: people apply to me to raise their dead as if I was king of the infernal regions.' He then gave Wang's wife a thrashing with his staff, which she bore without a murmur, and before a gradually increasing crowd of spectators. After this he produced a loathsome pill which he told her she must swallow, but here she broke down and was quite unable to do so. However, she did manage it at last, and then the maniac crying out, 'How you do love me!' got up and went away without taking any more notice of her. They followed him into a temple with loud supplications, but he had disappeared, and every effort to find him was unsuccessful. Overcome with rage and shame, Wang's wife went home, where she mourned bitterly over her dead husband, grievously repenting the steps she had taken, and wishing only to die. She then bethought herself of preparing the corpse, near which none of the servants would venture, and set to work to close up the frightful wound of which he died.

While thus employed, interrupted from time to time by her sobs, she felt a rising lump in her throat, which by and by came out with a pop and fell straight into the dead man's wound. Looking closely at it, she saw it was a human heart; and then it began as it were to throb, emitting a warm vapour like smoke. Much excited, she at once closed the flesh over it, and held the sides of the wound together with all her might. Very soon, however, she got tired, and finding the vapour escaping from the crevices, she tore up a piece of silk and bound it round, at the same time bringing back circulation by rubbing the body and covering it up with clothes. In the night she removed the coverings, and found that breath was coming from the nose; and by next morning her husband was alive again, though disturbed in mind as if awaking from a dream and feeling a pain in his heart. Where he had been wounded, there was a cicatrix about as big as a cash, which soon after disappeared.

Lilith and the Blade of Grass

(*Jewish*)

Once a Jew was seduced by Lilith and smitten by her charms. Yet he was sorely troubled by it, and so he set out for the tsaddik Rabbi Mordecai of Neschiz to ask for help.

Now the rabbi knew by clairvoyance that the man was coming, and he warned all the Jews of the town not to let him into their houses or give him a place to sleep. And so, when the man arrived and found nowhere to spend the night, he went away and lay down on a haystack in a barnyard. At midnight Lilith came to him and whispered, 'My love, come down to me from that haystack.'

'Why should I come to you?' asked the man. 'You always come to me.'

'My love,' said Lilith, 'in that haystack is a blade of grass that I'm allergic to.'

'Well, then,' said the man, 'why don't you show it to me? I'll throw it away and you can come.'

As soon as Lilith showed it to him, he took it and tied it round his neck, thus saving himself forever from her clutches.

Daughter of the Moon,
Son of the Sun

(Siberian)

All through the day the Sun rides through the sky in his golden sledge. At dawn it is drawn by Polar Bear, at midday by Buck Reindeer, and at dusk by Doe Reindeer. Many are the chores the Sun must attend to: granting life to all that lives, nourishing the green moss and trees, giving light and strength to all beasts and birds and to the Saami people, that they may grow strong and multiply.

Towards twilight, when the Sun gets weary, he sinks down to the sea; all he then wishes is to rest and sleep, to regain his powers for the coming day.

But one evening, as Doe Reindeer drew the Sun towards his watery couch, the Sun's handsome son Peivalke spoke up.

'Father, it is time for me to marry.'

'Have you chosen your bride?' asked the Sun, wearily.

'Not yet. I have tried my golden boots on all the earthly maids and not one would wear them. Their feet are so heavy and clumsy, they cannot follow me up to the sky.'

'Then you have sought wrongly,' said the Sun, with a yawn. 'Tomorrow I shall speak to the Moon: she has a daughter. Though she is poorer than us, the Moon's daughter does dwell in the heavens and will make you a worthy bride.'

So the Sun rose early as day dawned, just as his neighbour the moon was about to take her rest.

'Tell me, my pale companion,' he said, 'is it not true that you have a daughter? I have found a worthy husband for her – she is indeed fortunate, for he is none other than my own son Peivalke.'

The Moon's bright countenance grew dim.

'My child is still too young. When I hold her close I hardly notice she is there; a puff of wind would bear her off. How can such a mite marry your son?'

'It matters not,' said the Sun. 'My tent is spacious and bountiful. She will be nourished well and will soon grow strong. Come, bring her to my son.'

'Oh no!' cried the Moon, aghast, and swiftly drew a white cloud about her child. 'Your Peivalke would scorch her delicate skin. What is more, she is already promised to Nainas, the Northern Lights. There he is now walking proudly across the ocean down below.'

'So that's it then!' said the Sun, gruffly. 'You reject my son for those miserable coloured stripes? Lest you be unmindful, my humble companion, it is I who give life to all things. I am all-powerful.'

'Your power, neighbour, is but half the power there is,' murmured the Moon, softly. 'When dusk comes your powers recede into the night. And throughout the dark night? And the long winter? Where is your power then? Nainas shines on in winter too, piercing the gloom of night with his cheerful rays.'

These words only angered the Sun even more.

'I'll wed my son to your daughter, just see if I don't!' he blazed.

Thunder rolled across the heavens, the wind howled, the waves towered white with rage above the ocean, and the mountains shook in dread. The herds of reindeer huddled close and the Saami tribes trembled in corners of their summer shelters.

The Moon scurried away into the darkness of the night.

'I must keep my child safe from the Sun's angry gaze,' she thought.

Looking down from the sky she spied a small island in the middle of a lake where an old man and his wife lived.

'To that old pair,' the Moon said, 'I shall entrust my daughter. She will be safe there.'

By and by the Sun tired of his ranting: the thunder became still, and the wind's wail died, and the waves settled back into the sea. And it was just about that time that the old man and his wife went into the forest to strip birch bark for sandals. They were astonished to hear a tiny voice crying above their heads: 'Niekia, Niekia, help me, help me.'

And there on a branch of a fir tree they saw a silver cradle rocking to and fro. As the old man reached to take it down, he saw a child lying there; she was like any other save that she gleamed as moonlight, a silver pallor covering her tender skin.

The old pair carried the cradle home, overjoyed at their good fortune. They tended her carefully, brought her up as their own daughter, and she did all they told her dutifully. Yet every night, before she went to bed, she would leave the hut, raise her pallid face to the Moon, lift up her arms and shine more brightly than before. When in playful mood she would call 'Niekia, Niekia' and melt away to nothing, leaving but the merry echo of her laughter.

So the old folk called her Niekia.

As the days passed, Niekia grew into a tall and slender maid with a bright face as round as cloudberries, her fair plaits strung like silver threads. The lovely moon maiden learned to make quilts of reindeer hide and embroider them with beads and silver.

In the passage of time, word reached the Sun that on the island in that lake there lived a maid uncommon to the daughters of men. So he sent his son Peivalke to seek her out; no sooner did the radiant young Sun gaze upon the silver maid than he fell deeply in love with her.

'Earth maiden, try on these golden boots,' said Peivalke.

Niekia blushed, but did as she was bid. Straightaway, she cried out in pain: 'Oh, they are burning my feet! How hot they are.'

'You will get used to them,' smiled Peivalke, reassuringly.

But before his eyes she melted into a misty haze and the golden boots stood empty on the ground.

Wrapped in quivering moonbeams, Niekia hid in the forest until nightfall. Then, as the Moon rose in the sky, Niekia followed her mother's light through the forest and across the cold tundra. At last, as dawn was breaking, she came to the shores of the oceans, to a lonely hut standing on the barren strand. Without a thought, Niekia entered the hut and found it empty. It was so untidy that she at once fetched a pail of sea-water and set to washing the hut. Her work done, she turned herself into an old spindle, hung herself up on the wall, and fell asleep.

As twilight cast its dark shadows upon the shore, heavy footsteps woke Niekia and she saw a group of warriors enter, all clad in silver armour, and each more handsome and stronger than the next. They were the Northern Lights led by their eldest brother, Nainas.

'Our hut is so clean,' said Nainas in amazement. 'A good house-wife has visited us. Though I know not where she is hiding, I can feel the keen gaze of her eyes upon us.'

The brothers sat down to supper and when they had finished they began a mock battle among themselves, striking at one another with their sabres, making white sparks and crimson flashes that danced and soared into the sky. Then, tired from their sword-fight, the brothers sang songs about the bold warriors of the sky, each flying off in turn until at last only Nainas remained.

'Now, dear housewife,' he pleaded, 'please show yourself. Should you be of respected years, you shall be a mother to us. Should you be of middle years, you shall be our sister; and should you be yet young, you shall be my bride.'

'Here I am, judge for yourself,' said a soft voice behind him.

As he turned he saw a slim and lovely figure standing in the dim light of early dawn. And he recognized the lovely daughter of the Moon.

'Will you be my wife, Niekia?' he asked.

'Yes, Nainas,' she answered, so quietly he could barely hear her.

Just at that moment the first flush of dawn spread across the sky as the top of the Sun's head appeared.

'Wait for me here, Niekia,' cried Nainas, and was gone.

Every evening, Nainas and his brothers flew back to their home on the shore, fought their sword-battle and then, at sunrise, flew away again.

'Please stay with me just for one day,' Niekia begged Nainas.

'That I cannot,' said Nainas. 'Across the ocean I must engage in the battle of the skies. Should I remain, the Sun would pierce me right through with his shafts of fire.'

As she waited in her lonely hut, Niekia wondered how she might detain her dear Nainas. And in her solitude she sang a song to her beloved.

He is tall like mountain ash,
His hair covers his shoulders
Like squirrels' tails.
When he disappears
I lie down in my hut.
Oh, how long is a spring day?
But the evening comes
And through a hole in the hut
I see my love coming.
When he enters and looks at me
My heart melts
Like snow in the sun.

When she had finished, an idea came to her: she would make a quilt of reindeer hide, and embroider on it the stars and the Milky Way. That she did and, before the brothers returned home, she hung the quilt beneath the ceiling of the hut.

When night fell, Nainas flew home with his brother warriors. They played their games, had their supper, sang songs and lay down to rest. Nainas slept soundly. As dawn approached his eyes opened several times but, seeing the starlit sky with the Milky Way above him, he imagined it to be still night, too early to rise.

Niekia crept outside quietly some time after day had dawned, but forgot to close the hut door: in an instant, Nainas opened his eyes and saw the bright light of morning shining through the open door; he saw the Polar Bear pulling the Sun's golden sledge through the sky. At once he dashed from the hut calling his brothers after him.

But it was too late.

The Sun saw him, and sent down a shaft of fire that pinned him to the ground. Poor Niekia realized too late what she had done: she ran to her Nainas, shielding him from the Sun with her own body.

As she did so, Nainas struggled to his feet and flew off to safety in the heavens. The Sun seized Niekia by her plait, burned her with his fiery gaze and summoned his son Peivalke.

'You may burn me to a cinder, but I shall never marry Peivalke,' wept the daughter of the Moon.

In his fury, the Sun flung Niekia into the arms of her mother. And Mother Moon caught her, pressed her to her breast and still holds her safe and close to this day.

If you look closely at the moon, you will see the shadow of Niekia's fair face upon her mother's bosom. Niekia is there watching the pale glimmer over the ocean of the battle of the Northern Lights across the evening sky, and pining for her beloved Nainas.

The Loving Fox

(Japanese)

A man was once walking at twilight along Suzaku Avenue in Kyoto when he met an extraordinarily beautiful woman. She seemed happy enough to let him strike up a conversation with her, and from close up he found her even more alluring. Unable even to imagine letting the opportunity pass, he filled her ears with so many sweet nothings that he soon very nearly had what he burned for.

The woman tried to hold him off. 'Now that we've gotten this far,' she said, 'I'd like so much to go all the way! But you see, if we do you'll die.'

Much too excited to listen, the man kept pressing himself on her until she gave in. 'I really can't refuse you,' she said, 'since you insist so urgently. Very well then, I'll do whatever you wish and die in your place. If you want to show me gratitude, copy the Lotus Sutra and dedicate it for me.'

The man seemed not to take her seriously, and he finally consummated his desire. They lay in each other's arms all night long, chatting like old lovers. At dawn the woman got up and asked the man for his fan. 'I meant what I said, you know,' she told him, 'I'm going to die instead of you. If you want proof, go into the palace grounds and look around the Butoku Hall. You'll see.' Then she left.

At daylight the man went to the Butoku Hall and found there a fox lying dead with his fan over its face. He was very sorry. Every seven days after that he finished a copy of the Lotus Sutra and dedicated it for the fox's soul. On the night following the forty-ninth day he dreamed that she came to him, surrounded by angels, and told him that thanks to the power of the Teaching she was to be born into the Tōri Heaven.

The Story of Aristomenes

(Latin)

' "I had gone to Macedonia on business, as you probably know, and I was coming home after ten months with a tidy sum of money when, just before reaching Larissa, I was waylaid by bandits in a wild valley and robbed of practically everything but my life. Well, I managed to get away from them in the end and, almost at my last gasp, reached this town. Here I went to an inn run by a woman named Meroë. She was no longer young but extraordinarily attractive, and when I told her my sad story and explained how anxious I was to return home after my long absence, she pretended to be deeply sympathetic, cooked me a grand supper for which she charged me nothing, and afterwards pressed me to sleep with her. But from the moment that I first climbed into her bed my mind began to sicken and my will-power to fail. While I was still well enough to work for a living I gave her what little money I picked up by carrying bags, and then, as I grew weaker, I even presented her with the clothes that the kind robbers had left me to cover my nakedness. And now you see the condition into which bad luck and a charming woman have brought me."

' "Good God," I said, "you deserve all this and more, if possible, for having deserted your home and children and made yourself a slave to an old bitch like that!"

' "Hush, hush," he cried, a forefinger to his lips, looking wildly round in case we were overheard. "Say nothing against that marvellous woman, or your tongue may be your ruin."

' "Really!" I said. "Then what sort of innkeeper can she be? From the way you talk, anyone would think that she was an absolute empress possessed of supernatural powers."

' "I tell you, Aristomenes," he answered in lugubrious tones, "my Meroë is able, if she pleases, to pull down the heavens or uplift the earth; to petrify the running stream or dissolve the rocky mountain; to raise the spectral dead or hurl the gods from their thrones; to quench the bright stars or illuminate the dark Land of Shadows."

' "Come, come, Socrates, this is the language of melodrama! Ring down the curtain for pity's sake and let me have the story in plain words."

'He answered: "Will a single instance of her powers convince you? Or must you have two, or more? Her ability to make men fall passionately in love with her – not only Greeks, but Indians, and eastern and western Egyptians and even, if she pleases, the mythical inhabitants of the Antipodes – this is only a slight sample of her powers. If you want to hear of the greater feats that she has performed in the presence of reliable witnesses, I will mention a few. Well, first of all, one of her lovers dared have an affair with another woman; she only needed to pronounce a single word and he was transformed into a beaver."

' "Why a beaver?"

' "Because the beaver, when alarmed by the hunt, bites off its own testicles and leaves them lying by the river bank to put the hounds off the scent; and Meroë hoped that this would happen to him. Then there was the old innkeeper, her neighbour and rival, whom she transformed into a frog; and now the poor fellow swims around in one of his own wine casks, or buries himself in the lees, croaking hoarsely to his old customers: 'Walk up! Walk up!' And the barrister who had once been briefed to prosecute her: his punishment was ram's horns, and now you can see him any day in court bleating his case and making learned rebuttals, with the horrible things curling from his forehead. Finally, when the wife of another of her lovers spoke nastily about her, Meroë condemned her to perpetual pregnancy by putting a charm on her womb that prevented the child from being born. This was about eight years ago; and now the poor woman swells bigger and bigger every month until you would believe her to be on the point of bearing a young elephant."

' "But when all these things came to be generally known?"

' "Why, then there was a public indignation meeting, at which it was decided to stone her to death the next day. This single day's grace was enough for Meroë, just as it was for Medea when King Creon ordered her to quit Corinth. Medea, you remember, set fire to her supplanter's bridal head-dress; soon the whole palace was alight, and the new bride and Creon himself were both burned to death. But Meroë, as she confided to me the next morning when drunk, dug a trench and performed certain rites over it, and by the dark power of the spirits that she invoked, she laid a spell on the gates and doors of every house in Hypata, so that for forty-eight hours nobody could come out into the streets, not even by tunnelling through a house wall. In the end the whole town had to appeal to her from their windows, promising if she freed them never to molest her again but, on the contrary, always to defend her against harm; then she relented and removed the spell. But she took her revenge on the chairman of the meeting by spiriting away his house at midnight – walls, floors, foundations and all, with himself inside – to a town a hundred miles off. This place stood on top of a waterless hill – the townspeople had to rely on rain-water for all purposes – and the buildings were so closely crowded together that there was no space to fit the house in; so she ordered it to be flung down outside the town gates."

'"My dear Socrates," I said, "these are certainly very wonderful and terrible stories and I am beginning to feel a little scared myself; in fact, really frightened. Suppose that your old woman were informed by her familiar spirits of all that we have been saying? But what do you say to going to sleep at once? The night is still young and we could make an early start tomorrow morning, getting as far away from this damned hole as our legs will take us."

'While I was speaking, poor Socrates suddenly fell asleep, and began snoring loudly: the natural effect of a good meal and plenty of wine on a man in his exhausted condition. I locked and barred the bedroom door, pushed the head of my bed against the hinge, shook up the mattress and lay down. For a time I could not sleep, because of Socrates's uncanny stories, but about midnight when I had comfortably dozed off, I was awakened by a sudden crash and the door burst open with greater force than if a pack of bandits had run at it with their shoulders. Lock, bar and hinges all gave way together and my bed, which was a worm-eaten old camp-bed, a bit short for me and with one damaged leg, was tossed into the air and fell upside down, pinning me underneath it.

'Emotions are contradictory things. You know how sometimes one weeps for joy; well now, after this terrible awakening, I found myself grinning and joking to myself: "Why, Aristomenes, you have been transformed into a tortoise!" Though knocked flat, I felt fairly safe under the bed and poked my head out sideways, like a tortoise

peeping under his shell, to watch what would happen next. Presently in came two terrible old women; one of them carried a lighted torch in her hand, the other a sponge and a drawn sword. They stood over Socrates, who was still asleep, and the one with the sword said to the other: "Look sister Panthia, here is the man whom I chose to be my sweetheart – as condescendingly as the goddess Diana chose the shepherd Endymion, or Olympian Jove chose that pretty little Ganymede. And a wonderfully hot time I gave him, too. But he never returned my girlish passion and fooled me day and night. Now I have caught him not only spreading scandal about me but actually planning to run off! He fancies himself an Odysseus, does he, and expects me to howl and sob like Calypso when she awoke and found herself alone on her island?" Then she pointed at me and said: "And this creature peeping at us from under the bed is Aristomenes, who put him up to his mischief: but if he hopes to get safely away from me he is making the mistake of his life. I'll see that he repents too late of all the nasty insulting things he said about me earlier tonight, and of this new impertinent prying."

'I broke into a cold sweat and began to tremble so violently that my spasms made the bed rattle and dance over me. But Panthia said to Meroë – she could only have been Meroë: "Sister, shall we tear him to pieces at once, or shall we first tie strong twine around his privates and haul him up to a rafter and watch them being slowly cut through?"

'"No, no, dear, nothing of that sort! Let him be for a while. My darling Socrates will be needing a sexton tomorrow to dig a little hole for him somewhere or other." Still speaking, she turned Socrates's head on the pillow and I watched her drive the sword up to the hilt through the left side of his neck. Blood spurted out, but she had a small bladder ready and caught every drop as it fell. Socrates's windpipe had been sliced through, but he uttered a sort of cry, or indistinct gurgle, and then was silent. To complete the sacrificial rite in what, I suppose, was her usual manner, this charming woman thrust her hand through the wound, deep into my poor friend's body, groped about inside and at length pulled out the heart. But Panthia took the sponge from her and stopped the gapping wound with it, muttering as she did so:

Sponge, sponge, from salt sea took,
Pass not over the running brook!

Then they came across the room to me, lifted away the bed, squatted over me and staled long and vigorously in my face.

'After this they left me; and no sooner had they crossed the threshold than the door rose up by itself and bar, lock and hinges miraculously refixed themselves in their original positions. I lay prostrate on the floor, naked, cold and clammy with loathsome urine. "A new-born child must feel like this," I said to myself. "Yet how different his prospects are! I have my whole life behind me, not in front of me. Yes, I'm as good as dead, like a criminal on his way to the cross. For what will become of me tomorrow morning when they find Socrates's corpse with his throat cut? Nobody will believe my story. 'You ought at least to have cried out for help if you were no match for the women,' they will tell me. 'A big strong man like you, allowing a friend's throat to be cut before your eyes and not uttering a word!'" But the night was now nearly over and at last I made up my mind to steal out of the inn before daylight and run off. I took up my bundle of belongings, drew the bolts of the door and put the key in its lock, but the honest old door which during the night had opened of its own accord to let my enemies in, now refused to let me out until I turned the key this way and that a score of times and rattled hard at the handle. Once outside in the court-yard I called out: "Hey, porter, where are you? Open the gate, I want to be off before daybreak."

'He was lying naked on the bare ground beside the gate and answered, still half-asleep: "Who's that? Who's asking to get off at this time of night? Don't you know, whoever you are, that the roads are swarming with bandits? You may be tired of life, or you may have some crime on your conscience, but don't think that I'm such a pumpkin-headed idiot as to risk my life for yours by opening the gate and letting them in."

'I protested: "But it's almost morning. And anyhow, what harm could bandits do you? Certainly I think you are an idiot to be afraid of them. A team of ten professional wrestlers couldn't take anything worth having from a man as naked as you are."

'He grunted, turned over on his other side and asked drowsily: "How do I know that you haven't murdered the man you brought in yesterday afternoon – running off at this unearthly hour?"

'I shall never forget how I felt when he said this. I had a vision of hell gaping for me and the old three-headed dog snarling hungrily. I was convinced that Meroë had refrained from cutting my throat only because of her vicious intention to get me crucified. I went back to my room, determined to kill myself in my own way. But how was I to set about it? I should have to call on my bed to help me. So I began talking to it. I said coaxingly: "Listen, bed, dear little bed, the only true friend that I have left in this cruel world, my fellow-sufferer and the sole witness of my innocence – please bed, lend me some clean, wholesome instrument to put me out of my misery. For I long to die, dear bed!" Anticipating the bed's reply, I began to tug out a length of the rope with which its frame was corded, made one end fast to a rafter which stuck out above the window, and knotted the other into a running noose. I climbed on the bed, put my neck into the noose, and then kicked the bed away.

'My attempt at suicide was a failure. The rope was old and rotten and broke under my weight. Down I tumbled. I rolled gasping and choking against the body of Socrates which was lying on its mattress not far off. And at that instant in came the porter and shouted: "Hey you, you who a moment ago were rearing to get on in such frantic haste, what are you doing here, wallowing on that mattress and grunting like a pig?"

'Before I could answer, Socrates sprang up, as if suddenly awakened – whether by my fall or the porter's hoarse voice was not clear – and said sternly: "I have often heard travellers cursing porters and their surly ways, and upon my word, they have every right to do so. I was tired out, and now this damned fellow bursts into the room and shouts at us – I am sure with the notion of stealing something while our attention is distracted – and spoils the deepest sleep that I have had for months."

'At the sound of Socrates's voice I jumped up in an ecstasy of relief and cried: "No, no, you are the best porter in the whole wide world, and honest as the day! But look, look, here's the man whom in your drunken daze just now you accused me of murdering – my friend, whom I love as dearly as a father or brother." I hugged and kissed Socrates, but he pushed me away crossly, saying: "Ugh, you stink like the bottom of a sewer!" and began offering unkind suggestions as to how I came to be in such a mess. In my confusion I made him some sort of lame excuse – I forget what – and turned the conversation as soon as possible. Catching hold of his hand, I cried: "What are we waiting for? Why not start at once and enjoy the freshness of the early morning air?"

'"Why not?" he sniffed. So I shouldered my bundle once more, settled my bill with the porter, and Socrates and I were out on the road.

'When we had gone some little distance from the town and the whole countryside stood out clear in the rising sun, I took a long careful look at Socrates's throat to see where, if at all, the sword had gone in. But nothing showed and I thought: "Here's Socrates as well as ever he was and without a scratch on him. No wound, no sponge, not even a scar to show where the sword went burrowing in, only a couple of hours ago. What a vivid and fantastic dream! I was mad to drink so much." And I said aloud: "The doctors are right. If you stuff your stomach the last thing at night and then flood it with drink you are bound to have nightmares. That was why I slept so poorly last night after our celebration; I had such a frightful dream that I still feel as though I were spattered with human blood."

'Socrates laughed. "Blood indeed! The plain truth is that you soaked your bed and still stink of it. But I agree with you about the cause of nightmares. Last night I had a terrible one myself, now I come to remember it: I dreamed that my throat was cut and I had all the sensations of agony from the wound, and then someone pulled my heart out, which was such an unspeakable experience that it makes me feel ill even to think of it. My knees are trembling so violently now that I must sit down. Have you anything for me to eat?"

'I opened my haversack and took out some bread and cheese. "What about breakfast under that big plane tree over there?" I asked.

'As we sat down together I noticed that his healthy looks had faded and that, though he ate ravenously, his face was turning the colour of boxwood. I must have looked almost as pale myself because the vision of that terrible pair of furies had repossessed my mind, and all the terrors of the night returned with a sudden rush. I took a small bite of bread, but it stuck in my gullet and I could neither swallow it nor cough it up. I grew more and more anxious. Would Socrates survive? By this time a number of people were about, and when two men are travelling together and one dies mysteriously by the roadside suspicion naturally falls upon the other. He ate a huge meal, a great deal of bread and nearly a whole cheese, and then complained of thirst. A few yards off, out of sight of the road, a brook ran gently past the roots of the tree. It was bright as silver, clear as crystal, placid as a pond, "Come here, Socrates," I said. "This looks better than milk. Have a good drink of it." He got up walked along the shelving bank until he found a place that suited him, knelt down, bent his head forward, and began to drink greedily. But hardly had his lips touched the water when the wound in his throat opened wide and the sponge dropped out into the water followed by a small trickle of blood. He would have fallen in after it, if I had not caught at one leg and lugged him up to the top of the bank. He was stone dead when I got him there.

'After a hurried funeral service I scraped away the sandy soil and laid him in his eternal resting place, there by the brookside. Then, trembling and sweating with fear, I ran across the fields, continually changing my direction, stumbling on and on, always making for the wildest and most desolate country . . .'

That was the end of Aristomenes's story.

Ala and the Old Hag

(Central African: Congo)

Two young men were on their way to a dancing party. They were singing and full of good cheer. Suddenly there appeared an old woman who begged them: 'Please take me on your backs!'

One of the men said: 'I won't, you smell and you have dirty wounds!' The other one, his name was Ala, had pity on her, and took her on his back. As soon as the old witch had settled down on his back, she began to pinch him and to push her dirty feet into his sides. His whole body ached and he wandered about aimlessly, for she was beginning to get him in her power. After several hours, hunger gnawed his stomach and he lamented his fate. Thirst, too, visited him; it settled in his throat and made it ache.

At last they came to a river. Ala said: 'Old woman, climb down, let us drink!' But she said: 'You can drink with me on your back.' So he had to keep her on his back all the time.

After many hours, he found a dead buffalo, lying in the grass. Ala said: 'Woman, come down, let us skin this animal. Let me make a fire so we can cook the meat and eat it.' She said: 'Go on, skin it with me on your back!' At last he asked: 'Don't you want to eat?' She replied: 'Yes, and you will put some good strips of meat for me on your shoulders.'

Ala went on wandering about in the savannah with the woman on his back for three months. Finally he fell down and lay on the ground. The old hag stepped off his back and looked at him closely, for a long time. When she was at last satisfied that he was dead, she went away. Ala got up and ran, ran for his life and freedom. She turned and saw him go, but it was too late, she could not overtake him. She took off her legs and arms and rolled behind

85

him, like a boulder rolling down a river bed, when the rains have come.

Ala arrived home. His sister saw him and called out: 'Mother, Ala has come back!' Their mother said: 'Do not joke with a mourning mother.' It was Ala himself, only he was very weak. They killed an ox which he ate, then another, then another, six in all, until finally his strength had returned.

Suddenly the old hag appeared and claimed her mount. They treated her politely, and gave her a stool, asking her to wait until her steed would be ready. In the meantime they quickly dug a pit, and covered it with grass. Then they put a cauldron of water to heat over the fire. When all was ready, they said: 'Wouldn't you like to have a wash?' The old woman went across the patch where fresh grass had been put out – to dry, apparently, for thatching. A well-mannered person would not have walked across it. However, she did, and as the pit lay beneath it, she fell down into it. Quickly they poured the hot water over her so that she died. Then they filled in the earth on top of her.

Ala's body regained its strength gradually. Everyone agreed that the old woman had been a dangerous witch who had sucked out his strength. Ala had been lucky to escape.

The Queen's Ring

(Pomeranian)

A queen went out to walk in the meadows. The queen was very beautiful, but she was also very sad: because many months ago the king, her dear husband, had gone away to the wars; and in all these months the queen had no news of him.

'But he cannot be dead,' said the queen to herself. 'If he were dead I should surely know it.'

So, after she had wandered here and there, the queen sat down by a well to rest. She often came to the well, because it was at this spot that the king had given her his last kiss before he rode away. And it was here that he had put on her finger a diamond ring, and said, 'Keep this ring carefully, look at it often, and when you look at it think of how much I love you!'

Now, as she sat by the well, the queen took the ring from her finger and laid it against her cheek. 'Dear ring,' said she, 'dear ring, night and day I think of him who gave you to me! Dear ring, tell me, oh tell me where he is!'

Then, oh me, what happened? The ring slipped from the queen's hand and fell into the well.

'My ring, my ring!' cried the queen, leaning over the water. The well was deep, and the ring had sunk to the very bottom of it – what was she to do? She leaned over the water, she couldn't even see the ring, no, not the least sparkle of it. 'My ring, my ring!' She wept and wept.

Then out of the well clambered a big green frog.

'Why do you weep, beautiful queen?' said the frog.

'My ring, my ring!' cried the queen. 'I have dropped it into the well, and I cannot, cannot get it again!'

'But surely the queen is rich – she can buy another ring?' said the frog.

'No, no, *no!*' cried the queen. 'Not another ring like this, for this ring my dear husband gave to me before he went away.'

'And do you value it so much because of that?' said the frog.

'I value it above everything else in the world!' cried the queen.

'Well then,' said the frog, 'if you will give me what I ask, I will dive back into the well and bring up your ring.'

'I will give you anything you ask,' said the queen.

'Is that a promise?' said the frog.

'That's a promise,' said the queen.

So the frog dived back into the well, and soon came up again, holding the ring in one of its webbed hands.

How the ring sparkled! How the queen laughed, though the tears were still on her cheeks. 'Oh, thank you, thank you, dear frog,' she said. 'And now, what shall I give you?'

'Just a kiss on my mouth,' said the frog.

'Oh!' said the queen. 'Oh, I cannot give you that!'

'Why not?' said the frog.

'Because,' said the queen, 'you are . . .' She was going to say, 'so ugly and slimy', but no, that would be too ungrateful. So she said, 'A queen can kiss no one but the king her husband.'

'Then I will put the ring back where I found it,' said the frog. And he was about to jump into the water again, when the queen cried out, 'No, no, I will kiss you, I will kiss you!'

And she picked up the frog, shut her eyes, and kissed its cold gaping mouth . . .

'Now open your eyes, my dearest!' said a laughing voice. Whose voice? The voice of the king her husband! Yes, the frog had vanished, and there in its place stood the king, her husband, stooping to take her in his arms.

And this is the tale he told her: 'After the war was over, my darling, I was riding home at the head of our victorious troops when we lost our way in a thick mist. My men rode this way and that way, searching for the road. I could hear their voices and the sound of their horses' hoofs growing fainter and fainter; and when the mist lifted it was night, and I found myself alone, in front of a small house in a deep forest. I got off my horse and went into the house to ask for a night's lodging; and in the house I found a beautiful damsel seated on an ivory stool before a golden spinning-wheel, spinning silver thread.

'"What will you give me in return for a night's lodging?" said the beautiful damsel.

'"Whatever you ask," said I, "and whatever I can."

'"You can easily give me what I ask," said the beautiful damsel. "All I ask is a kiss."

'"But that is something I cannot give," said I. "I kiss no one but my own dear queen."

'Then the damsel sprang up from her ivory stool. But she was no longer beautiful. She was indeed a hideous witch. "You call yourself a king!" she screamed, "you are nothing but a cold-blooded frog!" And she struck me with her distaff. Then my limbs dwindled, and my body shrank, my mouth grew wide, my eyes goggled. Yes, she had turned me into a frog.

'"A frog you are, and a frog you shall remain, until some lovely woman of her own free will kisses you on your gaping mouth!" she shrieked. And she took me up by one leg and flung me out through the door.

'"I kiss no one but my own dear queen," I said again, as I crept away into the forest.

'Then I began my weary journey home. Days and nights, days and nights went by. I passed through many kingdoms. Journeying by day, resting by night in some hidden corner of great palaces or peasants' cottages, I saw many lovely women, both high-born queens and princesses, and lowly village maidens. Perhaps one of them would have taken pity on me and kissed me had I asked them. "But no," I told myself. "I never have kissed any woman but my own dear queen, and I never will kiss any woman but my own dear queen. And if it takes me the rest of my life, I will come at last to where she waits for me."

'And so, my darling, the poor little frog journeyed on and on, through great cities, and over wide moors, through rushing rivers, and dense forests, on and on and on, until, at last, that poor little frog came home into his own kingdom. And the rest you know, my darling.'

Then the king put the ring back on the queen's finger, and hand in hand they returned to their palace, where they lived happily ever after.

PART FOUR

Transformations

The Grinning Face of
an Old Woman

(Japanese)

People often went hunting to an old pond in the Minase Hills which was frequented by flocks of water-birds, but something in the pond would catch the hunters and many of them died.

Three brothers, personal guards at the retired emperor's palace on the Minase River, were just setting off hunting when someone warned them to stay away from the pond. One of the three, Nakatoshi, refused to believe the story, and feeling anyway that it would be unworthy of him not to brave the pond's dangers, he set off undaunted, with just one young attendant.

It was evening and too dark even to see the path, but Nakatoshi got through the hills, found the pond, and waited on the bank under the overhanging branches of a pine. Deep in the night the water trembled and waves rolled across the pond. The frightened Nakatoshi fitted an arrow to his bowstring. Next, a luminous mass rose out of the pond and flew over the pine. As soon as Nakatoshi drew his bow the thing flew back to the pond, returning only when he relaxed and removed the arrow from the string. This happened several times till Nakatoshi understood that his bow would be no use. He put it down and drew his sword instead. This time the luminous mass came so close that Nakatoshi saw in the light the grinning face of an old woman.

With the light so unexpectedly close and the form inside it so clear, he dropped his sword and attacked barehanded. When the thing tried to drag him into the pond, he braced himself against the roots of the pine and resisted until he could draw his dagger and stab it. The light went out.

A hairy beast lay dead at Nakatoshi's feet. It was a badger.

Nakatoshi carried it back to his room at the Minase Palace and went to bed. The next morning his two brothers came to find out how his expedition had gone.

'Look at that!' cried Nakatoshi, and threw the badger out to them.

They were deeply impressed.

The Red Woman

(*Irish*)

One time the Fianna were in Almhuin with no great work to do, and there came a very misty morning, and Finn was in dread that sluggishness would come on his men, and he rose up, and he said: 'Make yourselves ready, and we will go hunting to Gleann-na-Smol.'

They all said the day was too misty to go hunting; but there was no use in talking: they had to do as Finn bade them. So they made themselves ready and went on towards Gleann-na-Smol; and they were not gone far when the mist lifted and the sun came shining out.

And when they were on the edge of a little wood, they saw a strange beast coming towards them with the quickness of the wind, and a Red Woman on its track. Narrow feet the beast had, and a head like the head of a boar, and long horns on it; but the rest of it was like a deer, and there was a shining moon on each of its sides.

Finn stopped, and he said: 'Fianna of Ireland', he said, 'Did you ever see a beast like that one until now?' 'We never did indeed,' said they; 'and it would be right for us to let out the hounds after it.' 'Wait a while,' said Finn, 'till I speak with the Red Woman; but do not let the beast go past you,' he said. They thought to keep back the beast then, going before it; but they were hardly able to hinder it at all, and it went away through them.

And when the Red Woman was come up to them, Finn asked her what was the name of the beast she was following. 'I do not know that,' she said, 'though I am on its track since I left the borders of Loch Dearg a month ago, and I never lost sight of it since then; and the two moons that are on its two sides shine through the country all around in the night time. And I must follow it till it falls,' she said, 'or I will lose my own life and the lives of my three sons that are the best fighting men in the whole world.' 'We will take the beast for you if you have a mind,' said Finn. 'Do not try to do that,' she said, 'for I myself am swifter than you are, and I cannot come up with it.' 'We will not let it go till we know what sort of a beast is it,' said Finn. 'If you yourself or your share of men go after it, I will bind you hand and foot,' said she. 'It is too stiff your talk is,' said Finn. 'And do you not know,' he said, 'I am Finn, son of Cumhal; and there are fourscore fighting men along with me that were never beaten yet.' 'It is little heed I give to yourself or your share of men,' said the Red Woman; 'and if my three sons were here, they would stand up against you.' 'Indeed it will be a bad day,' said Finn, 'when the threat of a woman will put fear on myself or on the Fianna of Ireland.' With that he sounded his horn, and he said: 'Let us all follow now, men and dogs, after that beast that we saw.'

He had no sooner said that word than the woman made a great water-worm of herself, and made an attack on Finn, and she would have killed him then and there but for Bran being with him. Bran took grip of the worm and shook it, and then it wound itself round Bran's body, and would have crushed the life out of her, but Finn thrust his sharp sword into its throat. 'Keep back your hand,' said the worm then, 'and you will not have the curse of a lonely woman upon you.' 'It is what I think,' said Finn, 'that you would not leave me my life if you could take it from me; but go out of my sight now,' he said, 'and that I may never see you again.'

Then she made herself into a Red Woman again, and went away into the wood.

All the Fianna were gone on the track of the beast while Finn was talking and fighting with the Red Woman; and he did not know in what place they were, but he went following after them, himself and Bran. It was late in the evening when he came up with a share of them, and they still on the track of the beast. The darkness of the night was coming on, but the moons in the sides of the beast gave a bright light, and they never lost it from sight. They followed it on always; and about midnight they were pressing on it, and it began to scatter blood after it, and it was not long before Finn and his men were red from head to foot. But that did not hinder them, and they followed him on till they saw him go in at the foot of Cnoc-na-righ at the breaking of day.

When they came to the foot of the hill the Red Woman was standing there before them. 'You did not take the beast,' she said.

'We did not take it, but we know where it is,' said Finn.

She took a Druid rod then, and struck a blow on the side of the hill, and on the moment a great door opened, and they heard sweet music coming from within. 'Come in now,' said the Red Woman, 'till you see the wonderful beast.' 'Our clothing is not clean,' said Finn, 'and we would not like to go in among a company the way we are,' he said.

She put a horn to her mouth and blew it, and on the moment there came ten young men to her. 'Bring water for washing,' she said, 'and four times twenty suits of clothes, and a beautiful suit and a crown of shining stones for Finn, son of Cumhal.' The young men went away then, and they came back at the end of a minute with water and with clothing.

When the Fianna were washed and dressed, the Red Woman brought them into a great hall, where there was the brightness of the sun and of the moon on every side. From that she brought them into another great room; and although Finn and his men had seen many grand things up to that time, they had never seen any sight so grand as what they saw in this place. There was a king sitting in a golden chair, having clothes of gold and of green, and his chief people were sitting around him, and his musicians were playing. And no one could know what colour were the dresses of the musicians, for every colour of the rainbow was in them. And there was a great table in the middle of the room, having every sort of thing on it, one better than another.

The king rose up and gave a welcome to Finn and to his men, and he bade them to sit down at the table; and they ate and drank their fill, and that was wanting to them after the hunt they had made. And then the Red Woman rose up, and she said: 'King of the Hill, if it is your will, Finn and his men have a mind to see the wonderful beast, for they spent a long time following after it, and that is what brought them here.'

The king struck a blow then on his golden chair, and a door opened behind him, and the beast came through it and stood before the king. And it stooped down before him, and it said: 'I am going on towards my own country now; and there is not in the world a runner so good as myself, and the sea is the same to me as the land. And let whoever can come up with me come now,' it said, 'for I am going.'

With that the beast went out from the hill as quick as a blast of wind, and all the people that were in it went following after it. It was not long till Finn and his men were before the rest, in the front of the hunt, gaining on the beast.

And about midday Bran made the beast turn, and then she forced it to turn a second time, and it began to put out cries, and it was not long until its strength began to flag; and at last, just at the setting of the sun, it fell dead, and Bran was at its side when it fell.

Then Finn and his men came up, but in place of a beast it was a tall man they saw lying dead before them. And the Red Woman came up at the same time, and she said: 'High King of the Fianna, that is the King of the Firbolgs you have killed; and his people will put great troubles on this country in the time to come, when you yourself, Finn, and your people will be under the sod. And I myself am going now to the Country of the Young,' she said, 'and I will bring you with me if you have a mind to come.' 'We give you our thanks for that,' said Finn, 'but we would not give up our own country if we were to get the whole world as an estate, and the Country of the Young along with it.' 'That is well,' said the Red Woman; 'but you are going home empty after your hunt.' 'It is likely we will find a deer in Gleann-na-Smol,' said Finn. 'There is a fine deer at the foot of that tree beyond,' said the Red Woman, 'and I will rouse it for you.' With that she gave a cry, and the deer started out and away, and Finn and his men after it, and it never stopped till it came to Gleann-na-Smol, but they could not come up with it. Then the Red Woman came to them, and she said: 'I think you are tired now with following after the deer; and call your hounds off now,' she said, 'and I will let out my own little dog after it.' So Finn sounded a little horn he had at his side, and on the moment the hounds came back to him. And then the Red Woman brought out a little hound as white as the snow of the mountains, and put it after the deer; and it was not long till it had come up with the deer and killed it, and then it came back and made a leap in under the cloak of the Red Woman. There was great wonder on Finn; but before he could ask a question of the Red Woman, she was gone out of sight. And as to the deer, Finn knew there was enchantment on it, and so he left it there after him. And it is tired and empty the Fianna were, going back to Almhuin that night.

The Woman Who Turned Her Husband Into a Snake

(North American: Cochiti)

In Cochiti there were four sisters. They lived all together. The eldest was married. Her husband slept with his wife one night. Next day he slept with her sister. The third night with the third, the fourth with the fourth. When the fourth night was over he had slept with the four sisters. They were all pregnant. People talked about it. They said, 'Wonder who lay with those girls?' Even his wife did not know who had made her sisters pregnant.

When their babies were born, all four were born at the same time. They were all very small babies and they looked just like the brother-in-law. People talked about this. They said, 'The husband of the eldest sister lay with these girls.' His wife heard this. 'I didn't know my husband lay with all my sisters. He hasn't any sense.' She was angry. 'I shall do something to him.' She had a medicine stone. She didn't tell anyone what she was going to do. She went out with her husband, and they came to an *arroyo* bank. 'Look, I found something pretty.' 'Let me see.' 'I found it.' He liked it. She said, 'Stand over there. You may have it if you catch it.' She rolled it to him. He ran after it and caught it. As soon as he touched it he turned into a snake. She said, 'Go off now! See if you come across any good luck. I didn't know you were treating me the way you did. Now all you can eat is cornmeal and pollen.' The wife came back to her house. She left her sisters. Nobody knew which way she went.

Kertong

(Chinese)

Once upon a time there lived in Soochow a farmer so industrious that he not only kept his fields and pastures in neat array, but tended his house just as tidily. People in the village nearby laughed and said he had no need of a wife – the only work he allotted to anyone else was the cleaning of his water barrel, and for that he kept a large snail 'living-in', so to speak. There were times, however, that the farmer grew morose and wished for someone to share his life, someone who would be waiting for him at day's end, happy to welcome him home.

One bright morning during the fall harvest he had no time to wash up the dishes or tidy the house before going to the fields. When he returned home that evening he was astounded to find the dishes clean, the house in good order and, in addition, a pot of steaming hot rice waiting on the stove.

'It's not possible!' he exclaimed. 'I surely locked the door when I left this morning! Who could have come in to do this?' He searched the house, but there was no one to be found. 'Now there is a fine thing,' he mused. 'If I were to believe in fairy creatures, I would think . . .'

But he didn't think very long, for he was worn out after the day's hard work, and went to bed and to sleep soon after he had supped.

The next morning he got up as usual at cock's crow. But someone or something had been there before him. When he stepped into the kitchen, he found breakfast ready and his lunch nicely packed in a basket. Again he searched the house but found nothing and nobody. He went thoughtfully off to the fields, leaving his house in disorder but with carefully locked door.

Upon his return, he found the house in order and dinner prepared as before. From that day on, he never had to clean or tidy his house or cook his meals. Everything was done for him by his mysterious helper.

One morning he awoke before daybreak, before the cock crew, and lay thinking about the breakfast he was sure to find on the stove, when he heard little noises coming from the kitchen. Quietly he got out of bed and crept to the kitchen door. There, standing at the stove with her back to him, was the graceful figure of a young woman.

Rubbing his eyes for a better look, he moved forward – incautiously. He fell over a low stool. The maiden fled into the courtyard without a backward glance. He ran after her as fast as he could, but there was only a loud, hollow 'kertong' over near the water barrel, and not so much as a shadow of the maiden. Though he searched diligently over every inch of ground, he could find no slightest trace of her. He knew then that she had to be a fairy creature.

The farmer had an aged aunt who was well-versed in the ways of fairies, sprites and other such creatures, and he remembered her telling him one time that fairy creatures who took human form could retain their humanness if they were fed human food. It could do no harm to try.

Accordingly, he stayed up all that night, hiding behind the kitchen door in wait. Very early the next morning he heard a noise from the courtyard and the next instant saw the maiden enter the kitchen. As soon as her attention was entirely on the food she was preparing, he tiptoed from his hiding place and caught her in his arms. Without a word he forced a rice ball between her lips and made her swallow it.

'Creature! Dear elfin creature!' he cried.

'Let me go,' said the maiden quietly, 'else I shall never come again.'

'Then promise not to disappear?'

'Very well.'

Reassured, he let go, and she turned round to face him. He was overjoyed to see that she was very beautiful, and he stared at her for some time before he could recover himself. Then, with a start, he said with the utmost courtesy, 'Dear fairy creature, please sit down.'

'I am neither fairy nor elf,' said she tartly, 'and I don't care to be called "creature". I am here to help you, but if you treat me badly at any time, I shall leave you at once.'

'Oh, no! Please no!' He fell to his knees. 'Please do not go away. Stay and keep me company for ever!'

'Only if you do exactly as I tell you. First, get up off your knees.'

He scrambled to his feet and stood before her, eager to follow her simplest command.

'Every day,' she said, 'you will go to work as usual. When you leave, lock the door as you have always done. I shall care for you and your house as long as you keep silent about my existence. Do you understand?'

'Yes, yes, anything you say!' he promised. 'Anything!'

'You must never tell anyone at all about me!'

'I won't, I won't! I promise you!' From then on, he was never lonely. The maiden taught him songs to sing, and he sang them as he worked in the fields. She entertained him with enchanting stories. His clothes – jacket, trousers, shoes, socks – all were kept fresh clean and so meticulously mended that the stitches were not to be seen. He laughed easily now, and so readily joked with his friends and neighbours that they found him a good companion instead of the old bent stick he had been heretofore. They began to invite him to go with them to the tavern, but he always withstood their coaxings in favour of going home to his maiden.

One evening, however, to help celebrate the birth of a neighbour's grandchild, he went with several friends to a tavern. The wine flowed, and too much of it flowed down the farmer's throat, where it loosened his voice. Before he knew what was happening, he was telling his friends the whole story of the mysterious maiden who kept house for him. Even as he finished, he realized his appalling mistake and begged his friends not to repeat the story. 'For I shall be in deep trouble if it gets about.'

His friends shook their heads in grave doubt. 'What makes you think she is a *good* spirit? Suppose she is evil? Brother, consider! Your whole life may be ruined by this infatuation!'

'Spirits are risky,' said one of his friends in deep earnestness. 'Even the best of them are hardly to be trusted, not when they are inside one's house, preparing one's food. Who is to know when they might decide to stir in a little, well, a little bane, for instance, or something that will make you into a spirit exactly like *them?*'

'Yes,' said another. 'Just as you forced the rice ball down her throat, who knows when she might force something even worse down yours!'

'Not to be trusted!' they all agreed.

Disturbed, the farmer went home. He had defended the maiden against his friends' suspicious questionings, but the worm of doubt had crawled inside him.

He kept a close watch on the maiden's every movement, and took to coming home at unusual times and getting up extremely early in order to catch her unawares. Out of his spyings and sneakings, he was able to garner only one small fact: whenever the maiden disappeared in the courtyard, there was a small 'kertong', as if something had been dropped into the water barrel.

The next time he heard the 'kertong', then, he went to look into the barrel. There was only the big snail moving sluggishly at the bottom.

'Oh, no!' he whispered to himself, appalled. 'Surely she cannot be the spirit of the snail? Bewitched by a *snail?* Oh, no!'

He set off at once to see his old aunt. He told her everything and begged her to think of some way to save him from the snail spirit. His aunt, a wise old woman, counselled caution in a matter such as this, but her nephew insisted that the idea of being companioned by a snail was so repellent that he could no longer bear to look upon her, for he could think only of snail slime.

His aunt sighed. 'Then you have no need of my wisdom,' she said. 'You already know that pouring salt on a snail will kill it.'

He stared at her for a moment, and then turned and ran out of the door.

Back home, he pretended that everything was as usual. At nightfall, the maiden disappeared in the courtyard. When the farmer heard the 'kertong' he rushed to the water barrel with a cup of salt . . . but the snail was gone!

Bewildered, he slowly undressed and got into bed, daring to hope that his friends had been wrong.

Shortly after midnight he was awakened by a knock at the door. The maiden stood on his doorstep!

Completely forgetting his earlier suspicions, he received her joyfully – but the maiden recoiled from him with a shudder. 'Wretched man!' she said, and her voice struck cold into his heart. 'I have come only to take leave of you.'

'No!' he cried. 'Do not say it!'

Tears of anger and of hurt welled into her eyes and streamed down her face. 'I came to you to help you because you were a gentle, good man; I asked only that you tell no one. You broke that promise and because of your wagging tongue, you then tried to do me harm. You have repaid my kind offices with spiteful malice. You have broken the bond between us, and it cannot be patched like a torn shirt.'

The farmer struggled to beg her forgiveness, to offer his excuses, to implore her to stay, but before a single word could leave his tongue, he realized that it was too late.

She had vanished completely.

The farmer took up his old lonely life, and again cooked meals and cleaned the house and mended his own clothes when he wasn't in the fields, but now he had a new occupation. In memory of the snail spirit, he raised many a family of snails in his water barrel, daring to hope that one day he would again hear a happy 'kertong' in his courtyard.

If he did, of course, he never told anyone.

The Boy and the Hare

(Irish)

'Eh . . . There's another story about eh, years ago, when the landlord the Gages, they were the landlords, they owned the island, they used to take friends out from the mainland for a day's shooting on the island. You know, shooting the ducks and shooting the hares, and they had em . . . pheasants and all on the island. It was well stocked and eh, they were going to the Upper End to shoot some hares you see? So on the way up em . . . they met a small boy you see, and they said to him, they had dogs with them, and they said to him, "If you can find a whin bush with a hare in it, we'll get, you know, and tell us on the way back down, we'll give you a half-crown." You see?

'So em, you know, at that time a half-crown was a small fortune. The wee boy went home and he told his granny, and you know. And she say to him, "There's a hillock on the way to the Upper End, it's called Doads, and eh . . . ," she said to him, "you go up to Doads and wait for them coming back, and eh," she said, "you know the bush, the whin bush growing along the road," she says, "and in the whin bush there'll be a hare." You see? So, eh anyway the wee boy done this and eh the, eh, went up and waited for it. But now in telling his granny you know about eh, getting the half-crown for the hare and all, he forgot to tell them that the Gages had the dogs with them, these hounds with them for hunting the hares. So eh they . . . on the way down again the wee boy pointed out you know where the eh bush was with the hare in it. And they surrounded the bush you see, with the dogs and the hare bolted out of the bush and the dogs set off in pursuit. Eh . . . anyway the hare run down the hill, right down Doads and down the back where the church is up there, and back down and disappeared in this wee boy's granny's door you see. And eh when they caught up with it, the dogs were going mad, the door closed you see and the dogs were going mad eh . . . at the door, and the Gages run up and opened the door, and ah . . . there the granny was sitting at the fire, she hadn't a breath, she was gasping, at the fire and ah the wee boy says, to her, he says, "By God Granny," he says, "you beat the dogs," he says, "and I've got the half-crown." So, that was supposed to be, the granny could turn herself into a hare you see. So eh this is another of the tales.'

Roland

(German)

Once upon a time there lived a real old witch who had two daughters, one ugly and wicked, whom she loved very much, because she was her own child; and the other fair and good, whom she hated, because she was her stepdaughter. One day the stepchild wore a very pretty apron, which so pleased the other that she turned jealous, and told her mother she must and would have the apron. 'Be quiet, my child,' said she, 'you shall have it; your sister has long deserved death. Tonight, when she is asleep, I will come and cut off her head; but take care that you lie nearest the wall, and push her quite to the side of the bed.'

Luckily the poor maiden, hid in a corner, heard this speech, or she would have been murdered; but all day long she dared not go out of doors, and when bedtime came she was forced to lie in the place fixed for her; but happily the other sister soon went to sleep, and then she contrived to change places and get quite close to the wall.. At midnight the old witch sneaked in, holding in her right hand an axe, while with her left she felt for her intended victim; and then raising the axe in both her hands, she chopped off the head of her own daughter.

As soon as she went away, the maiden got up and went to her sweetheart, who was called Roland, and knocked at his door. When he came out she said to him, 'Dearest Roland, we must flee at once; my stepmother would have killed me, but in the dark she has murdered her own child: if day comes, and she discovers what she has done, we are lost!'

'But I advise you,' said Roland, 'first to take away her magic wand, or we cannot save ourselves if she should follow and catch us.'

So the maiden stole away the wand, and taking up the head dropped three drops of blood upon the ground: one before the bed, one in the kitchen, and one upon the step: this done, she hurried away with her lover.

When the morning came and the old witch had dressed herself, she called to her daughter and would have given her the apron, but no one came. 'Where are you?' she called. 'Here upon the step,' answered one of the drops of blood. The old woman went out, but seeing nobody on the step, she called a second time. 'Where are you?' 'Hi, hi, here in the kitchen; I am warming myself,' replied the second drop of blood. She went into the kitchen, but could see nobody; and once again she cried, 'Where are you?'

'Ah! here I sleep in the bed,' said the third drop; and she entered the room, but what a sight met her eyes! There lay her own child covered with blood, for she herself had cut off her head.

The old witch flew into a terrible passion, sprang out of the window, and looking far and near, presently spied out her stepdaughter, who was hurrying away with Roland. 'That won't help you!' she shouted; 'were you twice as far, you should not escape me.' So saying, she drew on her boots, in which she went an hour's walk with every stride, and before long she overtook the fugitives. But the maiden, as soon as she saw the witch in sight, changed her dear Roland into a lake with the magic wand, and herself into a duck, who could swim upon its surface. When the old witch arrived at the shore, she threw in breadcrumbs, and tried all sorts of means to entice the duck; but it was all of no use, and she was obliged to go away at evening without accomplishing her ends. When she was gone the maiden took her natural form, and Roland also, and all night long till daybreak they travelled onwards. Then the maiden changed herself into a rose, which grew amid a very thorny hedge, and Roland became a fiddler. Soon after up came the old witch, and said to him, 'Good player, may I break off your flower?' 'Oh! yes,' he replied, 'and I will accompany you with a tune.' In great haste she climbed up the bank to reach the flower, and as soon as she was in the hedge he began to play, and whether she liked it or not she was obliged to dance to the music, for it was a bewitched tune. The quicker he played, the higher was she obliged to jump, till the thorns tore all the clothes off her body, and scratched and wounded her so much that at last she fell down dead.

Then Roland, when he saw they were saved, said, 'Now I will go to my father, and arrange the wedding.'

'Yes,' said the maiden, 'and meanwhile I will rest here, and wait for your return, and, that no one may know me, I will change myself into a red stone.'

Roland went away and left her there, but when he reached home he fell into the snares laid for him by another maiden, and forgot his true love, who for a long time waited his coming; but at last, in sorrow and despair of ever seeing him again, she changed herself into a beautiful flower, and thought that perhaps someone might pluck her and carry her to his home.

A day or two after a shepherd who was tending his flock in the field chanced to see the enchanted flower; and because it was so very beautiful he broke it off, took it with him, and laid it by in his chest. From that day everything prospered in the shepherd's house, and marvellous things happened. When he arose in the morning he found all the work already done; the room was swept, the chairs and tables dusted, the fire lighted upon the hearth, and the water fetched; when he came home at noonday the table was laid, and a good meal prepared for him. He could not imagine how it was all done, for he could find nobody ever in his house when he returned, and there was no place for any one to conceal himself. The good arrangements certainly pleased him well enough, but he became so anxious at last to know who it was, that he went and asked the advice of a wise woman. The woman said, 'There is some witchery in the business; listen one morning if you can hear anything moving in the room, and if you do and can see anything, be it what it will, throw a white napkin over it, and the charm will be dispelled.'

The shepherd did as he was bid, and the next morning, just as day broke, he saw his chest open and the flower come out of it. He instantly sprang up and threw a white napkin over it, and immediately the spell was broken, and a beautiful maiden stood before him, who acknowledged that she was the handmaid who, as a flower, had put his house in order. She told him her tale, and she pleased the shepherd so much, that he asked her if she would marry him, but she said, 'No,' for she would still keep true to her dear Roland, although he had left her: nevertheless, she promised still to remain with the shepherd, and see after his cottage.

Meanwhile, the time had arrived for the celebration of Roland's wedding, and, according to the old custom, it was proclaimed through all the country round, that every maiden might assemble to sing in honour of the bridal pair. When the poor girl heard this, she was so grieved that it seemed as if her heart would break, and she would not have gone to the wedding if others had not come and taken her with them.

When it came to her turn to sing, she stepped back till she was quite by herself, and as soon as she began. Roland jumped up, exclaiming, 'I know the voice! that is my true bride! no other will I have!' All that he had hitherto forgotten and neglected to think of was suddenly brought back to his heart's remembrance, and he would not again let her go.

And now the wedding of the faithful maiden to her dear Roland was celebrated with great magnificence; and their sorrows and troubles being over, happiness became their lot.

The Snake Wife

(Japanese)

A beautiful woman appeared at the home of a man who was grieving over the death of his wife. They married and presently a child was born. When it came time, the wife asked her husband not to look under any circumstance. After making doubly sure, she went into the room to deliver her baby. The man could not endure his worry and looked in secretly. There he saw a great snake coiled around a baby. He was dumbfounded, but he withdrew and said nothing about it. The woman came out on the seventh day carrying a lovely little boy, but she was weeping bitterly. She said she could stay no longer because her true form had been seen. She scooped out her left eye and gave it to her husband. She told him to let the baby suck it if he cried. He cared for the baby by letting it suck the eye, but the eye began to grow smaller after a while until it was completely gone. The father put his child onto his back and went to the pond in the hills to look for his wife. The great snake appeared and took out her remaining eye and gave it to him. She asked that a bell be hung near the lake and rung at the sixth hour of the morning and evening. She hid in the lake again. The father furnished the temple by the pond with a bell and arranged to have time marked. When the child grew up, he learned about his birth and went to the pond to meet his mother. She appeared in human form as a blind woman. He put her on his back and carried her home and lived with her as a dutiful son.

The Old Woman in the Wood

(German)

Once upon a time a poor Servant Girl was travelling with her boxes through a wood, and just as she got to the middle of it she found herself in the power of a ferocious band of robbers. All at once they sprang out of the brushwood, and came towards her; but she jumped out of her cart in terror, and hid herself behind a tree. As soon as the robbers had disappeared with their booty she came from her hiding-place, and saw her great misfortune. She began to cry bitterly, and said to herself, 'What shall I do now, a poor girl like me; I cannot find my way out of the wood; nobody lives here, and I must perish with hunger?' She looked about for a road, but could not find one; and when evening came she sat down under a tree, and, commending herself to God, determined to remain where she was, whatever might happen. She had not sat there a long while before a little White Pigeon came flying towards her, carrying in his beak a small golden key. The bird put the key into the Girl's hand, and said, 'Do you see yon great tree? Within it is a cupboard, which is opened with this key, and there you will find food enough, so that you need not suffer hunger any longer.' The Girl went to the tree, and, unlocking it, found pure milk in a jug, and white bread fit to break into it; and of these she made a good meal. When she had finished, she said to herself, 'At home now the cocks and hens are gone to roost, and I am so tired I should like to go to bed myself.' In a moment the Pigeon flew up, bringing another gold key in his bill, and said, 'Do you see yon tree? Open it and you will find a bed within!' She opened it, and there stood the little white bed; and, after saying her prayers and asking God's protection during the night, she went to sleep. In the morning the Pigeon came for the third time, bringing another key, with which he told the Girl to open a certain tree, and there she would find plenty of clothes. When she did so, she found dresses of all kinds ornamented with gold and precious stones, as beautiful as any princess could desire. And here in this spot the Maiden dwelt for a time; while the Pigeon every day brought her what she needed; and it was a very quiet and peaceful life.

One day, however, the Pigeon came and asked the Maiden whether she would do an act of love for him. 'With all my heart!' was her reply. 'I wish you then,' said the Pigeon, 'to come with me to a little cottage, and to go into it, and there on the hearth you will see an old Woman, who will say, "Good-day!" But for my sake give her no answer, let her do what she will: but go past her right hand, and you will see a door which you must open, and pass into a room, where upon a table will lie a number of rings of all descriptions, and among them several with glittering stones; but leave them alone, and look out a plain one which will be there, and bring it to me as quickly as possible.'

The Maiden thereupon went to the cottage, and stepped in; and there sat an old Woman who made a great face when she saw her, but said, 'Good-day, my child!' The Maiden made no answer, but went towards the door. 'Whither are you going?' cried the old Woman, 'that is my house, and nobody shall enter it unless I wish!' and she tried to detain the Maiden by catching hold of her dress. But she silently loosened herself, and went into the room, and saw the heap of rings upon the table, which glittered and shone before her eyes. She threw them aside and searched for the plain ring, but could not find it; and while she searched she saw the old Woman slip in and take up a birdcage, with which she made off. So the Maid pursued her, and took the birdcage away from her. As she looked at it she saw the ring in the bill of the bird which was in it. She took the ring and ran home, joyfully expecting the White Pigeon would come and fetch the ring, but he did not. So she leaned herself back against her tree and waited for the bird; but presently the tree became as it were weak and yielding, and its branches began to droop. All at once the boughs bent round, and became two arms; and as the Maiden turned round, the tree became a handsome man, who embraced and kissed her, saying, 'You have saved me out of the power of the old Woman, who is an evil witch. She changed me into a tree a long while ago, and every day I became a White Pigeon for a couple of hours; but so long as she had possession of the ring I could not regain my human form.' Thereupon his servants and horses recovered also from the enchantment, for they likewise had been changed into trees; and once more they accompanied their master to his kingdom (for he was a King's son), and there he married the Maiden, and they lived happily ever afterwards.

The Leopard Woman

(Liberian)

A man and a woman were once making a hard journey through the bush. The woman had her baby strapped upon her back as she walked along the rough path overgrown with vines and shrubbery. They had nothing to eat with them, and as they travelled on they became very hungry.

Suddenly, emerging from the heavily wooded forest into a grassy plain, they came upon a herd of bush cows grazing quietly.

The man said to the woman, 'You have the power of transforming yourself into whatever you like; change now to a leopard and capture one of the bush cows, that I may have something to eat and not perish.' The woman looked at the man significantly, and said, 'Do you really mean what you ask, or are you joking?' 'I mean it,' said the man, for he was very hungry.

The woman untied the baby from her back, and put it upon the ground. Hair began growing upon her neck and body. She dropped her loincloth; a change came over her face. Her hands and feet turned into claws. And, in a few moments, a wild leopard was standing before the man, staring at him with fiery eyes. The poor man was frightened nearly to death and clambered up a tree for protection. When he was nearly to the top, he saw that the poor little baby was almost within the leopard's jaws, but he was so afraid that he couldn't make himself come down to rescue it.

When the leopard saw that she already had the man good and frightened, and full of terror, she ran away to the flock of cattle to do for him as he had asked her to. Capturing a large young heifer, she dragged it back to the foot of the tree. The man, who was still as far up in its top as he could go, cried out,

115

and piteously begged the leopard to transform herself back into a woman.

Slowly, the hair receded, and the claws disappeared, until finally, the woman stood before the man once more. But so frightened was he still, that he would not come down until he saw her take up her clothes and tie her baby to her back. Then she said to him, 'Never ask a woman to do a man's work again.'

Women must care for the farms, raise breadstuffs, fish, etc., but it is a man's work to do the hunting and bring in the meat for the family.

The Three Crones

(Italian)

There were once three sisters who were all young. One was sixty-seven, another seventy-five, and the third ninety-four. Now these girls had a house with a nice little balcony, in the very middle of which was a hole for looking down on people passing along the street. The ninety-four-year-old sister, seeing a handsome young man approach, grabbed her finest scented handkerchief and sent it floating to the street just as the youth passed under the balcony. He picked it up, noticed the delightful scent, and concluded, 'It can only belong to a very beautiful maiden.' He walked on a way, then came back and rang the doorbell of that house. One of the three sisters answered the door, and the young man asked, 'Would you please tell me if a young lady lives in this mansion, by chance?'

'Yes indeed and not just one.'

'Would you do me a favour and allow me to see the one who lost this handkerchief?'

'No, that is impossible. A girl can't be seen before she's married. That's the rule at our mansion.'

The youth was already so thrilled just imagining the girl's beauty that he said, 'That's not asking a bit too much. I'll marry her sight unseen. Now I'm going to tell my mother I've found a lovely maiden whom I intend to marry.'

He went home and told his mother all about it. She said, 'Dear son, take care and don't let those people trick you. You must think before you act.'

'They're not asking a bit too much. I've given my word, and a king must keep his promise,' said the young man, who happened to be a king.

He returned to the bride's house and rang the doorbell. The same crone answered the door, and he asked, 'Are you her grandmother?'

'That's right, I'm her grandmother.'

'Since you're her grandmother, do me a favour and show me at least a finger of the girl.'

'No, not now. You'll have to come back tomorrow.'

The youth said goodbye and left. As soon as he was gone, the crones made an artificial finger out of the finger of a glove and a false fingernail. In the meantime his eagerness to see the finger kept him awake all night long. The sun came up at last, and he dressed and ran to the house.

'Madam,' he said to the crone, 'I've come to see my bride's finger.'

'Yes, yes,' she replied, 'right away. You'll see it through the keyhole of this door.'

The bride pushed the false finger through the keyhole. Bewitched by its beauty, the young man kissed the finger and slipped a diamond ring on to it. Head over heels in love by then, he said to the crone, 'I must marry her forthwith, Granny; I can't wait any longer.'

'You can marry her tomorrow, if you like.'

'Perfect! I'll marry her tomorrow, on my honour as a king!'

Being rich, the three old women were able to get everything ready overnight for the wedding, down to the tiniest detail. The next day the bride dressed with the help of her two sisters. The king arrived and said, 'I'm here, Granny.'

'Wait a minute, and we'll bring her to you.'

Here she came at last, arm in arm with her sisters and covered with seven veils. 'Remember,' said the sisters, 'you may not look at her face until you are in the bridal chamber.'

They went to church and got married. Afterward the king wanted them all to go to dinner, but the crones would not allow it. 'The bride, mind you, isn't used to such foolishness.' So the king had to keep quiet. He was dying for night to come when he could be alone with the bride. The crones finally took her to her room, but made him wait outside while they undressed her and put her to bed. At last he went in and found the bride under the covers and the two old sisters still busying about the room. He undressed, and the old women went off with the lamp. But he'd brought along a candle in his pocket. He got it, lit it, and what should he see but an old withered crone streaked with wrinkles!

For an instant he was speechless and paralysed with fright. Then in a fit of rage he seized his wife and hurled her through the window.

Under the window was a vine-covered trellis. The old crone went crashing through the trellis, but the hem of her night-gown caught on a broken slat and held her dangling in the air.

That night three fairies happened to be strolling through the gardens. Passing under the trellis, they spied the dangling crone. At that unexpected sight, all three fairies burst out laughing and laughed until their sides hurt. But when they had laughed their fill, one of them said, 'Now that we've had such a good laugh at her expense, we must reward her.'

'Indeed we must,' agreed another. 'I will that you become the most beautiful maiden in the world.'

'I will,' said the second fairy, 'that you have the most handsome of husbands and that he love you with his whole heart.'

'I will,' said the third fairy, 'that you be a great noblelady your whole life long.'

At that, the fairies moved on.

At dawn the king awakened and remembered everything. To make sure it wasn't just a bad dream, he opened the window in order to see the monster he'd thrown out the night before. But there on the trellis sat the loveliest of maidens! He put his hands to his head.

'Goodness me, what have I done!' He had no idea how to draw her up, but finally took a sheet off the bed, threw her an end to grab hold of, then pulled her up into the room. Overjoyed to have her beside him once more, he begged her to forgive him, which she did, and they became the best of friends.

In a little while a knock was heard on the door. 'It must be Granny,' said the king, 'Come in, come in!'

The old woman entered and saw in bed, in place of her ninety-four-year-old sister, the loveliest of young ladies, who said, as though nothing were amiss, 'Clementine, bring me my coffee.'

The old crone put a hand over her mouth to stifle a cry of amazement. Pretending everything was just as it should be, she went off and got the coffee. But the minute the king left the house to attend to his business, she ran to his wife and asked, 'How in the world did you become so young?'

'Shhhhh!' cautioned the wife. 'Lower your voice, please! Just wait until you hear what I did! I had myself planed!'

'Planed! Planed? Who did it for you? I'm going to get planed too.'

'The carpenter!'

The old woman went running to the carpenter's shop lickety-split. 'Carpenter, will you give me a good planing?'

'Oh, my goodness!' exclaimed the carpenter. 'You're already dead-wood, but if I plane you, you'll go to kingdom come.'

'Don't give it a thought.'

'What do you mean, not give it a thought? After I've killed you, what then?'

'Don't worry, I tell you. Here's a thaler.'

When he heard 'thaler', the carpenter changed his mind. He took the money and said. 'Lie down here on my workbench, and I'll plane you all you like,' and he proceeded to plane a jaw.

The crone let out a scream.

'Now, now! If you scream, we won't get a thing done.'

She rolled over, and the carpenter planed the other jaw. The old crone screamed no more: she was dead as dead can be.

Nothing more was ever heard of the other crone. Whether she drowned, had her throat slit, died in bed or elsewhere, no one knows.

The bride was the only one left in the house with the young king, and they lived happily ever after.

PART FIVE:

Guardians of the Seasons and Elements

The First People and the First Corn

(North America: Amerindian)

Long ago, Klos-kur-beh, the Great Teacher, lived in the land where no people lived. One day at noon, a young man came to him and called him 'Mother's brother'.

Standing before Klos-kur-beh, he said, 'I was born of the foam of the waters. The wind blew, and the waves quickened into a foam. The sun shone on the foam and warmed it, and the warmth made life, and the life was I. See – I am young and swift, and I have come to abide with you and to help in all that you do.'

Again on a day at noon, a maiden came, stood before the two, and called them 'my children'. 'My Children, I have come to abide with you and have brought with me love. I will give it to you, and if you will love me and will grant my wish, all the world will love me, even the very beasts. Strength is mine, and I give it to whosoever may get me. Comfort also is mine, for though I am young, my strength shall be felt over all the earth. I was born of the beautiful plant of the earth. For the dew fell on the leaf, and the sun warmed the dew, and the warmth was life, and that life is I.'

Then Klos-kur-beh lifted up his hands towards the sun and praised the Great Spirit. Afterward, the young man and the maiden became man and wife, and she became the first mother. Klos-kur-beh taught their children and did great works for them. When his works were finished, he went away to live in the Northland until it should be time for him to come again.

The people increased until they were numerous. When a famine came among them, the first mother grew more and more sorrowful. Every day at noon she left her husband's lodge and stayed away from him until the shadows were long. Her husband, who dearly loved her, was sad because of her sorrow. One day he followed her trail as far as the ford of the river, and there he waited for her to return.

When she came she sang as she began to ford the river, and as long as her feet were in the water she seemed glad. The man saw something that trailed behind her right foot, like a long green blade. When she came out of the water, she stooped and cast off the blade. Then she appeared sorrowful.

The husband followed her home as the sun was setting, and he bade her come out and look at the beautiful sun. While they stood side by side, there came seven little children. They stood in front of the couple, looked into the woman's face, and spoke: 'We are hungry, and the night will soon be here. Where is the food?'

Tears ran down the woman's face as she said, 'Be quiet, little ones. In seven moons you shall be filled and shall hunger no more.'

Her husband reached out, wiped away her tears, and asked, 'My wife, what can I do to make you happy?'

'Nothing else,' she said. 'Nothing else will make me happy.'

Then the husband went away to the Northland to ask Klos-kur-beh for counsel. With the rising of the seventh sun, he returned and said, 'O wife, Klos-kur-beh has told me to do what you asked.'

The woman was pleased and said, 'When you have slain me, let two men take hold of my hair and draw my body all the way around a field. When they have come to the middle of it, let them bury my bones. Then they must come away. When seven months have passed, let them go again to the field and gather all that they find. Tell them to eat it. It is my flesh. You must save a part of it to put in the ground again. My bones you cannot eat, but you may burn them. The smoke will bring peace to you and your children.'

The next day, when the sun was rising, the man slew his wife. Following her orders, two men drew her body over an open field until her flesh was worn away. In the middle of the field, they buried her bones.

When seven moons had passed by and the husband came again to that place, he saw it all filled with beautiful tall plants. He tasted the fruit of the plant and found it sweet. He called it *Skar-mu-nal* – 'corn'. And on the place where his wife's bones were buried, he saw a plant with broad leaves, bitter to the taste. He called it *Utar-mur-wa-yeh* – 'tobacco'.

Then the people were glad to their hearts, and they came to the harvest. But when the fruits were all gathered, the man did not know how to divide them. So he sent to the Great Teacher, Klos-kur-beh, for counsel. When Klos-kur-beh came and saw the great harvest, he said, 'Now have the first words of the first mother come to pass, for she said she was born of the leaf of the beautiful plant. She said also that her power should be felt over the whole world and that all men should love her.

'And now that she has gone into this substance, take care that the second seed of the first mother be always with you, for it is her flesh. Her bones also have been given for your good. Burn them, and the smoke will bring freshness to the mind. And since these things came from the goodness of a woman's heart, see that you hold her always in memory. Remember her when you eat. Remember her when the smoke of her bones rises before you. And because you are all brothers, divide among you her flesh and her bones. Let all share alike, for so will the love of the first mother have been fulfilled.'

Mistress of Fire

(Siberian)

This story began a long time ago when all Selkups lived in four great tents on a single camping ground.

One day the men went to the forest to hunt, leaving the women and children behind in the tents. At the end of three days, the hunters had still not returned and one of the women came out of her *yurta* to chop some firewood. She brought logs into the tent, threw them on to the hearth and, lighting a fire, drew close to it with her baby at her breast. Soon the fire was crackling merrily while the mother warmed her baby by its glow.

All of a sudden, a spark flew up, fell on the child and burnt him. In his pain the baby screamed and the mother sprang up very cross with the fire.

'Ungrateful fire!' she cried. 'I give you logs to burn and you harm my child. You'll get no more from me. I'll chop you up instead, pour water on you and put you out.'

Leaving her baby in the cot and taking up an axe, she first chopped away at the flames and then, picking up a potful of water, she dashed it on to the burning embers.

'Just you try to burn anyone now!' she cried. 'I've put you out good and proper: not a spark's left.'

Sot it was: the fire burned no more. It was dark now in the tent and so cold that the baby began to wail even louder than before. The mother became frightened by what she had done and tried to light the fire again; and although she tried hard, she blew and puffed, all her efforts were in vain.

As the baby's cries continued, she ran to her neighbours for a light. But the moment she pulled back the tent flap, the fire on her neighbour's hearth went out and could not be re-kindled. The same happened at every tent, even though she would open the tent flap just a fraction: the moment she appeared, the fires would splutter and smoke and then go out altogether.

All her kinsfolk scolded her and one old woman told her she had plainly offended the Mistress of Fire.

The mother began to cry at her plight: there was now no fire anywhere in the camp, no one could light one, and it was dark and cold in the tents.

'Come, let us go to your tent, girl,' the old woman said. 'I wish to see what you have done to anger the Mistress.'

Back in her own tent, the baby was crying even more than ever and it was colder than anywhere else in the camp. The old woman took two sticks of wood and rubbed them together in an effort to start a fire; yet though she worked patiently to kindle some fire, nothing came of it. But then, to her surprise, she saw a faint light appear on the hearth; she bent lower and peered hard. At first she could scarcely see anything, it being so dark; then gradually she made out the figure of an old crone crouching there. As the woman stared, the old crone's lined and withered face grew bright and rosy, seeming to radiate a glow as from a fire.

And then she spoke: 'Do not try to light a fire for you will not succeed. The mistress of this tent has offended me gravely, and I cannot forgive her. She chopped at my head and threw water in my face.'

'I knew that silly girl had done something wicked,' said the old woman. 'Please do not be angry with us all, Fire Mistress, she is young and stupid and has caused us all to suffer. Give us fire, I beg you.'

The Fire Mistress was silent, unmoved by the woman's pleas. After a long pause she finally spoke again: 'All right, I shall grant you fire on one condition: that stupid girl must give me her son. From his heart I shall kindle a flame. Knowing this, she will always respect fire and never treat it thoughtlessly again.'

Turning to the young mother, the old woman said: 'Because of you all seven tribes of man remain without fire. How are they to survive? There is nothing for it: though the judgement be harsh, you must give up your son to save us all!'

The mother wept, remorseful at her thoughtless act and heartbroken at the judgement it had brought upon her. But there was nothing for it: if the tribes of man were to be saved she had to sacrifice her child. And so she did.

When she had given up her child, the Mistress herself towered over her like a huge flame and spoke thus: 'Know now, O Selkups, that you must never touch fire with any tool of iron unless you are in great need. And then you should seek my permission first. Mind my words well.'

With that she touched the logs with her fingertips, setting them alight. The flames immediately leapt up and spiralled up to the very roof of the sky as the Fire Mistress swept up the child and vanished with him into the flames. Neither were ever seen again.

'A legend will be born this day,' said the old woman to the grieving mother. 'From mouth to mouth the story will be told of how a fire was lit from the heart of your child. And it was done to save the Selkup tribes.'

Anancy and the Hide-Away Garden

(Afro-Caribbean)

The garden belongs to Old Witch-Sister. Nobody is really ever supposed to see this garden. But Anancy keeps on hearing about the garden grown on rocks.

'It's the world's most glorious garden,' people whisper to Anancy.

'If allowed at all, not more than one stranger is ever supposed to see the garden,' people also whisper to Anancy.

Anancy sets out alone to find the garden.

Anancy finds himself in a desert of rocks. He climbs up a hillside of rocks. Getting up to the top, Anancy breathes like a horse pulling hard.

At the flat top of the hill, the garden is open wide to blue sky. Anancy stands fixed in surprise. Anancy is amazed.

'True-true. This is the richest garden in the whole world!' Anancy whispers to himself. 'The garden is growing, is fruiting, is ripening, is blossoming. Look at fattest vegetables! Look at shining fruits and flowers! Look at a garden of all reds, all oranges and browns, all yellows and purples!'

Anancy walks along the edge of the garden. Anancy can't help keeping on talking to himself. 'What a garden of fat vegetables. What a garden of flowers that stay in your eyes. What a garden of little fruit trees ripening and blossoming. What a garden sweet-smelling of plenty-plenty!'

Anancy bends down. He examines the rocky ground. Roots are gone down, hidden in rocks, shaped like smooth mounds of earth.

Anancy stands. He looks in wonder at the colourful garden in bright hot sunshine. Anancy whispers, 'Sunshine takes roots. Sunshine takes roots and grows like garden.'

Anancy turns round. He goes back down the rocky hillside singing:

Sunshine 'pon rocks gets dressed up like garden.
Sunshine 'pon rocks gets dressed up like garden.
Seeds get wings in a breeze-blow.
Seeds get wings in a breeze-blow.
Catch them, pocket them, plant them back of house, O!
Piece-piece luck comes quiet in one-one.
Breeze-blow seeds raise up stone-land!
Oh, catch them, pocket them, plant them back of house.
Oh catch them, pocket them, plant them back of house.
Sunshine 'pon rocks gets dressed up like garden, O!

Anancy stops singing. As he walks along, he begins to think again how the garden is rich and fat and colourful.

Anancy begins to think the garden should be his. He begins to feel how it feels having the garden. Anancy begins to count up what the garden can do for him. He reckons up that the garden can get mountains of praises for him. And in the heat of the day, he can lie back in a shade in the beautiful garden. He can stay there and listen to birds singing, and go off to sleep.

'Old Witch-Sister needs nothing beautiful!' Anancy says aloud.

Then Anancy laughs a funny laugh of excitement. In himself now he feels, he knows the Hide-Away Garden shall belong to him – Anancy!

But, Anancy remembers – nobody can just take away the garden easily. For one thing, the garden has a Gardener-man. He cares for the garden. He's also watchman of the garden. Then, some mysterious ways work with the garden that cannot ever be explained. Any food stolen from the garden makes the eater keep being sick till the robber is found out. Then, of great-great importance, there is the flute-playing by Gardener-man, who walks with a stick taller than himself.

With his stick lying beside him, Gardener-man sits on a comfortable pile of rocks at sunset every day. Sitting there, he plays his flute to the garden. He gives the garden his music till darkness covers him.

While the flute is playing, Old Witch-Sister always comes and listens. Dressed in red completely, Old Witch-Sister creeps up into the garden, unseen. Sometimes she just listens and goes away again. Other times, she begins to dance straightaway, on a flat rock near

the centre of the garden. But there is one big-big rule you see, that must be kept.

Gardener-man must never-never play his flute over a certain length of time. If Gardener-man should ever go on with the music over a certain length of time, he will not be able to stop playing. Also, if Old Witch-Sister happens to be dancing, she too will not be able to stop dancing.

Anancy goes and sees his son.

'Tacooma,' Anancy says, 'I want you to get Bro Blackbird KlingKling to get nine Blackbird KlingKling-cousins together with himself. I want them to do a careful-careful clever job. I want them to hide, to listen, to learn Gardener-man's music of the flute, exact-exact. I want them to learn, to know, to remember every, every slightest bit.'

The Blackbird-people creep up and listen unseen, as Anancy asks. Bro Blackbird KlingKling and cousins have sharp ears. They take in every sound of Gardener-man's flute music, quick-quick.

Anancy sends a message to Gardener-man. The message invites Gardener-man to come and eat with him. But, you see, Anancy goes and collects Gardener-man himself. And because he's setting a trap for Gardener-man, just listen to that Anancy. 'Oh, Mister Gardener-man, I just happen to be passing this way. And my good memory says we are eating together. And as you know, Bro Nancy isn't a man to miss a friendly company a little longer. So I come and call for you.'

Gardener-man walks with his stick taller than himself beside Anancy, towards Anancy's house. At this exact time, Anancy's son Tacooma makes his way to the Hide-Away Garden.

Quick-quick. Tacooma collects up some food from the garden.

Sunset comes. The Blackbird-people come and sit in Gardener-man's place, on the pile of rocks. The Blackbird-people begin to sing Gardener-man's flute playing, all to the garden.

The Bird-people work the singing in groups of three. When one group is stopping, the other group comes in smart-smart. Like that, the Blackbird-people carry on and on with Gardener-man's music, perfect-perfect.

With really sweet throats of the flute, the Blackbird-people sing and sing to the garden. Flute music fills the garden and the whole sunset evening, sweeter than when the Gardener-man himself plays.

Dressed all in red, slow-slow, Old Witch-Sister creeps up into the garden. On her flat rock, Old Witch-Sister begins to dance, slow-slow. Her long red skirt sways about a little bit at first. The skirt begins to sway about faster. Then the skirt begins to swirl and swirl. From head to toe, with arms stretched wide, Old Witch-Sister spins and spins and spins. Darkness comes down. Darkness finds Old Witch-Sister swirling as fast as any merry-go-round.

Last to sing, on his own, Bro KlingKling takes over the flute-singing. As Bro KlingKling's voice spreads over the garden, Old Witch-Sister drops down dead, in a heap of red clothes. Then, at Anancy's house, Gardener-man is the only one to eat the stolen food from the garden. Same time as Old Witch-Sister, Gardener-man drops down dead too.

Anancy gets himself busy. Anancy sees to it that Old Witch-Sister and Gardener-man get buried as far apart as possible. He sees to it too that Gardener-man's walking stick is buried with him.

Then Anancy jigs about. Dancing, Anancy says:

Sunshine 'pon rocks gets dressed up like garden.
Catch them, pocket them, plant them back of house, O!

Anancy begins to plan making a feast for himself, family and friends. He begins to plan too how he'll get Bro Dog, Bro Pig and Bro Jackass to work the garden.

Next day, early-early, Anancy starts out with Dog, Pig and Jackass and others to see the Hide-Away Garden.

They come to the garden. Anancy cannot believe his eyes. Every fruit and vegetable and flower and blossom is dried up. Every leaf is shrivelled and curled crisply. Anancy whispers, 'The whole garden is dried up. The Hide-Away Garden is dead. Dead! Really dead!'

Anancy sings:

Whai-o, story done, O!
Whai-o, story done, O.
The garden dead.
The garden dead.
The garden dead, O!

Everybody is sad. Even people who have never seen the garden get sad and very sad.

'That should never ever happen again,' people say.
Nobody likes people who play bad tricks.

Johnny, Draw the Knife

(Oral Irish)

They always say, and it is a fact, you always get three very large seas coming, and then you'll get a calm spell, you'll get three small ones. They always come in threes. I know from having connections down the west coast, they say that they come in lots of seven. You get seven very big heavy seas coming in, then you'll get seven smaller ones. Up in this part of the world you always get three very big ones coming. So there's a saying, if you're ever caught like that now, this was round the back of the island, there's big reefs, what we call 'bows'. If you were talking to somebody, and they said they seen a 'bow' breaking what they would really mean is, one of the reefs, seen the big swell breaking on it . . .

There was a bow round the other side of the island, and there was three fishermen out on it, out fishing, and instead of rowing out round the back of this bow, they decided to go underneath it. It was a short way of doing things. Now, you can stop, as I've said before, the seas always come in lots of three, three big and three small ones, but somehow they miscounted it, and they say if you do that, there's one way of stop . . . saving yourself. If the sea is going to overwhelm you, which it will, if you get a very big one, if you have a penknife of steel in your pocket, anything sharp, of steel, you know, something that will penetrate the flesh, and cast it into the middle of the wave, you'll be quite safe.

These three men were out fishing, the other side of the island, they'd miscalculated this, and instead of three, instead of counting three big waves going in, they'd only counted two. So they were underneath the reef, and they seen the third wave rising, so they realized then that they had miscounted it and they knew they were

134

going to be overwhelmed, so John says to father (there was a father and son and a neighbour in the boat). He says to his father, he says, 'We're done for,' he says, 'there's no way we're going to get clear.' He says, 'There's no point in rowing,' he says, 'we're not going to get clear of that.' And the father says to him, 'Oh,' he says. 'Aye,' he says, 'pull away,' he says. His father was steering the boat, and the sea was coming after him and the boat was running ahead of it, and there was no way they could do it. So the father says, 'Don't worry,' he says, 'we'll be all right.' And he put his hand in his pocket and took out his knife and he opened the knife, and just as the sea was about to overwhelm him, he fired his knife into the centre of the wave, and it just went on by them, and they were all right. But, as it went by them, a woman appeared in the back of the wave, and she said as the sea was going by (this woman appeared, and the knife was stuck in her breast) and she says to them, she says to the father, 'Johnny,' she says, 'draw the knife.' And he says, 'I won't.' And she says, 'John, draw the knife.' And he says, 'I won't.'

So that was all right. The father didn't go back to sea again, so he explained to the son all about it . . . that the next one would have got them. So he says to him, he says, that he couldn't go back, because some misfortune would happen him in the boat, that this was his one chance, he had taken his chance, he had forfeited his chance, and that he couldn't do it again. So he would have to pay a price for it. Now if he had went back they say that the boat would have maybe capsized, or upset, or the sea would have taken them back, anyway, so this is why he never went back to sea.

So, they say that if this happens, you're supposed to take out your knife and throw it in the centre of the wave, but that's it. You'll save yourself, and you'll save everybody on the boat, but you must forfeit something, you must give up the fishing.

The Snow-Daughter and
the Fire-Son

(Icelandic)

There was once upon a time a man and his wife, and they had no children, which was a great grief to them. One winter's day, when the sun was shining brightly, the couple were standing outside their cottage, and the woman was looking at all the little icicles which hung from the roof. She sighed, and turning to her husband said, 'I wish I had as many children as there are icicles hanging there.' 'Nothing would please me more either,' replied her husband. Then a tiny icicle detached itself from the roof, and dropped into the woman's mouth, who swallowed it with a smile, and said, 'Perhaps I shall give birth to a snow child now!' Her husband laughed at his wife's strange idea, and they went back into the house.

But after a short time the woman gave birth to a little girl, who was as white as snow and as cold as ice. If they brought the child anywhere near the fire, it screamed loudly till they put it back into some cool place. The little maid throve wonderfully, and in a few months she could run about and speak. But she was not altogether easy to bring up, and gave her parents much trouble and anxiety, for all summer she insisted on spending in the cellar, and in the winter she would sleep outside in the snow, and the colder it was the happier she seemed to be. Her father and mother called her simply 'Our Snow-daughter', and this name stuck to her all her life.

One day her parents sat by the fire, talking over the extraordinary behaviour of their daughter, who was disporting herself in the snow-storm that raged outside. The woman sighed deeply and said, 'I wish I had given birth to a Fire-son!' As she said these words, a spark from the big wood fire flew into the woman's lap, and she said with a laugh, 'Now perhaps I shall give birth to a Fire-son!' The man

136

laughed at his wife's words, and thought it was a good joke. But he ceased to think it a joke when his wife shortly afterwards gave birth to a boy, who screamed lustily till he was put quite close to the fire, and who nearly yelled himself into a fit if the Snow-daughter came anywhere near him. The Snow-daughter herself avoided him as much as she could, and always crept into a corner as far away from him as possible. The parents called the boy simply 'Our Fire-son', a name which stuck to him all his life. They had a great deal of trouble and worry with him too; but he throve and grew very quickly, and before he was a year old he could run about and talk. He was as red as fire, and as hot to touch, and he always sat on the hearth quite close to the fire, and complained of the cold; if his sister were in the room he almost crept into the flames, while the girl on her part always complained of the great heat if her brother were anywhere near. In summer the boy always lay out in the sun, while the girl hid herself in the cellar: so it happened that the brother and sister came very little into contact with each other – in fact, they carefully avoided it.

Just as the girl grew up into a beautiful woman, her father and mother both died one after the other. Then the Fire-son, who had grown up in the meantime into a fine, strong young man, said to his sister, 'I am going out into the world, for what is the use of remaining on here?'

'I shall go with you,' she answered, 'for, except you, I have no one in the world, and I have a feeling that if we set out together we shall be lucky.'

The Fire-son said, 'I love you with all my heart, but at the same time I always freeze if you are near me, and you nearly die of heat if I approach you! How shall we travel about together without being odious the one to the other?'

'Don't worry about that,' replied the girl, 'for I've thought it all over, and have settled on a plan which will make us each able to bear with the other! See, I have had a fur cloak made for each of us, and if we put them on I shall not feel the heat so much nor you the cold.' So they put on the fur cloaks, and set out cheerfully on their way, and for the first time in their lives quite happy in each other's company.

For a long time the Fire-son and the Snow-daughter wandered through the world, and when at the beginning of winter they came to a big wood they determined to stay there till spring. The Fire-son built himself a hut where he always kept up a huge fire, while his

137

sister with very few clothes on stayed outside night and day. Now it happened one day that the King of the land held a hunt in this wood, and saw the Snow-daughter wandering about in the open air. He wondered very much who the beautiful girl clad in such garments could be, and he stopped and spoke to her. He soon learnt that she could not stand heat, and that her brother could not endure cold. The King was so charmed by the Snow-daughter, that he asked her to be his wife. The girl consented, and the wedding was held with much state. The King had a huge house of ice made for his wife underground, so that even in summer it did not melt. But for his brother-in-law he had a house built with huge ovens all round it, that were kept heated all day and night. The Fire-son was delighted, but the perpetual heat in which he lived made his body so hot, that it was dangerous to go too close to him.

One day the King gave a great feast and asked his brother-in-law among the other guests. The Fire-son did not appear till everyone was assembled, and when he did, everyone fled outside to the open air, so intense was the heat he gave forth. Then the King was very angry and said, 'If I had known what a lot of trouble you would have been, I would never have taken you into my house.' Then the Fire-son replied with a laugh, 'Don't be angry, dear brother! I love heat and my sister loves cold – come here and let me embrace you, and then I'll go home at once.' And before the King had time to reply, the Fire-son seized him in a tight embrace. The King screamed aloud in agony, and when his wife, the Snow-daughter, who had taken refuge from her brother in the next room, hurried to him, the King lay dead on the ground burnt to a cinder. When the Snow-daughter saw this she turned on her brother and flew at him. Then a fight began, the like of which had never been seen on earth. When the people, attracted by the noise, hurried to the spot, they saw the Snow-daughter melting into water and the Fire-son burn to a cinder. And so ended the unhappy brother and sister.

Mother Holle

(German)

Once upon a time there was a widow who had two daughters; one of them was pretty and clever, and the other ugly and lazy. But as the ugly one was her own daughter, she liked her far the best of the two, and the pretty one had to do all the work of the house, and was in fact the regular maid of all work. Every day she had to sit by a well on the high road, and spin till her fingers were so sore that they often bled. One day some drops of blood fell on her spindle, so she dipped it into the well meaning to wash it, but, as luck would have it, it dropped from her hand and fell right in. She ran weeping to her stepmother, and told her what had happened, but she scolded her harshly, and was so merciless in her anger that she said: 'Well, since you've dropped the spindle down, you must just go after it yourself, and don't let me see your face again until you bring it with you.'

Then the poor girl returned to the well, and not knowing what she was about, in the despair and misery of her heart she sprang into the well and sank to the bottom. For a time she lost all consciousness, and when she came to herself again she was lying in a lovely meadow, with the sun shining brightly overhead, and a thousand flowers blooming at her feet. She rose up and wandered through this enchanted place, till she came to a baker's oven full of bread, and the bread called out to her as she passed: 'Oh! take me out, take me out, or I shall be burnt to a cinder. I am quite done enough.'

So she stepped up quickly to the oven and took out all the loaves one after the other. Then she went on a little farther and came to a tree laden with beautiful rosy-cheeked apples, and as she passed by it called out: 'Oh! shake me, shake me, my apples are all quite ripe.'

She did as she was asked, and shook the tree till the apples fell like rain and none were left hanging. When she had gathered them all up into a heap she went on her way again, and came at length to a little house, at the door of which sat an old woman. The old dame had such large teeth that the girl felt frightened and wanted to run away, but the old woman called after her: 'What are you afraid of, dear child? Stay with me and be my little maid, and if you do your work well I will reward you handsomely; but you must be very careful how you make my bed – you must shake it well till the feathers fly; then people in the world below say it snows, for I am Mother Holle.'

She spoke so kindly that the girl took heart and agreed readily to enter her service. She did her best to please the old woman, and shook her bed with such a will that the feathers flew about like snowflakes; so she led a very easy life, was never scolded, and lived on the fat of the land. But after she had been some time with Mother Holle she grew sad and depressed, and at first she hardly knew herself what was the matter. At last she discovered that she was homesick, so she went to Mother Holle and said: 'I know I am a thousand times better off here than I ever was in my life before, but notwithstanding, I have a great longing to go home, in spite of all your kindness to me. I can remain with you no longer, but must return to my own people.'

'Your desire to go home pleases me,' said Mother Holle, 'and because you have served me so faithfully, I will show you the way back into the world myself.'

So she took her by the hand and led her to an open door, and as the girl passed through it there fell a heavy shower of gold all over her, till she was covered with it from top to toe.

'That's a reward for being such a good little maid,' said Mother Holle, and she gave her the spindle too that had fallen into the well. Then she shut the door, and the girl found herself back in the world again, not far from her own house; and when she came to the courtyard the old hen, who sat on top of the wall, called out:

> 'Click, clock, clack,
> Our golden maid's come back.'

Then she went in to her stepmother, and as she had returned covered with gold she was welcomed home.

She proceeded to tell all that had happened to her, and when the mother heard how she had come by her riches, she was most anxious to secure the same luck for her own idle, ugly daughter; so she told her to sit at the well and spin. In order to make her spindle bloody, she stuck her hand into a hedge of thorns and pricked her finger. Then she threw the spindle into the well and jumped in herself after it. Like her sister she came to the beautiful meadow, and followed the same path. When she reached the baker's oven the bread called out as before: 'Oh! take me out, take me out, or I shall be burnt to a cinder. I am quite done enough.'

But the good-for-nothing girl answered: 'A pretty joke, indeed; just as if I should dirty my hands for you!'

And on she went. Soon she came to the apple tree, which cried: 'Oh! shake me, shake me, my apples are all quite ripe.'

'I'll see myself farther,' she replied, 'one of them might fall on my head.'

And so she pursued her way. When she came to Mother Holle's house she wasn't the least afraid, for she had been warned about her big teeth, and she readily agreed to become her maid. The first day she worked very hard, and did all her mistress told her, for she thought of the gold she would give her; but on the second day she began to be lazy, and on the third she wouldn't even get up in the morning. She didn't make Mother Holle's bed as she ought to have done, and never shook it enough to make the feathers fly. So her mistress soon grew weary of her, and dismissed her, much to the lazy creature's delight.

'For now,' she thought, 'the shower of golden rain will come.'

Mother Holle led her to the same door as she had done her sister, but when she passed through it, instead of the gold rain a kettle full of pitch came showering over her.

'That's a reward for your service,' said Mother Holle, and she closed the door behind her.

So the lazy girl came home all covered with pitch, and when the old hen on the top of the wall saw her, it called out:

'Click, clock, clack,
Our dirty slut's come back.'

But the pitch remained sticking to her, and never as long as she lived could it be got off.

PART SIX

Witchy Devices: Cauldrons, Broomsticks and Trysts with the Devil

Hooch for Skye!

(Scottish)

Jack stayed with his mother in this wee croft away in the west corner of Skye. And he worked around the croft here and there. So on his visits to the village he used to see this old lady at the shop, when he went to the wee shop in the store. She was always in selling eggs and things, and he fell into talk wi' her one day. She asked him his name.

He said, 'Jack they call me.'

She said, 'Where do you stay?'

He said, 'I stay away down at the end of the island wi' my mother.'

She said, 'What does your mother do?'

'My mother,' he says, 'has a wee croft down there.'

'Oh aye,' she says, 'I ken your mother. I'll tell you, are ye busy?'

'No,' he said, 'my mother's wee puckle hay is cut and she's no doing very much just now.'

'Well, look,' she says, 'my old sister and me stay away down at the end o' the island, about ten miles from here. When ye go home would ye ask yer mother if she could let ye off a couple o' days to come down and give us a wee hand wi' the hay? Because we've an awful crop o' hay this year and we canna work it wirsels, seein' my old sister's gettin' kind o' bad in her legs.'

'Okay,' he says, 'I'll see my mother.'

She says, 'I ken yer mother fine but it's years and years since I've seen her.'

Very well, Jack goes away home wi' his mother's bits o' messages. Back he goes to the wee croft, into his house and his mother says, 'Well, laddie, ye're home.'

'Aye,' Jack says, 'I'm home, Mother. But Mother, a funny thing happened to me today down at the wee store where I was down at the shop. I met an old friend of yours, she's an old woman.'

'Oh,' she says, 'I ken who ye met up wi' – old Maggie. And she has an old sister Jeannie. I've never seen them for years. Jack, what was she saying to ye? Ye ken, there are a lot o' stories goes about the island about them pair.'

'Ah, Mother,' he said, 'she's a nice old woman, the nicest old woman! In fact, she wants me to come and work wi' her.'

'What!' says the mother, 'gang an' work wi' her? Well, Jack, laddie, but ye can please yersel' if you want to go and work with her or no. But wi' the cracks and tales that I've heard about them, they're supposed to be witches, the two o' them. And if ye're going –'

'Mother, it's for nae harm,' he says. 'The old woman only wants me to gang an' work for a couple of days wi' them at the hay. Ye ken I'm no doin' much here.'

'Oh well, it's up to yersel'. But,' she says, 'I'm telling you, you'd better just be careful and watch what they give ye to eat, and watch what they tell ye to do. And pay attention, because they're definitely witches!'

'Ach, Mother,' he says, 'witches! There's nae such a thing as witches nowadays.'

Anyway, the next morning his mother makes him up a bit piece and that, and he has a good bit to go, about ten mile o' a walk to the end o' the island. Away he goes, travels on and on and on; it was a lovely day, the sun was shining. He walks on, comes right down through a wee village and down to this wee croft at the side o' the shore. Up he goes an' knocks at the door. The old woman comes out to him.

'Oh, it's you John,' she says. (She cried him John at first.) 'Come on in! I'm just getting my old sister up, old Jeannie, and giving her her breakfast.' She sits him down to the table and gives him a good breakfast. She says, 'Go round the shed there and ye'll get a scythe.' It was all the scythes they used in the olden days for cutting their hay. 'And there's a sharpening stone for sharpening it hangin' in a leather case from the rafters. Ye'll get rakes and forks an' everything else ye need in the shed. I'll give ye a wee shout at dinner-time.'

'All right,' says Jack.

Jack got used to this farm working, kent all about it. It was just a wee two or three acres of hay. They kept yin cow and a puckle hens these two old sisters; they sold eggs and things. He worked away all day, cut all this hay for them. He nearly finished it.

The old sister came out and gave him a shout, 'Come on in, Jack! It's about dinner-time.'

In he comes, sits down. He looks. He's never seen the other old sister before, but she's sitting at the table. He looks at her.

'Aye,' Maggie says, 'you've never met my sister, Jack. That's my sister Jeannie there. She's kind o' deaf, she'll no hear ye. She's two-three years older than me. Her legs are kind o' bad.'

'Well,' he says, 'I didna get your hay finished. I dinna ken if it's going to come on rain or no. And there's a lot –'

'Dinna worry, laddie! Dinna go home tonight!' Maggie says. 'There's plenty of room for you – ye can stay here. I'll make you a nice bed at the kitchen fire. Your mother'll ken where ye are. She'll no worry about ye.'

'All right,' says Jack. But anyway, Jack goes away out again, works another half-day.

But he thought to himself, 'There's something funny about that old sister o' hers. She says she's older than her, but she looks younger than her. And the way I saw her moving her feet in alow the table, there's no much wrong wi' her legs! And she disna use a staff because there's no a staff lying against the table. There's something kind o' droll – I canna figure it out. But anyway I'll mind what my mother tellt me,' so he's thinking.

But he works on again till five o'clock. The old woman gives him a shout, takes him in, gives him his supper. Now it be coming on late in the year, the hay was late, it was about September month. The nights were coming in close. The two old women made a bed to Jack at the front o' the fire, put a big fire o' peats on. And they went away up the stairs to their bed. Jack fell asleep.

He's lying and the fire's burning down low, ken, when the peats burn down low it's just a red *griosach*, a red fire. And he hears the feet coming down, two old sisters coming walking down the stairs. They come right to the fire. And old Jeannie, the one who was supposed to be crippled says, 'He's sleeping, he'll no hear you, he's sleeping.'

Jack was lying, and he lifted the blanket a wee bit, he keeked out. This is the two old sisters, and the other ane is walking as good as you and me! They go over to the side o' the grate. And there's an oven at the side of the grate. They open the door of the oven, and they take out a red cowl. (That's a kind o' woolly bonnet or 'toorie' with a long tassel on it.) One pulls one right down over her hair, the other one takes another one out and she pulls it over *her* hair. And they say, 'Hooch for London!' They're gone – both of them were gone!

Jack got up, wandered around the house, lighted a lamp, searched the house upside down outside in, but na! Round to the byre, the cow was standing eating at the back of the byre. Right round the hayfield, he searched round the place. The two old sisters were gone, there was not a bit to be seen o' them! So he searched round and round every shed, every nook, into the hen house, round the fields, down to the well – not a soul to be seen. The two old sisters had completely vanished, he couldn't find them anywhere.

He goes back into the house, kindles up the fire and makes himself a cup of tea. 'Man,' he says to himself, 'I doubt my mother was right. Where could those two old women go to this time o' night?' He looks at the clock. It was dead on twelve o'clock when they left, and now it was near one in the morning. Still no signs o' them. 'Ach,' he says, 'it'll no matter. I canna explain it. Maybe my mother'll tell me. But anyway I'm going to see it through, I'm going to see what happens here. I'm no going home till I see what happens.'

But he put some more peats on the fire, went back to his bed and happed himself up. But he must have fallen asleep. He was sleeping for about a couple o' hours when he heard the door opening. In came the first sister, and in came the second sister walking as good as me and you! Each had a bag in their hand, a leather bag. They placed them down on the table. And it was 'clink'. With the way they clinked it was money that was in the bags.

So one says to the other, 'Jeannie, one for you, one for me. Put them back in the same place where we put the rest!'

'Right!' Away goes old Jeannie up the stairs with the two bags and puts them away.

Jack's lying, he never says a word. The other old sister comes over and she stands aside the fire, she listens to see if she could hear him. She says to herself, 'He's sleeping, he's never wakened, he disna ken the difference.' She went away up the stairs, closed the door and all was silent.

But anyway, Jack fell asleep and he must have slept on. The first thing that wakened him was the old wife giving him a shout in the morning. She said, 'Jack, it's time to get up, seven o'clock, rise and get your breakfast!'

'Okay,' he said, 'I'll get up.' Jack got up, put on his clothes, had a wash. The old wife came round, gave him a good breakfast, porridge an' milk an' eggs.

She said, 'How are you this morning, Jack? Did ye sleep well last night? Anything disturb ye during the night?'

'Not a thing disturbed me during the night,' he said, 'I slept like a lamb the whole night through.'

'That's good,' she says, 'you must have been working hard.'

But anyway, Jack goes out, sharpens his scythe. Out to the field, starts again, cuts away an' cuts away, finishes the hay. All the hay is lying out.

Old Maggie comes out, gives him a shout again. 'Come on in, Jack, it's about dinner-time!'

He comes, gets his dinner, sits an' cracks to them for a long long while. They ask him about his mother and all these things, about his croft, one thing and another until the dinner hour is up. 'Ah well,' he says, 'I'll have to go away back out an' get on with the work.'

So he went out and he started turning the hay. It was a lovely sunny day. He worked away till night-time again. He came in, had his supper. To make a long story short it came to bedtime again. The two old sisters bade him good-night. Jack made his bed by the fire and he lay down. He looked at the clock, an old wag-at-the-wall clock was what they had on the wall. Half past eleven . . . Jack's sound in bed.

But just on the chap o' twelve o'clock he hears the feet coming down the stairs again. Down they come. One says to the other, 'Is he sleeping?'

She says, 'He's sound. He must have worked hard today, but we'll make it worth his while. We'll give him a good pay.'

He's lying, Jack's lying, he hears every word. Up they go again to the grate, open the door of the oven. Out comes the two cowls, on to their heads, 'Hooch for London!' They're off, off they go!

Same thing happened again. Jack got up, searched the house upside down, went up the stairs. The door to their bedroom was locked. 'Now,' he said, 'I cannae break the door down – they'll ken I was up the stairs.' He searched the house upside and down and he found this key. He tried it and the door opened. He went into their bedroom, and round the whole room. And in alow the bed he pulled out this big box, a leatherbound trunk. It was packed with wee bags, and every single bag was full o' sovereigns, gold sovereigns! 'Hmm,' he said, 'there's as much money there as would do everybody in the Isle of Skye!' And he shoved it back in below their bed, shut the door, locked it, put the key back where he had found it. He went away back down, back to his bed, fell sound asleep. He never heard them coming back.

The next morning she came down and wakened him again. She said, 'Had you a good sleep last night, Jack?'

'Oh, I slept,' he said, 'I was tired, dead tired. I'll finish the hay today, and –'

'Ah, but you'll have to put it up in ricks for us,' she says, 'because it will be wet lying like that, and ye ken you'll have to put it in stacks for us and do a bit o' repairs before you go away home, fencing an' that. I can employ you for a week, ye can stay a week. Your mother kens where you are so she'll no worry about you.'

He's thinking to himself now, 'Where they go tonight, I'm going with them!'

'Oh but,' she says, 'I forgot to tell you, Jack, there's a lot o' clothes here about your size that belonged to my brother. He was just about your age when he was killed, and there's a lot o' stuff here that's nae use to me and my old sister. We'll look it out for ye and you'll take it home wi' ye, it'll do for working wi'. My brother was killed.'

He says, 'What happened to your brother?'

'Oh,' she says, 'he was killed down in London. Anyway, we'll no speak about that.'

So Jack works all day, comes in, has his dinner. Works on in the afternoon again, has his supper. And he comes back in, goes to his bed.

Twelve o'clock he hears the feet coming down the stairs. He says, 'Where they're going tonight I'm going with them!'

One old sister says to the other, 'I think he's sleeping, he's no moving.' Over to the side of the fire they go, open the door beside the wee grate, pull out the cowls – on their heads – 'Hooch for London!'

Jack gets up out o' the bed, runs to the fire, he opens the oven and there's one red toorie left. He pulls it on his head, 'Hooch for London!' he says. 'Hooch for London!'

He travelled through the air at about a hundred miles an hour wi' this cowl on his head and the two sisters in front o' him. They circled round London, and down – right through this window! And with the welt he got coming down, he didna ken any words to stop himself from landing, he was knocked out completely. See, they knew words for to cushion their blow, how to land, be he didnae. He landed after them. When he wakened up, you know where he was lying? He was lying inside a cellar in the Royal Mint, and he was

surrounded by thousands o' bags of gold sovereigns! And his toorie was gone. So were the two old sisters. They were gone. But this is where they had been going, robbing the mint every night. Two witches!

But Jack searched all around . . . the mint's locked, there's no way o' him getting out – impossible! So in the morning when the guards came down they got him sitting inside the mint. Now this was what had happened to their brother before, to the sisters' old brother. Oh, Jack's in a terrible state now – he disna ken what to do with himself!

So the guards they ask him how he got in. But he couldn't explain, he says he disna ken how he got in. So in those days for stealing out o' the mint, the penalty was death, sentenced to death. You were hanged in an open court out in the front o' the public square. Jack is arrested, taken out of the cellar o' the mint, taken up to the court, tried and sentenced to be hanged for robbing the Royal Mint. And so many dozens o' the bags of gold that had gone a-missing – he got the blame o' the lot.

But anyway, he lay in the jail for three days, till the day he was to be hanged. He was taken out, taken up the steps, the thirteen steps to the scaffold and put on the scaffold. The hangman came, put the rope round his neck. And the minister came up to say two or three words to him before they hanged him.

The minister says to Jack, 'John, you were sentenced to death for robbing the Royal Mint. Have you anything to say before ye get hanged?' When up the steps to the scaffold runs this old lady!

She says to the hangman, 'Yes, I've got something to say!' And she placed the cowl on Jack's head. 'Hooch for Skye!' she said. The two of them were off!

And when Jack wakened up he was lying at the side of the fire back in the two old sisters' croft. As he wakens up this old sister's shouting to him, 'Jack, get up! It's time to get on wi' your work!'

So Jack worked all week for the two old sisters, forgot all about it. He said, 'I must have been dreaming – that never really happened to me – I must have been dreaming. Or was my mother right . . . did I dream or did it really happen? But anyway I must ask them!' At the end of the week he said to the two old sisters, 'Was I ever out o' here?'

'No,' she says, 'Jack, ye werena out o' here. You worked well. You've been the best worker ever we had here, you did everything!'

'But,' he says, 'was I no away from here, this place, during the night or anything? Did anything funny happen?'

'Na! You slept like a lamb o' God,' she says. 'You never were away from this place. Every morning we came down at breakfast-time you were aye lying in your bed, and you were lying in your bed when we went to our bed at night. You've never been out of this place since you came – for a full week.'

'Ah well, that's funny . . . ach,' he says, 'it must hae been a dream I had. I dreamed that I landed in . . .' He tellt her the whole story, he landed in the mint and he was to be hanged till death. 'And you,' he says, 'came.'

'Ach, Jack,' she says, 'you've been dreaming! The same thing happened to my poor brother, he had a dream like that too. But that's the last we ever saw o' him.'

So the old sister went away to get something for Jack, something for his breakfast. And he opened the oven and he keeked in, and inside the oven were three red toories, inside the oven. He said, 'I wasna dreaming.' And he shut the door. She came back in.

'Well,' he says to the old sister, 'that's all your jobs finished now. I think it's about time that I went home to see how my old mother's getting on.'

'Ah, but Jack,' she says, 'my sister has made up that bundle o' clothes for you that belonged to my brother. I think they'll do ye, just the very thing, you're about his build. Wait, I'll go an get ye your pay!'

So they gave him this big bundle of clothes to take back with him for his work. The two sisters went up the stairs and the one came down. She's carrying these two wee leather bags in her hand. 'There,' she said, 'Jack, there's your pay. And that's as much that'll keep you and your old mother for the rest o' your days.'

And Jack went away home to his mother and stayed happy for ever after. And that's the last o' the wee story!

The Cauldron-Born

(Welsh)

I am Taliesin and I am a Poet. As such I know the power of words;
the building of one syllable upon another; the placing of the words
in certain order so that they make a single, incontestable truth . . .

Once, before all this, I had another name. I was called Gwion and
I was the servant of the Old One. No job too dirty or too mean for
Gwion, whether it was cleaning up after her half-wit son, Afagddu,
or stirring the black pot which hung over the fire when she was
brewing up some new mischief to plague the world of men. I used
to believe all the evils of the world came out of that cauldron; now I
know that only truth is to be found inside its cold rim – truth which,
whether it is acceptable or not, is still terrible to behold. Yet it has
no quality of good or evil; it is simply there, passionless and still like
a clear glass or a still pool between white trees . . .

One day the Old One came into the hut where she kept her few
scrawny pigs, her cauldron, and me, cuffed me about the head and
ordered me to prepare a fire and set up the cauldron for some new
work she intended to begin almost immediately. 'So waste no time,
youth, or you will see how I reward you!'

Such expressions of love I was well acquainted with, and knew
better than to ignore. I struggled to mount the huge black pot on to
its tripod and then set about laying a fire. Then I filled the cauldron
with water as I had been taught and got as far out of the way as I
could in the corner of the hut until I was needed again.

The Old One took five days to gather all the ingredients necessary
for this new potion, and I had to keep it simmering while she went
out to get them. At the end of nine days a stinking, viscous fluid
filled the pot, and the Old One left me again, with strict instructions

not to let the mixture boil over or do anything else to it. 'And don't touch any, or you'll regret it,' she said – though why she should think I might want to was a mystery to me.

There was certainly no intention in me to disobey. I had felt the wrath of Herself before, knew that her shapely white hands could cause greater torment than one would believe possible of anyone – let alone someone as beautiful as she, with her white, white skin and black hair . . . But I must have put too much kindling under the cauldron, because it began to bubble suddenly, and as I went to dampen it down, and came near the pot, several bubbles burst, and some drops – there may have been three – splashed on to my hand.

They were scalding hot and I yelped with the pain and put my hand to my mouth to suck it. Immediately the world turned around me and I fell into a dark roaring place where sound and sensation were too great to bear, and where I, Gwion, became lost – never to return. And what I saw there is what I must tell, for the drink was the drink of initiation, brewed for the Old One's monstrous son; and in its black bile I tasted and saw all the sickness and all the waste of the world, and the long, slow poison of the soul of mankind. And there, too, I saw the dawn of hope, the coming of one whose presence would change the world for all time – aye, even to its very end – though I knew naught of this then, nor for long after.

Sensations – Pain. Fear. Horror. Such fear as wraps one in cold like a mist: nebulous, nameless and unformed, but real as the pain of birth and dying. Pain dragged me down into a bottomless dark where meaning no longer held good and where the identity which made me Gwion left its existence behind. Horror of darkness, void, negative terror which spells an end to life, to hope, to belief in anything swept through me.

Then, light. A bursting forth of such brilliance that to look upon it unprepared was to be blinded. I was not so prepared, but I had sense enough to look away, to study it in the reflections of the eye – a half-light and a half-truth which were all I could bear.

Faces swam towards me out of the light. Some smiled. Some frowned. I recognized none of them. I saw men in agony, men transformed, men who wept and laughed at life. And I saw women of unearthly beauty, whose appearance was such that I grew afraid for my very soul and tried to look away.

Then I heard voices. Calling out. Screaming. Shouting. The sounds of battle and love, of birth and death of agony and pleasure, of joy and fear. I closed my light-seared eyes and tried to shut out the sounds. But nothing would avail, and I found that only by opening myself to everything could I somehow bear it. I let myself be filled up with sound and light and movement – all these sensations set forth in a dimension of understanding that made me aware of them to a degree almost impossible to bear.

So things stood. But for a moment only. For the time it takes to blink an eye, all knowledge and understanding were mine. And, as I entered this realm of infinite possibilities, I knew that the Old One was aware of me and of what had occurred. For now I shared a part of her knowledge and her life.

She was coming after me.

I fled through a timeless landscape – hill, river and wood flowing past and around me as though they had no substance and I waded in them. All the time I felt the presence of the Old One, like a shadow flying over the earth, closer and closer behind.

To aid my escape I put on the gloves and ears of the hare and sped with the hare's speed; but I knew that she followed me still with the tongue and teeth of the greyhound, which ran fast as I. So I donned the feet and tail of the otter and sped through a watery world where startled fish broke on either side of my head. But as a hound the Old One sniffed my passage and came after me, so that I was forced to take to the wings of the bird. Even there she came; a hawk striking at my feathered back. And so at last to elude her I became a grain of wheat in a heap of chaff. But I knew, with my strange new awareness, that I was caught; and sure enough the Old One took me in a hen's beak and swallowed me down. Then she became herself and I found myself asleep in the fluid darkness of her womb. In this darkness I began to dream.

Of a shadow, which gave forth light, showing me a desolate place where no grass grew, where the trees were leafless and the ground cracked and dry. Then, into that waste, came a tendril of green which sent forth shoots, until a spiderweb of green lay across the dead earth . . .

Of a man, descending on a spiral stair, deeper and deeper below the world of light and day. In his hand a flickering lantern that showed only walls enslimed with fungus. At the bottom of the shaft a room deep in human filth, and crouching among it, an old blind woman, deathless and hideous, obscene, crouching and crouching, demanding that he kiss her flayed face and running sores. Sucking the life in him like a terrible spider . . .

Of earth herself: the great womb, teeming with all these images and more, far more than I can tell. Blind and dark, I crawled through the hot passageways within her vast bulk, my hands encountering nameless things that moved beneath me . . .

Then suddenly an absence of darkness into which I stumbled, blind. At first no difference, nothing I could name as light. But a warm hand, full of life, lifting me up; wings (or petals) enfolding me, and a warmth that was also a voice, neither male nor female, somehow inside my head, uttering words that were instantly transformed into images. An experience of the pains of creation, containing dark as well as light – tenderness and purity invoked . . .

All these things swirling together. And more. And yet more. And yet more still – all different, all the same, man and woman the same, death and birth the same. A great conjoining. A birth. My own birth cry in the heavens as I fell from the womb of the Old One into the light of the world whose soul I had seen die and be reborn . . .

And waking, shivering, on the mountainside, the cup still clutched in my numb fingers, the spiralling maze stilling at last beneath my gaze . . .

It is these things which seal the lips of the initiate, not the promise made at the door to the Mysteries. I, Taliesin, once Gwion, now reborn, Cauldron-born of the Old One whose ways have no more terror for me, born of the drink all must drink, know these things.

The Witches' Sabbath

(Norse)

But then there was a woman on a farm at Dovre who was also a witch. It was a Christmas Eve. Her hired girl was busy washing a brewing vat. In the meantime the woman took out a horn and anointed the broom, and all at once she flew up through the chimney. The girl thought this was quite a trick, and took a little salve and rubbed it on the vat. Then she also set out, and did not stop until she came to Bluekolls. There she met a whole flock of witches, and Old Erik himself. The devil preached to them, and after he had finished, he looked over to see if they had all come. Then he caught sight of the girl, who was sitting in the brewing vat. He did not know her, for she had not written in his book. And so he asked the woman who was with her if the girl would sign. The woman thought she would. Old Erik then gave the girl the book and told her to write in it. He wanted her to write her name, but she wrote what schoolchildren usually write when they try out their pens: 'I am born of God, in Jesus' name!' And then she was able to keep the book, for Old Erik was not the one to touch it again.

Now there was an uproar and a commotion on the mountain, as you might know! The witches took whips and beat on whatever they had to ride on, and they set out helter-skelter. The girl did not wait; she also took a whip, beat on the vat, and set out after them. At one place they went down and rested on a high mountain. Far below them was a wide valley with a big lake, and on the other side was another high mountain. When the witches had rested, they laid on the whips and swooped over the mountain. The girl wondered if she could also fly over it. At last she beat on the vat and came over on the other side too, both safe and sound.

'That was the devil of a hop for a brewing vat!' she said, but at the same moment she lost the book. And then she fell down and came no farther, because she had spoken and called him, even though she had not written her name in the book. She had to go the rest of the way on foot, wading through the snow, for she did not get a free ride any more, and there was many a mile to go.

The Birch Besom

(Scottish)

Once when I was intae Ireland and I'd pulled my wagon into a back-road beside Letterkenny and I was stayin there for a couple o nights, I was jist makin supper when an auld man was passin. 'Hallo there,' he said, 'How're ye gettin on? Ye've a good fire there.'

'No bad, man,' I says. 'Ye can have a seat there.'

So I gave him a cup o tea an he sat there, an I says, 'Dae ye stay here?'

'Oh yes,' he says, 'I stay at the top o the town. I'm a blacksmith an I've a blacksmith's shop.'

'Oh,' I says.

'And it's a queer way I got that blacksmith's shop.'

'What dae ye mean?' I says.

'Well,' he says, 'when I was a young lad just like yourself, I was on the road. I saw the blacksmith an I heard him chappin away intil this blacksmith's shop. I just dandered over and I says hallo to him and the blacksmith lookit up an he says, "Hallo there," and I says tae him, "Are ye needin onybody for a helper?"

'He says, "Are you a blacksmith?"

' "Well," I says, "I served two years in a blacksmith's shop."

' "Oh well," he says, "I'm needin a man, right enough. But I dinna make very much here in the blacksmith's shop. Just a few horses an that, and a plough or two."

' "Oh," I says, "I dinny need much because I havenae a home, I've no place to go."

' "Oh well," he says, "I've got a place next door there. It's a wee hoose. Ye can stay there an I'll pay ye aboot ten bob a week. Will that do ye?" ' "Oh," I says, "that'll do fine." '

Well, time it rolled on and he was a very good blacksmith, this young lad. One night the auld man was roarin. So he went in and this was the old man lying on the sofa and he looked up and said, 'Hey Paddy, is there something wrong wi me? I'm losin ma breath.'

'What can be wrong wi you?' says the young man. 'Ye were aa right the day.'

'I'm not a young man,' he says, 'If I go, I'll leave the blacksmith's shop tae you.'

'Och away,' says the young man, 'Ye're no tae speak like that.'

But he got worse and worse and the young man sent for the doctor and the doctor shook his head. 'He's full o bronchitis,' he said. 'Every tube in his breast is choked and I can't cure him. We may ease him, but we can't cure him.'

A couple of days after that he died, so the young man got him buried and he carried on wi the blacksmith's shop. He had the whole lot tae hissel now.

The old man that was talking to me told me what happened next. 'The very same thing happened again. I was workin one day intae the blacksmith's shop and it was about eleven o'clock, when in walked a young fellow and he says, "Have ye anything tae sort or have ye got a horse tae shoe or onythin?"

'"Naw," I says, "I have not."

'"I was lookin for a job," he says, "I've got no home and I'm an orphan."

'So I agreed to pay him ten bob a week and gie him the house next door, just as the old blacksmith had done wi me.

'"Oh," he says, "that'll be grand."

'So the young man took his jacket off. "Ye can start the morra," I says. '"Na, na," he says, "I'll start the day."

'He was the best blacksmith that ever I saw. He could do anything, an they caaed him Mick. Well, we workit like that for about five years and I was gettin kind o aulder. I said tae Mick, "I think I'll go down to Belfast the day."

'"What'll ye do in Belfast?" Mick said.

'"Well, tae tell ye the truth I widna tell nae ither body but yersel. I'm goin to look for a wife. I'm sick o makin ma supper an ma denner an ma breakfast masel."'

So the next day came round and he went down to Belfast and he went tae dances an pubs an everywhere till he was in a guest house and the landlady said tae him, 'Where do ye come from, Paddy?'

'I come from Letterkenny,' he says.

'Oh Letterkenny,' she says, 'And what are ye doin here? Ye've been here about three or four days.'

'Well,' he says, 'tae tell ye the truth, I'm lookin for a wife.'

'Och,' she says, 'there's plenty of them knockin about. Just wait a couple of hours and I'll get ye one.'

So he's sittin waitin, ye know, and this lassie comes in an she comes owre an spoke slow tae him an hearkened tae him. The landlady says tae him, 'How would that one do?'

'Ach, ye're jokin,' he says. 'That woman wouldnae take me! She's only about twenty or twenty-one.'

'It doesnae matter,' she says. 'She's no home an she's orphaned.'

'Oh well,' he says, 'she's the same as masel.'

So she went over an spoke tae the lassie an the lassie came over an spoke tae him an the two of them combined wi each ither an she came home wi him tae Letterkenny. Mick was workin away there and when the blacksmith came in Mick says, 'Well, did ye land lucky?'

'I did,' he says, 'a beauty she is. But we're not married yet.'

So Mick came and looked at her. 'By God,' he says, 'if she's as good as she looks, she'll be a topper. Generally when they've the good looks, they're a bad wumman.'

Paddy says, 'Well, she knows the door if she's bad.' They went and got married next day by special licence.

Time rolls on and oh! she was a good woman, a good baker and a good woman for makin grub. One night, however, she was oot tae the toon and she came back soakin wet, the water was rinnin oot her. 'My God,' says Paddy, 'why did ye go out on a day like that? Did ye no take your umbrella or your waterproof coat?'

She says, 'Ach, I forgot aa aboot them. It was a good day when I went away.' The next night she says, 'Paddy I don't feel so well.' She turned worse in the middle o the night so they sent for the doctor. The doctor came an he says, 'My goodness, she's turned an she's got pneumonia. Have you got any poultices?' In those days it was oatmeal poultices, so they made poultices all night, but the woman died the next mornin.

So Paddy went to Mick an he said, 'She's dead.'

'Oh no,' says Mick.

'Yes,' he says. 'It's wi her goin out wi no coat, no shawl, nor nothin.'

They sat up three nights wi her an had the funeral an they went to the funeral in a jauntin car.

So Paddy's sittin noddin comin hame an he says, 'It wasnae a bad funeral.'

'Oh,' Mick says, 'it was a good funeral.'

So they travels on and Paddy's just aboot sleepin when Mick pulled up the horse. He says, 'Paddy.'

Paddy lookit owre. 'What's wrong?' he says.

Mick says, 'Dae ye see what's comin? If I'm no far mistaken, there's somethin queer gaun on here.'

So they sat there an this person come right up tae them. It was his wife! Her they burit that day! 'My God,' says Paddy, 'it canny be her.'

'Yes, it's her right enough,' Mick says.

She says, 'Whit are ye daein here? Ye better get hame an get the kettle on.' She had a basket on her arm full o messages, so they went hame an put the kettle on. Paddy went across an felt her arms and her shoulders, an she says, 'What are you doin?'

'Oh nothin at all,' he says.

Mick says tae him on the side, 'The best thing we can do is go down to the priest,' so they went down and told him the whole story. 'Well,' says the priest, 'that's impossible. Ye burit her the day. She canny be up at the hoose.'

'Well,' says Paddy, 'come up an ye'll see.' So the three o them came tae the hoose an they pit the priest in. 'Hallo,' he says.

'Hallo, Father,' she says.

'How are you gettin on?' he says.

'Oh I'm champion,' she says, 'couldnae be better.'

So they come oot an the priest spoke tae Paddy and Mick. 'Wait till tomorrow mornin,' he says, 'an we'll take up the coffin an see what's in it.'

So the next mornin they went down to the graveyard an got the gravedigger an they dug the grave up. An do you know what was in the coffin? A birch besom! Aye, a birch besom. An that woman lived for about twelve year after.

The Broom is Busy

(Haitian)

Boki was watching Alse Odjo with a twig broom sweep the floor. The twig-ends were breaking off and Alse Odjo kept sweeping them up. 'You losing broom all over the floor!' Boki said, 'I see that broom creating its own work!'

'Just like everyone on this island!' Alse Odjo said back. 'That's the island way,' she didn't laugh. 'This broom born and raised here, you know.'

But Boki was not there just for talk, he was going with Alse Odjo to the hut of old Boukinez that fortune teller woman, that woman. They were going to bring two of her fortune guesses back to her. They went to turn two guesses back to Boukinez because no one before had bothered to walk guesses back, were they right or wrong the guesses and did she long to know what happened to them? They arrive at her hut. Boki says to her, 'We are two guesses come back.'

Boki says, 'Do you remember me, I'm Boki?' she nods yes she does, 'Remember you guessed for me a future dressed in fortune and laugh?' she nods yes again and says, 'Yes, I wanted that to be true yes.' Boki says, 'Well, madam, I must honest tell you now I am poor on this island many years now, often I see in a dream clouds passing through my heart and are bread then, true as I tell it. So each morning I carry out my crate porch and sit on it trying to be happy I don't need to buy butter for that kind of breakfast bread no no!'

Boki says, 'How did the world get this way can you say toward this?' he says to Boukinez.

She nods yes and no, then Alse Odjo steps up, 'And do you remember me, I'm Alse Odjo?' old Boukinez nods yes again, 'You guessed I'd find a music to cure us all!' Boukinez is nodding. 'Well, madam, I must tell you many years have passed through my flutes and they are tired, and all I can do is send my one goat to walk out clacking on the xylophone wood dock to try and cure us all, that funny goat, his one long spigot horn no good water pouring from it ever, and he got one short horn too! Tell me how did the world make him that way?'

All morning on her porch they talked her guesses, she remembered more of them from years gone by, and they kept saying to each other, 'How did the world do that?' End of morning they were all nodding alike, the goat watched this puzzled. And all along Alse Odjo was sweeping the porch of old Boukinez, leaving twigs. Boukinez she closed her eyes to hear them roll by breeze over the porch floor. She was laughing inside to herself because she knew later, after Boki and Alse Odjo gone, she'd try to catch those twigs with her feet, staying in her chair.

The Horned Women

(Irish)

A rich woman sat up late one night carding and preparing wool, while all the family and servants were asleep. Suddenly a knock was given at the door, and a voice called – 'Open! Open!'

'Who is there?' said the woman of the house.

'I am the Witch of the One Horn,' was answered.

The mistress, supposing that one of her neighbours had called and required assistance, opened the door, and a woman entered, having in her hand a pair of wool carders, and bearing a horn on her forehead, as if growing there. She sat down by the fire in silence, and began to card the wool with violent haste. Suddenly she paused and said aloud: 'Where are the women? They delay too long.'

Then a second knock came to the door, and a voice called as before – 'Open! Open!'

The mistress felt herself constrained to rise and open to the call, and immediately a second witch entered, having two horns on her forehead, and in her hand a wheel for spinning the wool.

'Give me place,' she said; 'I am the Witch of the Two Horns,' and she began to spin as quick as lightning.

And so the knocks went on, and the call was heard, and the witches entered, until at last twelve women sat round the fire – the first with one horn, the last with twelve horns. And they carded the thread, and turned their spinning-wheels, and wound and wove, all singing together an ancient rhyme, but no word did they speak to the mistress of the house. Strange to hear, and frightful to look upon were these twelve women, with their horns and their wheels; and the mistress felt near to death, and she tried to rise that she might call for help, but she could not move, nor could she utter a word or a cry, for the spell of the witches was upon her.

Then one of them called to her in Irish and said – 'Rise, woman, and make us a cake.'

Then the mistress searched for a vessel to bring water from the well that she might mix the meal and make the cake, but she could find none. And they said to her – 'Take a sieve and bring water in it.'

And she took the sieve and went to the well; but the water poured from it, and she could fetch none for the cake, and she sat down by the well and wept. Then a voice came by her and said – 'Take yellow clay and moss and bind them together and plaster the sieve so that it will hold.'

This she did, and the sieve held the water for the cake. And the voice said again – 'Return, and when thou comest to the north angle of the house, cry aloud three times and say, "The mountain of the Fenian women and the sky over it is all on fire."'

And she did so.

When the witches inside heard the call, a great and terrible cry broke from their lips and they rushed forth with wild lamentations and shrieks, and fled away to Slieve-namon, where was their chief abode. But the Spirit of the Well bade the mistress of the house to enter and prepare her home against the enchantments of the witches if they returned again.

And first, to break their spells, she sprinkled the water in which she had washed her child's feet (the feet-water) outside the door on the threshold; secondly, she took the cake which the witches had made in her absence, of meal mixed with the blood drawn from the sleeping family. And she broke the cake in bits, and placed a bit in the mouth of each sleeper, and they were restored; and she took the cloth they had woven and placed it half in and half out of the chest with the padlock; and lastly, she secured the door with a great cross-beam fastened in the jambs, so that they could not enter. And having done these things she waited.

Not long were the witches in coming back, and they raged and called for vengeance.

'Open! Open!' they screamed. 'Open, feet-water!'

'I cannot,' said the feet-water, 'I am scattered on the ground and my path is down to the Lough.'

'Open, open, wood and tree and beam!' they cried to the door.

'I cannot,' said the door; 'for the beam is fixed in the jambs and I have no power to move.'

'Open, open, cake that we have made and mingled with blood,' they cried again.

'I cannot,' said the cake, 'for I am broken and bruised, and my blood is on the lips of the sleeping children.'

Then the witches rushed through the air with great cries, and fled back to Slieve-namon, uttering strange curses on the Spirit of the Well, who had wished their ruin; but the woman and the house were left in peace, and a mantle dropped by one of the witches in her flight was kept hung up by the mistress as a sign of the night's awful contest; and this mantle was in possession of the same family from generation to generation for five hundred years after.

The Goodwife of Laggan

(Scottish)

One fine day Razay set out to the Isle of Lewes to hunt the deer that
were abundant there. He took his followers with him, the flower of
the young men of Razay. It was a beautiful day and the sport was
admirable. It had never been so good, and they hunted till sunset
and spent the evening in great merriment in their hunting lodge,
dining off roasted venison and good whisky, with songs and music
and tales, until late into the night. But while they were sleeping the
wind got up, and they wakened to a squally and blusterous day.
Razay was anxious to get home and ordered the crew to prepare
the boat. Many of them were doubtful whether the crossing was
possible, but danger was a spur to their laird, so he led them all
down to the jetty, but many of them were still doubtful, so Razay
broached a keg of whisky, and their spirits began to rise, though
several were still doubtful. Whilst they were debating an old crone
hobbled up to them, and Razay appealed to her as bound to know
the place. 'Ay, ay,' said she, 'I've been here this eighty year, and it's
as smooth as the back of your hand in comparison to the days when
my father would cross the water; aye and my husband too and my
young son, and come back as safe as if they were rocking in their
cradle. But they've no seamanship these days and are feared if the
wind gives but a wee whistle. I've aye heard tell that Razay's lads are
the greatest cowards in all Scotland, and I can see it's true the day.'

   At that taunt the most cautious man among them would not have
held back for the wealth of the Indies. They pushed out from the
jetty and hoisted sail, and the wind caught them and whirled them
out to sea, while the storm doubled and trebled itself, with lightning
and thunder and torrents of rain, so that there was no putting in to

shore again. Razay kept his brave heart and made his way to the tiller, and the hearts of his crew began to rise as he kept her head steadily to point of Aird on Skye. They had almost begun to hope when a great black cat crawled up on to the boat and began to climb the mast. Another came and another until they covered the rigging and blackened all the lee side of the boat. Last came an enormous beast and climbed the main mast. Razay called out to the crew to kill it, but as they made towards it all the cats with one movement heeled over the boat, and every man on board was engulfed in the sea and was drowned.

On that very day one of Razay's greatest friends, so keen a sportsman that he was generally called the Hunter of the Hills, and like him a determined enemy of the witches, was warming himself in his hunting lodge in the forest of Gaich, in Badenoch, listening to the howling of the storm outside. His two dogs lay stretched by the fire at his side and his gun was propped up in the corner of the bothy. As he sat, half-dozing, the door opened by a narrow crack and a poor, miserable, drenched cat stole into the room. The dogs bounded up, their hackles rising, and made for the creature, but to his surprise, she spoke with a human voice. 'Oh, great Hunter of the Hills,' she said, 'I appeal to you for protection. I know your hatred of my kind, but spare a poor jaded wretch, who flies to you for protection from the cruelty of her sisterhood!'

The Hunter was touched. Though from her speech he judged her to be a witch, yet he was too generous to oppress an enemy brought so low. He made his dogs lie down, and told her that she might sit by the fire and dry herself. But she held back and shivered. 'Your dogs are still angry,' she said, 'I am afraid they will tear me to pieces. I have a long hair here. I pray you to put it round them and bind them together.' The Hunter became still more suspicious. He took the strange, long hair and pretended to tie the dogs, but he put it round one of the rafters of the bothy; and the cat stole in and sat by the fire. Presently the Hunter noticed that the cat was growing larger and larger.

'A bad death to you, you nasty beast,' he said laughing, 'you are getting very large.'

'Aye, aye,' said the cat, chuckling too. 'My featheries are swelling as they dry.'

The Hunter said nothing, but watched the cat, who continued to grow larger and larger till suddenly he saw the Goodwife of Laggan sitting in front of him.

'Now, Hunter of the Hills,' she said, 'your hour of reckoning is at hand. You and Macgillichallum of Razay were the greatest enemies of my devoted sisterhood. We have reckoned with Razay. He lies a lifeless corpse at the bottom of the sea. And now, Hunter of the Hills, it is your turn.' And at that she seemed to enlarge yet more terribly and to grow as ugly as a devil, and sprang at him. But the dogs were not bound by the hair and they sprang to defend their master. They fastened on the witch's breasts, she tried to escape from them, shrieking loudly: 'Fasten hair! Fasten!', for she fancied that the hair was wound round the dogs. The hair fastened until the two rafters round which the Hunter had thrown it snapped like matchwood, but still the dogs tore at the witch, who dragged them with her out of the house and did not let go till she had torn every tooth out of their heads. When she got loose she flew away as a raven. Her wailing died away and the dogs crawled back to their master, and as he stroked and praised them they licked his hands and died. The Hunter wept over them as if they had been his own children. Then he buried them and went sadly home. His wife was out, and he waited some time till she got back. 'Where have you been, my love?' he said. 'On a sad errand,' she replied, 'I have been to visit the Goodwife of Laggan, who has been struck by a sudden illness, and is not expected to live through the night. All the neighbours are with her.' 'That's sad hearing,' said her husband. 'What is it ails the worthy woman?' 'It seems she was out on the moss cutting peats and the storm came down, so that she was soaked through, and was struck with a sudden colic.' 'It is only fitting that I should go to see her,' said the Hunter. 'Let us have dinner quickly and go.'

They soon reached the room, where all the neighbours were surrounding her bed, mourning the sufferings of one whom they had always regarded as a good neighbour and a worthy woman. The Hunter made his way through the crowd and stripped back the blankets so that they all could see the marks of the dogs' teeth on her breasts and arms. 'Look at this vile witch!' he said. 'This very day she compassed the death of Macgillichallum of Razay and tried to murder me.' And he told the whole story of what had happened. Everyone there was both amazed and convinced, for the marks of the dogs' teeth were plain on her body. All were prepared to drag her out and execute her without further trial, but the old witch pled with them to spare her human vengeance, for terrible sufferings awaited her from the fiend who had cheated and allured her, and who was now mocking at her torments. 'Take warning from me,' she said, 'and have no traffic with the Master whom I have served so long.' And she went on to tell them the whole story of her apprenticeship to evil and of all the terrible things she had done, ending with the account of the death of Razay and the foiled attempt upon his friend. And when she had told all she died.

That same night one of her neighbours was returning home from Strathdearn and just entering the dreary forest of Monalea in Badenoch, when he met a woman dressed in black, running at a great speed, and as she approached him she asked him how far it was from the kirkyard of Dalarossie, and if she could reach it before twelve o'clock. He said he thought that she could if she continued at that pace. She sped on, lamenting as she ran. He had not gone many miles when he met a great black dog, snuffing along the track, and shortly after he met another. Shortly after him there was a strong black man on a fine, fleet, black courser, who paused to ask him if he had seen a woman going that way. He replied that he had, running very fast. 'And were there two black dogs after her?' said the black stranger. 'There were,' said the traveller, 'two great dogs.' 'And do you think that the dogs will overtake her before she reaches the kirkyard of Dalarossie?' 'They should at any rate be hard on her heels,' said the traveller. With that the stranger gathered his reins and galloped away, and the traveller hurried towards home, for it was an uncanny encounter in an uncanny place. He had not gone far however when the black rider overtook him with the woman across his saddle bow and two dogs hanging one on her breast and one on her thigh. 'Where did you overtake her?' asked the traveller. 'Just as she was entering the kirkyard of Dalarossie,' said the black huntsman, and galloped away.

When the traveller got home and heard the story of the witch of Laggan he had no doubt that the woman in black was the soul of the witch flying for protection from the demons to whom she had sold herself to the kirkyard of Dalarossie, which is so sacred a place that any witch who visits it, dead or alive, is freed from her contract with Satan.

Baba Yaga

(Russian)

A certain peasant and his wife had a daughter. The wife died; the husband married another woman, and had a daughter with her also. His wife conceived a dislike for her stepdaughter and the orphan had a hard time. Our peasant thought and thought, and finally took his daughter to the woods. As he drove in the woods, he beheld a little hut standing on chicken legs. The peasant said: 'Little hut, little hut, stand with your back to the woods, and your front to me!' The hut turned around. The peasant entered it and found Baba Yaga: her head was in front, her right leg was in one corner, and her left leg in the other corner. 'I smell a Russian smell!' said Yaga. The peasant bowed to her and said: 'Baba Yaga the Bony-legged One, I have brought you my daughter to be your servant.' 'Very well, serve me, serve me!' said Yaga to the girl. 'I will reward you for it.' The father said farewell and returned home.

Baba Yaga gave the girl a basketful of yarn to spin, told her to make a fire in the stove, and to prepare everything for dinner. Then she went out. The girl busied herself at the stove and wept bitterly. The mice ran out and said to her: 'Maiden, maiden, why are you weeping? Give us some gruel: we shall return your kindness.' She gave them some gruel. 'And now,' they said, 'stretch one thread on each spindle.' Baba Yaga came back. 'Well,' she said, 'have you prepared everything?' The girl had everything ready. 'And now wash me in the bath!' said her mistress. She praised the maiden and gave her several beautiful dresses.

Again Yaga went out, having set more difficult tasks for her servant. Again the girl wept. The mice ran out. 'Lovely maiden,' they said, 'why are you weeping?' Give us some gruel: we shall return your kindness.' She gave them gruel, and again they told her what to do and how. Baba Yaga upon her return again praised the maiden and gave her even more beautiful dresses.

One day the stepmother sent her husband to see whether his daughter was still alive. The peasant drove into the woods; when he came to the house on chicken legs, he saw that his daughter had become very prosperous. Yaga was not at home, so he took the maiden with him. As they approached their village, the peasant's dog began to bark: 'Bow! wow! wow! A young lady is coming, a young lady is coming!' The stepmother ran out and struck the dog with a rolling pin. 'You're lying!' she said. 'You should bark, "Bones are rattling in the basket!"' But the dog kept barking the same thing as before. The peasant and his daughter arrived. The stepmother began to press her husband to take her daughter to Baba Yaga. He took her.

Baba Yaga set a task for her and went out. The girl was beside herself with spite, and wept. The mice ran out: 'Maiden, maiden,' they said, 'why are you weeping?' But she did not even let them speak; she struck them with a rolling pin and scolded them roundly and did not do her work. Yaga came back and became angry. Another time the same thing happened. Then Yaga broke her in pieces and put her bones in a basket.

Now the stepmother sent her husband for his daughter. The father went and brought back only her bones. As he approached his village, his dog barked on the porch: 'Bow! wow! wow! Bones are rattling in the basket!' The stepmother came running out with a rolling pin: 'You're lying!' she said. 'You should bark, "A young lady is coming!"' The husband arrived; and then the wife moaned and groaned.

There's a tale for you, and a crock of butter for me.

PART SEVEN:

Hungry Hags:
Cannibals and Blood-Suckers

Vikram and the Dakini

(Indian)

There was once a king called Vikram. He wasn't your king nor was he my king but he was a famous king, a long time ago. Everyone knows about him, so you must know something about him too. If nothing else, then at least his name. Well, once a woman in his guardianship died while her husband, a priest, was on pilgrimage. When the priest returned, Vikram said, 'Guard her body until I return with an antidote to death.'

Vikram travelled through jungles, wildernesses, rivers and deserts trying to find the secret of restoring life. In one wilderness an old hag came up and threw her arms around him weeping and saying, 'Oh my son, my son, I've missed you so much. I didn't think I would ever see you again.'

Vikram told the woman kindly, 'I'm not your son.'

'Don't you work for so-and-so Raja?' she asked. Vikram said no, he didn't and explained he was looking for the secret of restoring life.

The hag said, 'Once Yama takes someone away he never gives him back. Don't even think about it. But you and my son share a face. Replace him with such-and-such a Raja. He lives over in that direction – and send him back to me. Do this in the name of Kali. She will repay you.' And she stood there, shaking her head and muttering and mumbling.

It was on Vikram's tongue to remind her he had a quest of his own, but he took pity on the old hag and agreed.

Well, Vikram travelled on another eleven months and though he didn't find out about the secret of reviving the dead, he did find the old hag's son. The man who shared Vikram's face said that his job was to carry sacks of gold for the king who distributed it to his people each morning. It seemed an honourable job so Vikram said, 'Can I change places with you, because your mother is getting terribly old and wants you with her.'

So the young man changed places with Vikram. That was how Vikram started working with the king. And he noticed while he was working that the king looked terribly wan and exhausted, and the moment he had finished distributing the sacks of gold to his subjects, he would stagger into a temple nearby and fall into a deep sleep that was more like a coma than normal slumber. That was why Vikram kept a close watch on the king; he was a kind man and he wanted to help him if he could.

That night the king awoke, washed himself from the holy pond and cleansed himself as if for a prayer. Then he set off towards the edge of the city. And here was a cremation-ground and there, just by the end of it, was the jungle and the white temple of Kali gleaming in the darkness. Well, if you can believe it, Vikram was actually quite frightened for the first time in his life as he saw the king walk towards a dark figure suspended from a corpse hanging off a tree on the edge of the crematorium. The figure was of a fearsome woman. She was sucking with a slobbering, greedy noise, with little yelps and groans of pleasure, for all the world like an infant suckling from her mother's breast. But that is natural – she's a baby suckling on milk; this was a *dakini*, suckling on the blood of a young, dead corpse. Nor was it just any *dakini*. She was a chosen handmaiden of Herself, the great and powerful, the terrifying Kali herself. But Vikram did not know this as the king rapidly approached the witch and stopped her feasting on the blood. As the horrible creature fell back, a great shower of blood escaped from the opening in the corpse and splattered her face and body and she sucked greedily at the drops on her face and body letting out howls of protest and deprivation. Then, seeing it was the king, she dropped her howl to a whimper and cowered down a moment before turning to lead him to Kali. Because you know, everyone knows Kali is goddess of demonesses and witches as well as saints and kings and ordinary folk and paupers. Of everyone.

'Well, if he's going to visit Kali, he must be okay,' thought Vikram. Because as you know all kings are Kshatriyas and Kshatriyas worship Kali, the goddess of war. Either as Durga when she rides a tiger, or as Chandi swallowing drops of the Demon General's blood or as Kali dancing intoxicated with blood on the corpses of the demons she has slain. Whatever you call her, she's the Power. But when she's

Kali, or Bhavani or Chandi, she loves blood. You know, when you can see her tongue hanging out, a beheaded demon held in one hand, a necklace of skulls around her neck, and a skirt of severed hands. The Terrifying, the Destructress, the Swallower of Men from the cavernous dentata at both ends. And why not – the womb of the world, the Creatress, what she can thrust out, she can suck in – why not? Isn't that true? Once she concealed a sword in there, you know – but her Lord Shiva turned his massive *linga* into a thunderbolt! What revels those two have! They make the Earth shake. But that's another story, though maybe Vikram was thinking some of these things when he saw what he saw –

The king prostrated himself to the goddess and asked for her blessing, then climbed on to the platform before her. She put her teeth to his heart and drank deeply of his blood. She sucked and inhaled it until her face and hands were bloody and her clothes heavily marked. Vikram was watching in absolute silence, putting away everything he saw safely in his mind.

He saw Kali lean back and look at the king who still had a little life left in him. The *dakinis* prowled around hoping to lick up some droplets of a living man's blood from the ground. Away from gibbet and executioner's block, their desire was as cavernous as their bellies. Kali leant back sated, eyes ecstatically closed, savouring the fresh blood, sniffing the faint whiff of it lingering in the air. The *dakinis* placed the king in a cauldron full of oil and cooked him to a crisp. Then they drew him out and served him to Kali who devoured every morsel of him. But she did not eat with wildness or abandon. She was careful that not a single bone was so much as chipped. It was dawn by the time she'd finished picking his bones, every shred of meat, muscle and offal. Then she spread out his skeleton and her *dakinis* skulked around cleaning and wiping him. Meanwhile Kali herself reached for a jug of golden liquid and sprinkled it over his bones. Some gristle and muscles began to appear over the skeleton. Then she splashed on more liquid and he began to flesh out until the flesh grew right back to normal and the veins and vessels embedded in it began to quicken with a little blood.

Anyway, the king stood before Kali after a while, then bowed to her and praised her and she reached into her bloodstained robe and pulled out a crumpled bloody cloth like a great big handkerchief and unfurled it. As she dusted it, piles of gold fell to the ground and the king fell to his knees and scooped it up into bags.

Then he bowed low before her and took his leave. Soon his subjects began to gather and everything was the same as it had been the day before and the day before that. Only Vikram knew it was the last day for the nightly goings-on. He had a plan, you see. Vikram drugged the king's drink that night and made his way to the crematorium. But before that he cut gashes in the flesh of his arms and legs and put salt and chilli paste in them to keep him awake because it was now many hours since he had slept and he knew he had to be alert for his plan to work.

Well, he got to the crematorium and found a howling, blood-sucking *dakini* and she took him as before to the World-birther Kali to begin her game. Just before she had a chance to focus her gaze on him, he threw himself with a mighty leap on to the platform before her and she immediately bowed her head and sunk her teeth into his soft flesh, nuzzling a bit to find the spot where his heart was fullest with blood, and began to suck. Vikram felt himself go faint but the pain from the salt and chilli in his veins was so intense that it would keep even the dead awake, so he stayed alert. Kali smacked her lips and leant back.

'There is a new and fresh taste in this blood,' she mused, 'I have not tasted it before.'

As she sat savouring Vikram's blood, her face smeared red, he leapt straight into the boiling cauldron of oil. He wasn't going to wait for those *dakinis* to take charge of him. Who knows, they might recognize him? Then when he was cooked and served to Kali and she had picked the bones and every shred of flesh on them was gone, the *dakinis* cleansed the skeleton and Kali reached for the salver of golden liquid.

And afterwards, as she prepared to sprinkle the elixir on his bones, she stroked her full belly and smiled with the pleasure of secrets only she knew.

'I have been eating you for eleven months, Raja,' she said, 'but there is a succulence and piquancy about you today that I've never tasted before.' She laughed loudly.

The *dakinis* crouched and cackled and gurgled, knowing their mistress was on the verge of a triumph, but they were not privy to her secrets.

'Since you were so deliciously saucy and spicy today,' said Kali playfully, 'I will grant you a wish.'

'Three wishes,' said Vikram quickly, delighted that the goddess was falling for his trick.

Kali laughed. 'You are as saucy as you taste. I like that in a king. Three wishes then. What is the first?'

'Give me the elixir of life.'

Kali poured the golden liquor lavishly over Vikram, then when he sat up wholed, she handed him the salver with the remaining liquid.

'Enough for one life,' she laughed. 'The second wish now.'

'Give me your gold-making scarf,' demanded Vikram.

'You shall have it. Your third wish.'

Vikram inhaled deeply and brought together all the courage he had.

'Bequeath your blessings to this kingdom and its king, then leave forever.'

Kali had laughed with all of Vikram's requests as if they pleased her to the core of her heart. Now she laughed a deeper, most joyful laugh and said – 'My work here is done, Vikram, I intend to leave anyway.'

And she disappeared.

That was when Vikram realized she had known all along who he was!

After that, Vikram hurried back to the kingdom and gave the king the scarf of gold. The king thanked him and gave him a royal caval-cade to accompany him home. On his way back, he stopped to thank the old woman who had sent him on this mission. But there was no old woman there. It had been Kali all the time.

You see, Vikram had been a true worshipper of Kali all his life and when he found himself in trouble, she made everything happen like this to help him out. That was one of the times she stole a march over the wily old Death-god Yama. And that liquid in the salver brought the priest's wife back to life! What games those up there play with us! Sometimes they shower flowers; at other times they hail down arrows.

181

The Old Eagle-Hawk Woman

(Aboriginal)

In the dreamtime an old woman named Ngaroomba lived among the rocks. This old woman was of the Maledna tribe and was the mother of two girls who lived with her.

And the old woman would come out of her place among the rocks and begin singing a song. And the girls would dance and cause a cloud of dust to go up into the sky.

One day two boys came along to this place and saw what they thought was smoke rising into the sky. Towards evening the two boys began to come up to where the girls were dancing. And the two girls saw the boys and said to the old woman, 'Mother, here are two boys.'

'Oh,' said the old woman, 'you had better go over and have a talk with them.'

And later the old woman said to the two boys, 'You can camp with us tonight.' And each boy and girl lay down together on either side of the fire.

And at midnight the old woman got up and took a huge stone and, with it, killed both of the boys while they slept.

And in the night the two girls woke up calling to their mother, 'Mother, we want some meat to eat.' But the old woman said to them, 'You must go out hunting,' and sent them off on a walkabout.

And when the girls were gone, the old woman made a ground oven and cooked both the boys in it, and then she ate them both. And the old woman made her feet like the pads of a dingo. Then she made tracks all about the camp and tracks leading off out of the camp. And when the two girls came back she told them that the wild dogs had been and eaten the two boys.

And the old woman made the girls dance and raise a cloud of

dust and bring many young boys to her camp for a long time. And the old woman killed and ate over a hundred blackfellows in this way.

Now, two boys of the Kurrababa tribe came upon this camp when the old woman and the girls were away. And as the two boys were looking around the camp, they saw many spirits of blackfellows wandering about. And the two boys went away out of the camp and waited until it got late. Then they came back and were met by the two girls. And the two girls told them that they could come into the camp.

And in the night, the two boys got up and put a hollow log alongside each of the girls. Then they sat apart from the flickering light of the fire and watched. And they saw the old woman steal up with a huge stone between her hands. And when she came to where the first girl was sleeping, the two boys leapt out of the darkness and fell upon her with their boomerangs.

And before the old woman was dead, the elder of the two boys said to her, 'You should not have eaten blackfellows. You should have eaten goanna, wallaby or blue-tongue lizard.'

And the two brothers broke up the old woman with the stone she had carried. And the old woman afterwards turned into the eagle-hawk.

Then the two brothers said, 'We must turn into flying-foxes.' But to the two girls they said, 'You shall turn into two crimson-winged parrots, and you shall fly, calling through the trees to feed on the flowers.'

The Two Children and the Witch

(Portuguese)

There was once a woman who had a son and a daughter. The mother one day sent her son to buy five reis' worth of beans, and then said to both: 'My children, go as far out on the road as you shall find shells of beans strewed on the path, and when you reach the wood you will find me there collecting fire-wood.'

The children did as they were bid; and after the mother had gone out they went following the track of the beans which she went strewing along the road, but they did not find her in the wood or anywhere else. As night had come on they perceived in the darkness a light shining at a distance, easy of access. They walked on towards it, and they soon came up to an old woman who was frying cakes. The old woman was blind of one eye, and the boy went on the blind side and stole a cake, because he felt so hungry. Believing that it was her cat which had stolen the cake, she said, 'You thief of a cat! Leave my cakes alone; they are not meant for you!' The little boy now said to his sister, 'You go now and take a cake.' But the little girl replied, 'I cannot do so, as I am sure to laugh.' Still, as they boy persisted upon it and urged her to try, she had no other alternative but to do so. She went on the side of the old woman's blind eye and stole another of her cakes. The old woman, again thinking that it was her cat, said, 'Be off! Shoo you old pussy; these cakes are not meant for you!' The little girl now burst out into a fit of laughter, and the old hag, turning round then, noticed the two children, and addressed them thus: 'Ah! Is it you, my dear grandchildren? Eat, eat away, and get fat!' She then took hold of them and thrust them into a large box full of chestnuts, and shut them up. Next day she came close to the box and spoke to them thus: 'Show me your little fingers, my pets, that I may be able to judge whether you have grown fat and sleek.' The children put out their little fingers as desired. But the next day the old hag again asked them: 'Show your little fingers, my little dears, that I may see if you have grown fat and plump!' The children, instead of their little fingers, showed her the tail of a cat they had found inside the box. The old hag then said: 'My pets, you can come out now, for you have grown nice and plump.' She took them out of the box and told them they must go with her and gather sticks.

The children went into the wood searching one way while the old hag took another direction. When they had arrived at a certain spot they met a fay. This fay said to them: 'You are gathering sticks, my children, to heat the oven, but you do not know that the old hag wants to bake you in it.' She further told them that the old witch meant to order them to stand on the baker's peel, saying: 'Stand on this peel, my little pets, that I may see you dance in the oven'; but that they were to ask her to sit upon it herself first, that so they might learn the way to do it. The fay then went away.

Shortly after they had met this good lady they found the old witch in the wood. They gathered together in bundles all the fire-sticks they had collected, and carried them home to heat the oven. When they had finished heating the oven, the old hag swept it carefully out, and then said to the little ones, 'Sit here, my little darlings, on this peel, that I may see how prettily you dance in the oven!' The children replied to the witch as the good fay had instructed them: 'Sit you here, little granny, that we may first see you dance in the oven.' As the hag's intention was to bake the children, she sat on the peel first, so as to coax them to do the same after her; but the very moment the children saw her on the peel they thrust the peel into the oven with the witch upon it. The old hag gave a great start, and was burnt to a cinder immediately after. The children took possession of the shed and all it contained.

My Sweet Witch

(Central African: Congo)

A young man, Matsona, loved a girl whose name was Kitsumuna, and every night he brought her palm-wine. One day she told him: 'Tomorrow you may not come, come the night after.' The young man thought that strange, but he did not suspect the real reason, which was much worse than he thought: she was a witch! However, the young man decided to go and visit his sweetheart anyway, but just as a precaution he took some palm-nuts and put them in his loincloth.

He then went out and knocked at her door. She appeared very embarrassed at seeing him, but she could not refuse to let him in.

So he made love to her; but suddenly, in the middle of the night, he heard the voice of her father, the village chief, calling from above. It was in reality the chief's spirit, perched on top of the hut roof.

The chief entered the hut the way a bat would fly down from the roof; her mother followed and several other villagers came flying in, all bodiless. When the spirits were all present, the chief ordered his daughter Kitsumuna to come and sit with them. She was embarrassed because she knew that her lover could hear every word, although no one would be able to see in the dark night, not even witches.

Her father, the chief, gave her a piece of meat and told her to eat it. She dropped it clumsily, and the other witches too dropped their witches' meat. Therefore the chief witchmaster decided that not everyone in the village was asleep, and that someone must be over-hearing them. So he flew up, out of the hut and over the village, and sprinkled sleeping water over the huts to make quite sure that all the innocent people would be soundly asleep.

After his return to the witches' coven, it appeared that the magic water had still not worked on everyone, for when he tried to pour the sauce made with human blood, he spilt it. This proved that the sleepless person must be hiding in the girl's own hut. They searched it and finally found Kitsumuna's suitor Matsona.

He was invited by the chief to join the coven, and at once received a piece of meat. He knew very well what that meant: he had to contribute a human body at some future coven; the price for joining was to become a murderer. Since, however, the price for not joining was to become a victim, he had very little option.

He found a shrewd way out of this dilemma: seeing that his girl-friend's mother was one of the coven he said, like a well-brought-up young man: 'Of course I accept the meat with pleasure, but I really could not eat in the presence of my mother-in-law.'

They all agreed that this was impolite, even among witches, so he was allowed to eat sitting in a corner behind the bed, with his back turned to the others. In this manner he was able to take the palm-nuts from his pocket and eat them instead so that everyone could hear him chew. His girlfriend was of course very happy that her lover had joined the coven. She did not know that he had buried the food she had given him in the mud floor of the hut. After the meal the chief said: 'Now you must let us have one of your relatives, your mother for instance, or your grandmother.' The young Matsona said he agreed because he knew that that was expected of him.

Shortly afterwards the girl's grandmother died. The villagers suspected that she had not died of old age and urged the chief to send for a diviner. Matsona was the person sent to find a diviner, and on his way he passed through a nearby village where his future brother-in-law, Katsumuna's brother, lived. Matsona told him what his errand was, that he had been sent to find a diviner to investigate the mysterious death of Katsumuna's grandmother.

Her brother said: 'She is my own grandmother too. If her death has been caused by witchcraft, I must come and smell out the evil-doers. As you know, I am myself a diviner. I am grateful to you for telling me all this. I will come with you now, and on my arrival in the village, I will stay with you to begin with, merely as a future relative, so that I have time to sound the situation out without arousing suspicion.'

When the appointed day for the divining ritual arrived, the chief assembled all the inhabitants in the village square. The diviner then asked them to go and stand in groups, dividing free men from slaves, descendants from in-laws, and so on. The chief was beginning to feel uneasy, for he sensed that the wise diviner had perceived where the root of the trouble lay, so the chief's heart was burning with anxiety. Finally, the diviner had narrowed down his suspects to a single family, all the time singing:

Bapfumu wau ntanda
Baana wau ntanda . . .
Free men their rank,
slaves their rank . . .

In this manner he singled out the family of the chief, and dismissed all the others as acquitted. The chief, his wife and the members of the coven had to drink poison as a divine judgement, and they all died, including Katsumuna.

The Curse

(Armenian)

Once upon a time my grandmother's grandfather's father was walking through the town, deep in thought, when suddenly he looked up and saw a female elk running with the liver of a human being in her hands and a bunch of little elk children racing after her, yelling for food.

'Mama, food!' they cried one after another.

'All right, all right, wait until I get to the river where I can dip this liver into water. You know that you can't eat it yet,' the mother said, running in the direction of the river.

Now this ancestor of mine was a good man, and when he saw this sight, he shuddered. He knew that the liver was that of a human being and that, according to tradition, when it was dipped into water, the person to whom it belonged would die immediately. He had to stop the female elk – yet what was he to do? Suddenly he remembered stories of elks and recalled that they could be stopped from doing evil if a needle was pinned to their clothes.

Quick as thought, this ancestor removed the pin which held his turban together and stuck it on the elk mother's clothes. The woman stopped in her tracks. When the elk children saw their mother caught, they left her and ran swiftly away.

'Remove the pin and I will do anything you ask,' the elk begged the man.

'Whose liver is this?' the man asked.

The dwarf did not answer. When he asked her again, she told him that it was the liver of one of the young brides of the town who had just borne a child.

'Oh, you take the liver of an innocent young bride when you

know well enough that just as soon as you dip it into water, she will die. And yet, when you are caught, you expect pity. Why should I pity you? Take the liver and put it back into the body from which you wrenched it. Hurry, and when you have done that, return to me,' he commanded. The young bride, from whose body the liver had been torn, was in great agony and near death; but when the elk replaced her liver, she began to breathe easily and soon recovered.

The elk returned to her captor and begged him to release her. 'Let me go. I have children to feed; I must take care of them,' she said.

'You ask me to give you your freedom so that you can take care of your children, yet you would leave that young, new-born child an orphan to satisfy the appetites of your children.'

The elk was put to work in the home of her captor. She did all the cooking, baking, cleaning and serving. As she was an excellent worker, she never lagged in her duties although she always asked people to remove the pin from her clothes. But as everyone knew of her evil deed, no one would free her. So she worked year after year, always begging for her release. Finally after seven years, she approached her master once more: 'Remove the pin and set me free. I will not bother you or harm you or seven generations of your family,' she promised.

'But if I let you go, I know that you will harm us in one way or another.'

'If you set me free, I will not harm seven generations of your family. I will only cause all of your wooden spoons to break easily.' Soon the mother elk was liberated and kept her promise. She has not yet harmed the people in our family, but true to her curse, in Armenia our spoons did break easily.

Two Children and a Witch

(Melanesian)

On the island of Mele in the New Hebrides, a married couple had two children – a son and a daughter. The boy's name was Bogifini and the girl was Bogitini.

One day the parents said to the children, 'We are going gardening. Be good children while we are away. Do not go near the sea. There is a Witch, Likele, who lives near the salt-water, who likes to catch little boys and girls. Watch out, or she'll get you.'

The children promised to be good, and not to go near the salt-water. They shivered with fright at the thought of Likele.

'We won't go near the salt-water,' they both said.

So the mother and father took up their large pointed digging sticks, rested them on their shoulders and away they went to their food gardens.

No sooner had they gone than a beautiful red and gold butterfly came fluttering by. How beautiful it looked in the bright tropical sunshine! It flew round and round, alighted for a moment on a flower; then it took flight again, darting here and there.

Bogifini called, 'Look, Bogitini, look at the beautiful butterfly!'

They both ran after it to try to catch it. The butterfly would settle on a leaf or flower for a moment; then it would fly off again, and away the children went jumping over stones, and struggling through long grass; on and on they chased the butterfly. The boy and girl forgot their promise to their parents, and they forgot their fear of the Likele.

Soon the children were running merrily towards the beach. Far out over rock pools flew the butterfly. It was low tide. There was sand, and there were rocks and coral with pools of water in it.

Soon the children forgot the butterfly.

'Look Bogifini,' said Bogitini. 'Look at these lovely fish. Oh, so many of them! Let's catch them.'

They caught them in their hands: little fish one and a half inches long.

'Oh, we can't hold them,' they said. 'We need a basket.'

So off they both raced home. They picked up their mother's fishing baskets – one for each of them. Their mother had made the baskets neatly woven of leaves, and closed at the top, so that no fish could leap or wriggle out.

Bogitini and Bogifini soon filled both baskets with the tiny fish. They felt very happy indeed. Naughty children! They had quite forgotten their promises, and their fear of Likele.

As they walked back over the rocks, splashing happily through shallow pools, they saw an alarming sight. It was the dreaded witch, Likele, lying on a rock with her head tilted back into the water. She was washing her hair in a rock pool. She had long frizzy hair. She lifted her head and shook out the water.

'Ha! ha!' she cried. 'What have we here? Come here, my sweet little pets! Come here!'

The children were rooted to the spot in terror.

'Come here!' she repeated. 'What have you got in those baskets?'

She opened the baskets, took out all the fish, threw them down her throat, swallowed them all, and then picked up poor little Bogitini and swallowed her – all except one of Bogitini's fingers. One little finger, bitten off by Likele, fell unnoticed on the sand.

Bogifini rushed to a coconut tree and walked up it. With his hands round the trunk, and the flat of his feet squarely on the trunk just below, he quickly walked up the tree.

'Mother! Father!' he called. 'Mother! Father!'

'I think I hear one of our children calling, husband,' said the mother.

'Nonsense!' said her husband. 'I can't hear anything. Get on with your work, or I'll beat you with a stick, lazy woman!'

'Mother! Father!' came the call on the breeze. This time they both heard it. They ran to see what was the matter. Then the mother saw her son among the leaves of a coconut tree.

'Oh, my parents,' said Bogifini, 'we were naughty children.'

'Come down!' they cried. He slid down the tree.

'The witch swallowed my sister,' said the boy. He began to sob. Tears rained down the father's cheeks. The mother was more practical.

She had a stone axe in her hand. She had been using it to cut weeds away from her yam plants.

'Where is this Likele?' she said. 'Let us find her.' Soon she caught sight of the horrible creature. 'Ah! Likele, where is my daughter?'

'Your daughter?' said Likele. 'What's this talk about a daughter? I didn't see any little girl.'

The father had stopped weeping. He had a long reed spear in his hand. It had points made of sharks' teeth.

'Don't lie to me,' he said. And seizing Likele with his left hand, he held her down, and with his right hand, he drove the point of his spear right through her throat.

In a moment the witch was dead. The mother slit Likele's stomach open with the sharp edge of her axe. Out stepped dear little Bogitini. How they all rejoiced to see her again! They were so happy to be together once more.

El-Muzayyara

(Egyptian)

One night Idrees was returning from Barshoom, which is about three kilometres from here. He was riding his mare. He took the main road. There at the bridge he heard a voice calling, 'Oh, Idrees; oh, Idrees.'

He looked around and did not see anyone. He thought that it was the wind or something and kept on going. The voice called again, 'Oh, Idrees, come and help me.'

He looked towards the voice and saw a woman standing by the canal with a water jar in front of her; she couldn't raise it to carry it over her head.

Idrees dismounted and walked to her. He saw that she was not from our village. He asked her, 'What are you doing here at this hour?'

She answered, 'I am from over there,' turning her head towards the eastern part of the village. 'We are neighbours. I just had to get water, and time passed and it became too late. Wouldn't you let me mount behind you and ride to my house?'

Idrees said, 'All right.'

He put her behind him on the mare and went on. A short while later, he noticed that she was restless. He looked behind him, only to see her getting her breast out. It was an iron breast, with fire glowing at the nipple. He immediately realized that she was the *muzayyara* – her hair came down to her knees (they are beautiful) – and she was going to kill him. He poked his mare with all his might and caused it to rear up, while he held tightly to the reins. She (the *muzayyara*) fell to the ground, and he flew away like the wind.

As he got farther away, he heard her biting her finger and grum-
bling, 'Akh! Son of a dog, you got away from me!' Her eyes were
sparkling with fire.

PART EIGHT

Trials and Contests

The Bewitched Churn

(Irish)

Near the townland of Scarawalsh there lived an old woman of bad repute with her neighbours. She was seen, one May eve, skimming a well that lay in a neighbouring farm, and when that was done, she went into the adjoining meadow, and skimmed the dew off the grass. One person said he heard her muttering, 'Come all to me, and none to he.' In a day or two, the owner of the farm, coming in from the fields about noon, found the family still at the churn, and no sign of butter. He was a little frightened, and looked here and there, and, at last, spied a bit of stale butter fastened to the mantel beam of the open fireplace.

'Oh, you may as well stop,' said he, 'look what's there!' 'Oh, the witch's butter,' said one of the girls, 'cut it off the mantelpiece.' 'No use,' said another, 'it must be a charmed knife, or nothing. Go and consult the fairy man, in the old ruined house. If he doesn't advise you, nobody can.' The master of the house took the advice, and, when they had milk enough for another churning, this is what they did.

They twisted twigs of the mountain ash round their cows' necks, they made a big fire, and thrust into it the sock and coulter of the plough; they fastened the ash twigs round the churn, and connected them to the chain of the plough-irons; shut door and windows, so that they could not be opened from without; and merrily began the churning.

Just as the plough-irons were becoming red-hot, someone tried the latch of the door, and immediately they saw the face of the witch outside the window. 'What do you want, good woman?' 'The seed of the fire, and I want to help you at the churning. I heard what happened to you, and I'm rather lucky.' Here she roared out; for the burning plough-irons were scorching her inside. 'What ails you, poor woman?' 'Oh I have a terrible colic! Let me into the fire for mercy's sake, and give me a warm drink.' 'Oh, musha, but it's ourselves are sorry for you; but we could not open door or window now for St Mogue himself; for 'fraid the witch 'ud come in and cut our quicken gads, or pull out the plough-irons, or even touch the churn-staff. She got a bit of butter out of the fresh churning the other day; and took a sod out of our fire; and till she brings back the butter and the sod we must labour away. Have patience, poor woman; when we see a sign of the butter we'll open the door for you, and give you such a warm tumbler of punch, with caraways in it, as would bring you back from death's door. Put more turf on, and keep the irons at red heat.' Another roar ensued, and then she ejaculated, 'Oh, purshuin' to all hard-hearted naygurs, that 'ud see a fellow-creature dying in misery outside of their door! Sure, I was coming to yous with relief, and this is the sort of relief you'd give me. Throw up the window a bit, and take those things I made out for yous. Throw the bit of butter you'll find in this sheet of white paper into the churn, and this sod of turf into the fire, and cut away the bit of butter on the mantel beam with this knife, and give it back to me, till I return it to the knowledgeable woman I begged it from for yous.'

The direction being followed, the butter began to appear in heaps in the churn. There was great joy and huzzaing, and they even opened the door to show hospitality to the old rogue. But she departed in rage, giving them her blessing in these words, 'I won't take bit nor sup for yez. Yez have thrated me like a Hussian or a Cromwellian, and not like an honest neighbour, and so I lave my curse, and the curse of Cromwell on yez all!'

Rabbi Joshua and the Witch

(Jewish)

In their travels through Babylon, Rabbi Joshua ben Hanania and Rabbi Eliezer ben Hyrcanus arrived at a town in which there was to be found but a handful of Jewish families. It had been years since these Jews had contact with their brethren. Still, they were true to their tradition, and the fathers taught their sons all that they had been taught. So it was that when Rabbi Joshua and Rabbi Eliezer happened to pass two of these Jewish children playing in the street, they saw them making piles of sand, and one of them set one pile aside and said, 'This one shall be for the tithe.'

Now when they heard this, the two sages knew at once that the children must be Jewish, and they were very surprised that there were any Jews in that city. They asked one of the children to lead them to the Jewish quarter, and when they got there the rabbis knocked on the door of the first house they saw. When the family living there found that fellow Jews had come to visit them, they were overjoyed, and they welcomed the rabbis to stay as their guests.

That evening the rabbis joined their hosts for dinner. The meal was quite delicious, but the rabbis observed that before any dish was served to them, the host would first carry it into a nearby room. Rabbi Eliezer became suspicious about this and asked why it was done. Then the host told them that his old father was in that room, and that he had vowed not to leave there until rabbis should return to that city.

Now since both visitors were rabbis, they told the host to invite his old father to join them, and he gladly went to do so. When the old man came, his eyes filled with tears at the sight of rabbis in the city again at last. Then Rabbi Joshua asked him why he had made such a strange vow to remain in his room. And the old man replied, 'I am growing old, and I want to know that my son will be a father before I depart from this world. But my son is childless, and I vowed to remain in that room until sages arrived who could pray that God bless him with a son.'

Both rabbis were moved at the old man's explanation, and Rabbi Eliezer asked Rabbi Joshua to try to help him if he could. Rabbi Joshua agreed to do his best, and he asked their host, the old man's son, to bring him some flax-seed. When the seed was brought, Rabbi Joshua spread it upon the table. Then he took some drops of water in his fingers and scattered them upon the seeds. All at once, much to the amazement of everyone who was watching, the seeds began to grow.

In the space of a moment the flax was fully grown, as if it had taken root in the table-top. Then, while all watched in wonder, Rabbi Joshua reached deep into the flax and grabbed a bunch in his hand. And as he raised his hand up from out of the flax he pulled out first the locks of hair of a witch, then her head, and finally her whole body. Everyone in the room stared at that witch with complete astonishment. But Rabbi Joshua continued to hold her by the hair, and he stared in her eyes and said: 'I order you to break the spell you have cast over this man, so that he may have a child of his own.' And the witch trembled with fear before Rabbi Joshua's anger, and confessed that she had indeed made a charm and cast such a spell, but she pleaded that she could not break the spell, since she had cast the bewitched charm into the depths of the sea. Then Rabbi Joshua said to her, 'In that case, you will remain imprisoned in this wooden table until the spell is broken!' And he let go of the witch's hair, so that she sank back into the table, beneath the sprouted flax – which suddenly withered, so that only the seeds were to be seen, scattered on the table as they had been in the first place.

Then everyone knew that the old man's son had indeed been the victim of the witch's spell and mourned because the spell could not be broken. But Rabbi Joshua did not abandon hope. Instead he asked the childless man to take them to the shore of the sea in that city. And when the man did so, Rabbi Joshua stood there and invoked the presence of Rahab, the Prince of the Sea. And he called upon Rahab to recover the lost charm at once, so that the spell could be broken. And lo and behold, suddenly the charm rose to the surface of the water and floated to shore, directly at Rabbi

Joshua's feet. He opened it, took out the parchment on which the spell was written, and burned it, and the spell was broken once and for all. At that very same instant, the witch imprisoned in the table was set free, and went running out of that house as fast as she could, never again to be seen in that city.

Before the year was out the old man's son became a father. The family was overjoyed, particularly the grandfather, who lived long enough to see his grandson enter into the yoke of the *mitzvot*. And the name of that child was Judah ben Bathyra, and he himself became one of the sages and studied under Rabbi Joshua, who gladly taught him everything he knew.

The Witchmaster's Advice

(North American: Ozark)

The story goes that a hillman was just falling asleep when a pretty girl appeared with a bridle in her hand. In a twinkling she turned the poor fellow into a pony, leapt on his back, and rode him wildly through the woods. Later on she hitched him to a tree at the mouth of a cave, and he saw a group of 'furriners' carrying big sacks of money into the cavern. Finally she rode him back home, and he woke up next morning all tired out and brier-scratched. This happened night after night, and the hillman consulted a famous witchmaster. The witchmaster advised him to mark the tree to which he was tied at night, so that he could find it again in the daytime. Then, said the witchmaster, it would be an easy matter to waylay the witch and kill her with a silver bullet, and afterwards they could get the treasure in the cave. So the next night, being transformed into a horse, the hillman drapped as many drappin's as he could to mark the place and started in to chaw a big blaze on the sapling to which he was tied. 'I chawed an' I chawed,' he said, 'an' all of a sudden come a hell of a noise an' a big flash o' light. Then I heerd a lot o' hollerin', an' it sounded like my old woman was a-doin' the hollerin'. Quick as a wink I seen I was home again, an' it seemed like' – here the hillman stole a furtive glance at his wife, who sat stolidly smoking by the fireplace – 'it seemed like I'd went an' benastied the bed-blankets, an' dang near bit the old woman's leg off!'

The Son of Seven Queens

(Indian)

Once upon a time there lived a King who had seven Queens, but no children. This was a great grief to him, especially when he remembered that on his death there would be no heir to inherit the kingdom.

Now it happened one day that a poor old fakir came to the King, and said, 'Your prayers are heard, your desire shall be accomplished, and one of your seven Queens shall bear a son.'

The King's delight at this promise knew no bounds, and he gave orders for appropriate festivities to be prepared against the coming event throughout the length and breadth of the land.

Meanwhile the seven Queens lived luxuriously in a splendid palace, attended by hundreds of female slaves, and fed to their hearts' content on sweetmeats and confectionery.

Now the King was very fond of hunting, and one day, before he started, the seven Queens sent him a message saying, 'May it please our dearest lord not to hunt towards the north today, for we have dreamt bad dreams, and fear lest evil should befall you.'

The King, to allay their anxiety, promised regard for their wishes, and set out towards the south; but as luck would have it, although he hunted diligently, he found no game. Nor had he more success to the east or west, so that, being a keen sportsman, and determined not to go home empty-handed, he forgot all about his promise, and turned to the north. Here also he was at first unsuccessful, but just as he made up his mind to give up for that day, a white hind with golden horns and silver hoofs flashed past him into a thicket. So quickly did it pass that he scarcely saw it; nevertheless a burning desire to capture and possess the beautiful strange creature filled

205

his breast. He instantly ordered his attendants to form a ring round the thicket, and so encircle the hind; then, gradually narrowing the circle, he pressed forward till he could distinctly see the white hind panting in the midst. Nearer and nearer he advanced, till, just as he thought to lay hold of the beautiful strange creature, it gave one mighty bound, leapt clean over the King's head, and fled towards the mountains. Forgetful of all else, the King, setting spurs to his horse, followed at full speed. On, on he galloped, leaving his retinue far behind, keeping the white hind in view, never drawing bridle, until, finding himself in a narrow ravine with no outlet, he reined in his steed. Before him stood a miserable hovel, into which, being tired after his long, unsuccessful chase, he entered to ask for a drink of water. An old woman, seated in the hut at a spinning-wheel, answered his request by calling to her daughter, and immediately from an inner room came a maiden so lovely and charming, so white-skinned and golden-haired, that the King was transfixed by astonishment at seeing so beautiful a sight in the wretched hovel.

She held the vessel of water to the King's lips, and as he drank he looked into her eyes, and then it became clear to him that the girl was no other than the white hind with the golden horns and silver feet he had chased so far.

Her beauty bewitched him, so he fell on his knees, begging her to return with him as his bride; but she only laughed, saying seven Queens were quite enough even for a King to manage. However, when he would take no refusal, but implored her to have pity on him, promising her everything she could desire, she replied, 'Give me the eyes of your seven Queens, and then perhaps I may believe you mean what you say.'

The King was so carried away by the glamour of the white hind's magical beauty, that he went home at once, had the eyes of his seven Queens taken out, and, after throwing the poor blind creatures into a noisome dungeon whence they could not escape, set off once more for the hovel in the ravine, bearing with him his horrible offering. But the white hind only laughed cruelly when she saw the fourteen eyes, and threading them as a necklace, flung it round her mother's neck saying, 'Wear that, little mother, as a keepsake, whilst I am away in the King's palace.'

Then she went back with the bewitched monarch, as his bride, and he gave her the seven Queens' rich clothes and jewels to wear, the seven Queens' palace to live in, and the seven Queens' slaves to wait upon her; so that she really had everything a witch could desire.

Now, very soon after the seven wretched hapless Queens had their eyes torn out, and were cast into prison, a baby was born to the youngest of the Queens. It was a handsome boy, but the other Queens were very jealous that the youngest amongst them should be so fortunate. But though at first they disliked the handsome little boy, he soon proved so useful to them, that ere long they all looked on him as their son. Almost as soon as he could walk about he began scraping at the mud wall of their dungeon, and in an incredibly short space of time had made a hole big enough for him to crawl through. Through this he disappeared, returning in an hour or so laden with sweetmeats, which he divided equally amongst the seven blind Queens.

As he grew older he enlarged the hole, and slipped out two or three times every day to play with the little nobles in the town. No one knew who the tiny boy was, but everybody liked him, and he was so full of funny tricks and antics, so merry and bright, that he was sure to be rewarded by some girdle-cakes, a handful of parched grain, or some sweatmeats. All these things he brought home to his seven mothers, as he loved to call the seven blind Queens, who by his help lived on in their dungeon when all the world thought they had starved to death ages before.

At last, when he was quite a big lad, he one day took his bow and arrow, and went out to seek for game. Coming by chance past the palace where the white hind lived in wicked splendour and magnificence, he saw some pigeons fluttering round the white marble turrets, and, taking good aim, shot one dead. It came tumbling past the very window where the white Queen was sitting; she rose to see what was the matter, and looked out. At the first glance of the handsome young lad standing there bow in hand, she knew by witchcraft that it was the King's son.

She nearly died of envy and spite, determining to destroy the lad without delay; therefore, sending a servant to bring him to her presence, she asked him if he would sell her the pigeon he had just shot.

'No,' replied the sturdy lad, 'the pigeon is for my seven blind mothers, who live in the noisome dungeon, and who would die if I did not bring them food.'

'Poor souls!' cried the cunning white witch; 'would you not like to bring them their eyes again? Give me the pigeon, my dear, and I faithfully promise to show you where to find them.'

Hearing this, the lad was delighted beyond measure, and gave up the pigeon at once. Whereupon the white Queen told him to seek her mother without delay, and ask for the eyes which she wore as a necklace.

'She will not fail to give them,' said the cruel Queen, 'if you show her this token on which I have written what I want done.'

So saying, she gave the lad a piece of broken potsherd, with these words inscribed on it – 'Kill the bearer at once, and sprinkle his blood like water!'

Now, as the son of seven Queens could not read, he took the fatal message cheerfully, and set off to find the white Queen's mother.

Whilst he was journeying he passed through a town, where every one of the inhabitants looked so sad, that he could not help asking what was the matter. They told him it was because the King's only daughter refused to marry; so when her father died there would be no heir to the throne. They greatly feared she must be out of her mind, for though every good-looking young man in the kingdom had been shown to her, she declared she would only marry one who was the son of seven mothers, and who ever heard of such a thing? The King, in despair, had ordered every man who entered the city gates to be led before the Princess; so, much to the lad's impatience, for he was in an immense hurry to find his mother's eyes, he was dragged into the presence chamber.

No sooner did the Princess catch sight of him than she blushed, and, turning to the King, said, 'Dear father, this is my choice!'

Never were such rejoicings as these few words produced. The inhabitants nearly went wild with joy, but the son of seven Queens said he would not marry the Princess unless they first let him re-cover his mothers' eyes. When the beautiful bride heard his story, she asked to see the potsherd, for she was very learned and clever. Seeing the treacherous words, she said nothing, but taking another similar-shaped bit of potsherd, she wrote on it these words – 'Take care of this lad, giving him all he desires,' and returned it to the son of seven Queens, who, none the wiser, set off on his quest.

Ere long he arrived at the hovel in the ravine where the white witch's mother, a hideous old creature, grumbled dreadfully on reading the message, especially when the lad asked for the necklace of eyes. Nevertheless she took it off, and gave it him, saying, 'There are only thirteen of 'em now, for I lost one last week.'

The lad, however, was only too glad to get any at all, so he hurried home as fast as he could to his seven mothers, and gave two eyes apiece to the six elder Queens; but to the youngest he gave one, saying, 'Dearest little mother! – I will be your other eye always!'

After this he set off to marry the Princess, as he had promised, but when passing by the white Queen's palace he saw some pigeons on the roof. Drawing his bow, he shot one, and it came fluttering past the window. The white hind looked out, and lo! there was the King's son alive and well.

She cried with hatred and disgust, but sending for the lad, asked him how he had returned so soon, and when she heard how he had brought home the thirteen eyes, and given them to the seven blind Queens, she could hardly restrain her rage. Nevertheless she pretended to be charmed with his success, and told him that if he would give her this pigeon also, she would reward him with the Jogi's wonderful cow, whose milk flows all day long, and makes a pond as big as a kingdom. The lad, nothing loth, gave her the pigeon; whereupon, as before, she bade him go ask her mother for the cow, and gave him a potsherd whereupon was written – 'Kill this lad without fail, and sprinkle his blood like water!'

But on the way the son of seven Queens looked in on the Princess, just to tell her how he came to be delayed, and she, after reading the message on the potsherd, gave him another in its stead; so that when the lad reached the old hag's hut and asked her for the Jogi's cow, she could not refuse, but told the boy how to find it; and bidding him of all the things not to be afraid of the eighteen thousand demons who kept watch and ward over the treasure, told him to be off before she became too angry at her daughter's foolishness in thus giving away so many good things.

Then the lad did as he had been told bravely. He journeyed on and on till he came to a milk-white pond, guarded by the eighteen thousand demons. They were really frightful to behold, but, plucking up courage, he whistled a tune as he walked through them, looking neither to the right nor the left. By and by he came upon the Jogi's cow, tall, white and beautiful, while the Jogi himself, who was king of all the demons, sat milking her day and night, and the milk streamed from her udder, filling the milk-white tank.

The Jogi, seeing the lad, called out fiercely, 'What do you want here?'

Then the lad answered, according to the old hag's bidding, 'I want your skin, for King Idra is making a new kettle-drum, and says your skin is nice and tough.'

Upon this the Jogi began to shiver and shake (for no Jinn or Jogi dares disobey King Idra's command), and, falling at the lad's feet, cried, 'If you will spare me I will give you anything I possess, even my beautiful white cow!'

To this the son of seven Queens, after a little pretended hesitation, agreed, saying that after all it would not be difficult to find a nice tough skin like Jogi's elsewhere; so, driving the wonderful cow before him, he set off homewards. The seven Queens were delighted to possess so marvellous an animal, and though they toiled from morning till night making curds and whey, besides selling milk to the confectioners, they could not use half the cow gave, and became richer and richer by the day.

Seeing them so comfortably off, the son of seven Queens started with a light heart to marry the Princess; but when passing the white hind's palace he could not resist sending a bolt at some pigeons which were cooing on the parapet. One fell dead just beneath the window where the white Queen was sitting. Looking out, she saw the lad hale and hearty standing before her, and grew whiter than ever with rage and spite.

She sent for him to ask how he had returned so soon, and when she heard how kindly her mother had received him, she nearly had a fit; however, she dissembled her feelings as well as she could, and, smiling sweetly, said she was glad to have been able to fulfil her promise, and that if he would give her this third pigeon, she would do yet more for him than she had done before, by giving him the million-fold rice, which ripens in one night.

The lad was of course delighted at the very idea, and, giving up the pigeon, set off on his quest, armed as before with a potsherd, on which was written, 'Do not fail this time. Kill the lad, and sprinkle his blood like water!'

But when he looked in on his Princess, just to prevent her becoming anxious about him, she asked to see the potsherd as usual, and substituted another, on which was written, 'Yet again give this lad all he requires, for his blood shall be as your blood!'

Now when the old hag saw this, and heard how the lad wanted the million-fold rice which ripens in a single night, she fell into the most furious rage, but being terribly afraid of her daughter, she controlled herself, and bade the boy go and find the field guarded by eighteen millions of demons, warning him on no account to look back after having plucked the tallest spike of rice, which grew in the centre.

So the son of seven Queens set off, and soon came to the field where, guarded by eighteen millions of demons, the million-fold rice grew. He walked on bravely, looking neither to the right or left, till he reached the centre and plucked the tallest ear, but as he turned homewards a thousand sweet voices rose behind him, crying in tenderest accents, 'Pluck me too! Oh, please pluck me too!' He looked back, and lo! there was nothing left of him but a little heap of ashes!

Now as time passed by and the lad did not return, the old hag grew uneasy, remembering the message 'his blood shall be as your blood'; so she set off to see what had happened.

Soon she came to the heap of ashes, and knowing by her arts what it was, she took a little water, and kneading the ashes into a paste, formed it into the likeness of a man; then, putting a drop of blood from her little finger into its mouth, she blew on it, and instantly the son of seven Queens started up as well as ever.

'Don't you disobey orders again!' grumbled the old hag, 'or next time I'll leave you alone. Now be off, before I repent my kindness!'

So the son of seven Queens returned joyful to his seven mothers, who, by the aid of the million-fold rice, soon became the richest people in the kingdom. Then they celebrated their son's marriage to the clever Princess with all imaginable pomp; but the bride was so clever, she would not rest until she had made known her husband to his father, and punished the wicked white witch. So she made her husband build a palace exactly like the one in which the seven Queens had lived, and in which the white witch now dwelt in splendour. Then, when all was prepared, she bade her husband give a grand feast to the King. Now the King had heard much of the mysterious son of seven Queens, and his marvellous wealth, so he gladly accepted the invitation; but what was his astonishment when on entering the palace he found it was a facsimile of his own in every particular! And when his host, richly attired, led him straight to the private hall, where on royal thrones sat the seven Queens, dressed as he had last seen them, he was speechless with surprise, until the Princess, coming forward, threw herself at his feet, and told him the whole story. Then the King awoke from his enchantment, and his anger rose against the wicked white hind who had bewitched him so long, until he could not contain himself. So she was put to death, and her grave ploughed over, and after that the seven Queens returned to their own splendid palace, and everybody lived happily.

The Caellie Bheur

(Scottish)

Once the Hag of the Ridges, Caellie Bheur, captured the Sweetheart of Spring. She went down from her home on Ben Wyvis to the plains of Skye between the Red Hills on the east and the Great Loch on the west. There, she flung a brown fleece at the girl and said, 'Wash this brown fleece white or you'll never go free.'

The maiden washed and scrubbed but the fleece showed no sign of turning white. Meanwhile the Caellie herself boiled her clothes in Corryvrecken, her terrifying cauldron – clean as clean and shining white – and flung them over Storr to bleach and dry. Many days and nights went by and the weather in Skye remained terrible as it always was while the Caellie stayed. Then Spring decided he must fight with her. But the Caellie was an awesome hag and, naturally, Spring could not hold his own. Scrub, scrub, scrub, his sweetheart washed fleece again. Her fingers were worn, she was pale and sickly and despaired of getting the brown fleece white.

So Spring went to the Sun and told him his story. The Sun, being passionate and fiery, was incensed by the old hag and full of pity for Spring. In his intensity he flung his spear down on the moor where the Caellie was strolling. As the flaming spear struck the ground, it scorched the earth and blistered it and a ridge was formed six feet wide and six feet deep. The frightened hag buried herself beneath the roots of a holly bush. The maiden was free and joyfully reunited with Spring. But the ridge went on expanding until finally it erupted. Out of it flowed a glistening, molten mass which blazed and sparked for months. Then it dimmed from flaming red to glowing gold and smoked and spat until it became the Fire Hills.

To this day, the mountains blaze and glow proving that the Sun defeated the Caellie that cold season. And she's never managed to get snow on the Fire Hills.

Hag-Rog

(Canadian)

An old woman went to her doctor suffering from stomach pains and cramps and sleepless nights and all manner of ailments. The new-fangled machines in smart new hospitals showed up nothing wrong.

'Can *you* do anything for me?' she asked him.

The doctor asked the old woman, 'What do you think is causing all this?'

'My neighbour from two houses down,' she replied. 'Some say she's a witch.'

Well now, after twenty years in that community, the old doctor knew the antidote to that ill. He'd learned about 'hag-rog' long ago and it was very powerful medicine. So he told his patient the only way to cure it. She was to piss into a bottle then cork it firmly so that not a single drop escaped even if it were held upside down. Then she was to put it under her bed.

The old woman did that and as soon as she did, her stomach pains ceased, then her cramps, then she began to sleep well again. But her neighbour became ill. You could hear her screams of pain and frustration in the street. She went to the doctor complaining that she could not piss and this caused her great distress. It was right there in her bladder, just waiting to come out but could not. Not even a few little drops of it. As if it had been corked.

'Tell your patient,' she demanded, 'to uncork the bottle under her bed immediately.'

'I will,' the doctor reassured her, 'if you take off the spell you've put on her.'

So the neighbour cast off her malicious spell and the doctor's patient emptied her bottle, and the witch started pissing again. And how she pissed! She pissed buckets for a whole week. She'd do a little bit of work then run off happily to relieve herself, then a little bit more, then run off again. After a week she was back to normal. That witch never tangled with the old lady again.

Biddy Early, the Priest and the Crow

(Irish)

'Biddy was sick an' very bad. Now I can't tell you whether 'twas the way this parish priest was sent for or that he heard about her being sick, but anyway he went to the house when she was in bed, an' he went into the room to hear her confession. An' where he was hearing her confession at the back o' the house, there was a big ash tree outside, an' generally in nearly all the old houses there were very small windows. But the small window, anyway, was at the back o' the room, an' facing the tree. An' there was a crow outside in the tree an' the crow having Caw! Caw! Caw! all the time while the priest was hearing her confession.

'But after the confession Biddy says to him, "Father," says she, "could you bring in that crow to the end o' the bed?"

' "I'll try, anyway," says he.

'He started to pray an' read out of a book. The crow was all the time outside in the tree having Caw! Caw! Caw! out of him. But when the priest finished reading out o' the book, "I'll bring her in," says Biddy.

'She sat up in the bed an' she lifted up the pillow an' took out her magic bottle from under it. An' whatever she said, or whatever she did, the back window was open an' the crow flew in an' perched on the end o' the bed an' started to Caw! Caw! Caw! Biddy says to the priest, "That's what you couldn't do, now. Will you put out the crow now?" says she to him again.

'He started to pray an' pray. The crow started on the end o' the bed, Caw! Caw! Caw! all the time. "Well, I'll put her out," says Biddy.

'She held the bottle out in her hand with the neck of it facing the crow, an' the crow flew out the window again an' up on the tree an' started Caw! Caw! Caw! above in the tree again.

'She gave the bottle to the priest. "There 'tis for you, now," says she, "an' you'll have the same powers as I had."

'But what did the priest do with it only threw it into Kilbarron lake, an' 'tis supposed to be there yet.'

Petie Pete versus Witch Bea-Witch

(Italian)

Petie Pete was a little boy just so tall who went to school. On the school road was a garden with a pear tree, which Petie Pete used to climb and eat the pears. Beneath the tree passed Witch Bea-Witch one day and said:

Petie Pete, pass me a pear
With your little paw!
I mean it, don't guffaw,
My mouth waters, I swear, I swear!

Petie Pete thought, her mouth waters not for the pears but for me, and refused to come down the tree. He plucked a pear and threw it Witch Bea-Witch. But the pear fell on the ground right where a cow had been by and deposited one of its mementoes.

Witch Bea-Witch repeated:

Petie Pete, pass me a pear
With your little paw!
I mean it, don't guffaw,
My mouth waters, I swear, I swear!

But Petie Pete stayed in the tree and tossed down another pear, which fell on the ground right where a horse had been by and left a big puddle.

Witch Bea-Witch repeated her request, and Petie Pete thought it wiser to comply. He scampered down and offered her a pear. Witch Bea-Witch opened up her bag, but instead of putting in the pear, she put in Petie Pete, tied up the bag, and slung it over her shoulder.

After going a little way, Witch Bea-Witch had to stop and relieve herself; she put the bag down and went behind a bush. Meanwhile, with his little teeth as sharp as a rat's, Petie Pete gnawed the cord in two that tied up the bag, jumped out, shoved a heavy rock into the bag, and fled. Witch Bea-Witch took up the bag once more and flung it over her shoulder.

O Petie Pete,
To carry you is a feat!

she said, and wound her way home. The door was closed, so Witch Bea-Witch called her daughter:

Maggy Mag! Marguerite!
Come undo the door;
Then I ask you more:
Put on the pot to stew Petie Pete.

Maggy Mag opened up, then placed a cauldron of water over the fire. When the water came to a boil Witch Bea-Witch emptied her bag into it. *Splash!* went the stone and crashed through the cauldron. Water poured into the fire and spattered all over the floor, burning Witch Bea-Witch's legs.

Mamma, just what do you mean
By boiling stones in our tureen?

cried Maggy Mag, and Witch Bea-Witch, dancing up and down in pain, snapped:

Child, rekindle the flame;
I'll be back in a flash with something tame.

She changed clothes, donned a blonde wig, and went out with the bag.

Instead of going on to school, Petie Pete had climbed back up the pear tree. In disguise, Witch Bea-Witch came by again, hoping he wouldn't recognize her, and said:

Petie Pete, pass me a pear
With your little paw!
I mean it, don't guffaw,
My mouth waters, I swear, I swear!

But Petie Pete had recognized her and dared not come down:

Pears I refuse old Witch Bea-Witch,
Who would bag me without a hitch.

Then Witch Bea-Witch reassured him:

I'm not the soul you think, I swear,
This morning only did I leave my lair.
Petie Pete, pass me a pear
With your little paw so fair.

She kept on until she finally talked Petie Pete into coming down and giving her a pear. At once she shoved him down into the bag.

Reaching the bushes, she again had to stop and relieve herself; but this time the bag was tied too tight for Petie Pete to get away. So what did he do but call 'Bobwhite' several times in imitation of quail. A hunter with his dog out hunting quail found the bag and opened it. Petie Pete jumped out and begged the hunter to put the dog into the bag in his place. When Witch Bea-Witch returned and shouldered the bag, the dog inside did nothing but squirm and whine, and Witch Bea-Witch said:

Petie Pete, there's nothing to help you,
Bark like a dog is all you can do.

She got home and called her daughter:

Maggy Mag! Marguerite!
Come undo the door;
Then I ask you more:
Put on the pot to stew Petie Pete.

But when she went to empty the bag into the boiling water, the angry dog slipped out, bit her on the shin, dashed into the yard, and gobbled up hens left and right.

Mamma, have you lost your mind?
Is it on dogs you now want to dine?

exclaimed Maggy Mag. Witch Bea-Witch snapped:

Child, rekindle the flame:
I'll be back in a flash.

She changed clothes, donned a red wig, and returned to the pear tree. She went on at such length that Petie Pete fell into the trap once more. This time there were no rest stops. She carried the bag straight home where her daughter was waiting on the doorstep for her.

'Shut him up in the chicken coop,' ordered the Witch, 'and early tomorrow morning while I'm out, make him into hash with potatoes.'

The next morning Maggy Mag took a carving board and knife to the henhouse and opened a little hen door.

Petie Pete, just for fun,
Please lay your head upon this board.

He replied:

First show me how!

Maggy Mag laid her neck on the board, and Petie Pete picked up the carving knife and cut off her head, which he put on to fry in the frying pan.

Witch Bea-Witch came back and exclaimed:

Marguerite, dear daughter,
What have you thrown in the fryer?

'Me!' piped Petie Pete, sitting on the hood over the fireplace.

'How did you get way up there?' asked Witch Bea-Witch.

'I piled one pot on top of the other and came on up.'

So Witch Bea-Witch tried to make a ladder of pots to go after him, but when she got half-way to the top the pots came crashing down, and into the fire she fell and burned to ashes.

Notes

1. The Seven Sisters

This is my version of a story from my childhood retold for this anthology. The colloquial phrases, asides and story-tellers' formulae here, turn up regularly, for example, 'the jungles and deserts, rivers and mountain-lands . . . no sign of Adam or his progeny'. The reference to Adam in the second half suggests Muslim origin – unsurprising since the cultural mix in the field of stories is very deep-rooted.

The name Indravati does not, strictly speaking, mean 'daughter of Indra' – 'vati' suffixed to a name indicates possession. Such nice points, however, are peripheral to the storyteller – often illiterate – absorbed in her interpretation of the story. The Raja Inder of this story is a corruption of the superior god of the major Vedic triad replaced in the middle ages by the current supreme triad of Brahma-Vishnu-Shiva. Each of the many strands, sects and sub-sects of Hinduism gives prominence to its preferred god, goddess or pair from the rich and varied Hindu pantheon, so derision of the gods of one group by another – even in religious texts – is quite familiar. Indra – Inder in the language of the common folk – turns up in stories as a fairy king and a lecherous fellow. Many gods at one time or another have been described as sexually incontinent which explains the insemination of vegetation, animals and all manner of things. I took liberties in my version by articulating the sexy bits which I always sensed simmering beneath the surface of the sanitized versions told to me as a child. Ribald, intensely sexual and uninhibited texts do exist in Hindi literature of the medieval period, particularly the graphic pieces about the meetings of the rustic god Krishna and the married milkmaid Radha. The lust of witches is famed in India, as elsewhere in the world, so it appeared legitimate to express the lasciviousness of the seven sisters. It explains the motivation of the witches to possess the prince – something which was never clear to me as a child.

2. Finn's Madness

Finn Mac Cumhal (pronounced 'Mac Cool') was a great Irish hero of the Celtic tradition. He was brought up by two magical women, one of whom taught him the arts, the other his battle skills. He gained foresight after his thumb was scalded to the bone by the juices of the Salmon of Knowledge (cf. Gwion in 'The Cauldron Born'). Finn headed up about five thousand chieftains and warriors and, after a lifetime of heroism, passed over into the Other World where he slumbers, awaiting the final awakening. He is thus a wounded god (Jesus Christ archetype). The most obvious parallel is with Arthur who awaits resurrection after being carried away to Avalon by Morgan Le Fey.

During his adventures Finn tangled with many a magical woman. The Dagda with whom Daireann identifies herself, are a fairy tribe from among the Tuatha de Danaan who inhabit Tier na N'Og, the Land of the Ever Young. (See 'Coonlagh Ruadh and the Fairy Maiden,' p.17)

(*Gods and Fighting Men,* Lady Gregory, Ireland, John Murray, 1904, p. 231)

3. The Nixy

Andrew Lang describes this story simply as 'Eastern European' and he credits it to Kletke (who wrote in German). It is probably Hungarian, although examples of it exist all over the world. A Jewish version tells of a certain relation of the Baal Shem Tov who relentlessly casts his sins into the water. In revenge, the waters arose to engulf his son on the boy's thirteenth birthday but he was kept out of its reach because the Baal Shem Tov (out of consideration for the man's pious wife) had forewarned them of the event. (*Classic Hassidic Tales,* Meyer Levin, Dorset Press, 1931)

The nixy is clearly a water-witch. The hares, toads and frogs of this story are all witch-connected, so is the spinning wheel. As in many tales about witches, the evil is balanced by the good: the deceitful nixy and the kind old witch.

The rash promise motif probably originates from ancient human sacrifice rites.

(*The Yellow Fairy Book,* Andrew Lang, London, Longmans Green and Co., 1894, p.99)

4. The Maiden on the Loreley

Clearly based on the sirens of Greek myths, this maiden is altogether more forlorn and haunting than her more famous sisters. Here the nymphs are the victims of modernisation. The maiden's exile and loss of power reflects a diminishing belief in supernatural beings. Treacherous water-sprites and monsters possibly originated with men's fear of the waters and what was held in their depths. In many cultures crossing the seas was taboo. As the sea became more familiar and less fearsome, the creatures too waned in potency.

(*Legends of the Rhineland*, August Antz, translated by Kathlyn Rutherford, Bonn, Wilhelm Stolfuss Verlag, undated, p. 23)

5. Coonlagh Ruadh and the Fairy Maid

This is transcribed from storyteller Pat Ryan's tape of some of his favourite fairytales. It is probably a nineteenth-century piece and a literary version appears in Lady Wilde's collection, *Ancient Legends, Mystic Charms and Superstitions of Ireland* (1925). Pat heard the story, which includes songs, from his great-aunt Catherine. Seamus Ennis, the famous musician and story-teller, has a similar version. The fairy maid here is familiar, for example from Keats' *La Belle Dame Sans Merci*. Once the knight has seen her he sickens until he is either reunited with her or dies. This form of enchantment, very particular to Celtic based stories, enjoyed a revival in the work of the English Romantics. In Persio-Indian fairytales fairies freely abduct men with whom they fall in love. The apple has ancient Celtic associations with the Silver Bough of the underworld.

(From audio-tape *Tales of Old, British and Irish Fairytales*, Pat Ryan, London, Sheba Audio Productions, 1985)

6. The Marriage of Sir Gawain

The solution to the riddle was originally 'Sovereignty' now degenerated to imply that every woman wants her way. The motif of an ugly, old woman turning into a beautiful young one after kissing or lying with a young man is common in Celtic tales. There are many simple morals here – facing the undesirable, not judging by appearance and the transforming power of love. The hag here is the lost British goddess, Sovereignty, also known as the Loathly Lady. Her encounters with heroes allow her to judge whether they are worthy of being king. Acceptance of her loathly form indicates willingness to accept the tribulations of rulership along with the privileges. The Caelli Bheur, Morgan and the Morrigu each assume a loathly form for this purpose, but of her own will and not, as in this story, under the spell of another. One interpretation locates the Loathly Lady in the realm of the solar-lunar myth, an essential theme of witch-lore with its waxing-waning moon associations.

(*The Tale of Sir Gawain*, Neil Phillips, London, Beaver Books, 1989, p.40)

Part Two: WISE OLD WOMEN

1. I Love You More Than Salt

This rare Cinderella variant comes from Duncan Williamson, the celebrated Scottish storyteller, transcribed by his wife Dr Linda Williamson from the oral version. According to Duncan, travelling folk were not keen on witches and so he does not often name them in his stories. Here too, he describes the witch as an old woman in the first instant. In several other stories she appears in the guise of 'hen-wife', bird-woman, or a tall or magical woman. There is precedent for this in other cultures. The Celts did not name the fairy-folk, preferring to refer to them as the 'good people', and fairies in Brittany were called 'Mere Commere'.

In most Baba Yaga and Mother Holle variants the heroine finds that serving the witch and tending her animals brings rewards though these women retain a mystical and threatening aura about them. The witch-in-the-woods of this story in unambiguously a 'helper'. She may well be a very early model for the Fairy Godmother made famous by Perrault in his courtly telling of Cinderella. The Fairy Godmother seems to have no origins other than in the Italian *Pentamerone* of Giambattista Basile where a fairy helper emerges from a tree. It would appear that the insertion of 'God' between 'fairy' and 'mother' somehow endorses the acceptance of gifts from an occult source – particularly a witch, so long demonized by the church. Or perhaps 'God' is simply a corrupt form of 'good', in which case the pagan connection with fairies and the Mother Goddess once again comes into play. The mother figure is of course a crucial part of many Cinderella variants – a tree may grow from her grave or she may communicate with her daughter and find ways of feeding her.

This version is very realistic. The abandoned Princess is not magically supported but taken in by an old woman. The Princess's transformation into a dirty beggarmaid is a disguise. The only magic here is the withdrawal of salt – a strange nature miracle. Salt is meaningful in the context of fairytales since it is a talisman against spells. It was used to protect babies from birth-fiends, pilfering fairies and other spirits, none of whom eat salt. In alchemical theory, salt comprises the third major substance along with sulphur and quicksilver. It is believed to stabilize and ground the others. The loss and return of the salt in this story certainly brought the pompous old king down to earth!

(*Tell me a Story for Christmas*, Duncan Williamson, Edinburgh, Canongate Publishing, 1987, p.80)

2. The Tale Of the Merchant, the Crone and the King

This is Richard Burton's translation of the celebrated Arab classic about Scheherazade's marathon storytelling session to save her life. According to

Burton, this is the Eighth night. It appears in *The Supplemental Nights* to *The Book of the Thousand Nights and One Night*, which was published in a limited edition for private circulation only, since it was considered to be 'obscene'. The crone here either has strong supernatural powers or is quite formidably brilliant since she satisfies the logic of the irrational.

(*A Thousand and One Arabian Nights* Vol. I, translated by Sir Richard Burton, London, Burton Club, 1886, p.235)

3. The Four Gifts

Here again are women representing good and bad mothers – an avaricious task-mistress and a patient guide and protector who nevertheless lets Tephany learn through her own mistakes. Tephany appears to desire qualities strikingly similar to those of witches – sexual gratification, excessive beauty, wit and independence, but they prove to be beyond the control of a 'poor peasant girl'. Andrew Lang makes the age-old patriarchal points when he puts the words into the mouths of Tephany and the witch at the close of the story:

'I desire nothing but to be the poor peasant girl I always was, working hard for those she loves.'

And the witch's response:

'You have learned your lesson and now shall lead a peaceful life and marry the man you love.'

Somehow one is left with the feeling that poor Tephany has been short-changed, even though we are assured her husband learned to share in the work.

The story is reminiscent of 'The Old Woman in the Vinegar Bottle' type, where a fish is asked to grant increasingly greater favours but the asker ends up scarcely better off than she started – though she is infinitely richer morally.

(*The Lilac Fairy Book*, Andrew Lang, London, Longmans Green and Co. Ltd., 1910, p.299)

4. Habetrot

This is one of many tales in which subterfuge is rewarded. A lazy spinner story with a satisfying ending where a secret sisterhood is at work. Old Habetrot asks for no reward – not even like the famous Norwegian story of 'The Three Aunts' who wished to be acknowledged as a relative. In both stories, the lass liberates herself after acknowledging her association with coarse and ugly women, suggesting that it is important for women to reclaim their weak and ugly sides as well as the good in them. Spinning has been a womanly pursuit for centuries. It is an act of creation, demanding imagination and is associated with notions of power and control. The Fates and other controllers of destiny are identified with spinning. And it was from women that many great stories are believed to have originated. Perhaps such stories baulk against the notion of female docility and industriousness coupled with beauty and meekness. Men can take their pick – a beautiful, pampered wife or an ugly, industrious one.

Kate Briggs has recorded an interesting sequel to the 'Tom Tit Tot' tale from East Anglia in 'The Gipsy Woman', *British Folk Tales and Legends, A Sampler*. Here, after the death of Tom Tit Tot the Queen once again finds herself faced with a spinning ordeal. A gipsy woman agrees to do the spinning in exchange for the queen's best dress and asks her to arrange a feast and invite her. The woman appears beautifully dressed, stains the clothes of the other guests with black oil and confesses that her fingers are deeply and permanently marked with spindle grease. Thus the lazy queen wins a reprieve from spinning again.

(*A Dictionary of Fairies*, Kate Briggs, London, Penguin, 1979, p.213)

5. Unfortunate

The heroine of this story changes her destiny by following her nurse's advice to nurture and nourish it. She succeeds through her strong instinct for survival. The balance of opposites in the two Destinies – one beautiful, the other hideous – and the two mother figures – the queen passive and the nurse active – is again notable.

The motif of a witch who responds to nurturing occurs in the first extant myth where the Sumerian Erishkigal, a Demeter paradigm, moans in anguish after transforming the goddess Inanna into a lump of meat, skewered on a meat hook. Their grandfather sends down two creatures who mimic her agony and Erishkigal, overwhelmed by their sympathy, agrees to return Inanna from the Underworld.

(*The Book of Curses and Enchantments*, Ruth Mannings-Saunders, London, Magnet Books, 1979, p. 16)

6. Biddy Early's Flying Magic

This is one of the more general stories associated with Biddy Early. Born in Faha in 1798, Biddy spent most of her long life in Kilbarron, Co. Clare. She was recognized for her healing powers and her ability to take on the establishment, becoming known as the Wise Woman of Co. Clare. Lady Gregory foretold that Biddy would become the apocryphal focus for many of the magical stories that existed around her time. Eddie Lenihan comments, 'Biddy is purported to have done . . . what an oppressed peasantry would themselves wish to have done if they had dared, for example, standing up to the police or the landlord or putting the priest in his place.' He adds, 'Biddy was a real person of flesh and blood, since there is a danger that with her passing into the lore of general currency she may become a semi-mythological figure.'

She charged nothing for her help and is clearly remembered as a witch, albeit a good one. Eddie Lenihan found during his researches that people were frightened to talk about Biddy even as recently as the 1980s, which suggests a belief that her powers survive beyond the grave.

Eddie emphasises that this tale must not be interpreted as a piece of charlatanism. The word 'fly' is used metaphorically.

(*In Search of Biddy Early*, Edmund Lenihan, Dublin, The Mercier Press, 1987, p. 45)

Part Three: WITCHES IN LOVE: POSSESSIVE WOMEN AND DEVOTED WIVES

1. The Morrigu

The title Morrigu or Morrighan means Great Queen. She is the ancient warrior triple-goddess of Ireland, Macha-Neimann-Badb. Her totem is the battle-crow. She can fly, shape-shift and heal and is conspicuously similar to both Morgan Le Fey (Arthurian Cycle) and Modron (Mabinogian) and therefore also to Sovereignty. (See note on 'The Marriage of Sir Gawain'.) It is as Sovereignty that she meets and challenges Cuchulain, the champion of the King of Ulster and hero of the Ulster Cycle, whose status roughly corresponds to that of Gawain with Arthur. He used his death-inflicting spear, Gae Bolg, and in this story defends Ulster single-handedly against Maeve of Connacht because his warriors have been laid low due to Macha's curse. The battle is the result of the Cattle Raid of Cooley instigated by Queen Maeve, the enemy of the King of Ulster. Cuchulain wins the battle but fails Morrigu's test of kingship.

(*Cuchulain of Muirthemne*, Lady Gregory, London, John Murray, 1902, p. 211)

2. The Painted Skin

Strange Tales completed in 1679 by the Chinese scholar born P'u Sung-ling and variously known as Liu-Hsien, Liu Ch'uan, is the Chinese equivalent in fame and prestige as *The Arabian Nights*.

The witch-spirit in the painted skin wishes to gain control of Wang in order to acquire his vitality and be reborn as a human. Her savage ripping out of Wang's heart is not dissimilar to the scorned witches in the 'Story of Aristomenes' (p. 77). But as so often happens in these stories, the priest wins.

(*Strange Tales from a Chinese Studio*, translated by Herbert A. Giles, Cambridge, Cambridge University Press, 1908, p. 47)

3. Lilith and the Blade of Grass

There is a wealth of literature about Lilith in such sources as the Jewish Zohar and Midrash. Essentially, she was Adam's first mate and expressed annoyance at having to lie beneath him during copulation. As a result, she was banished to Earth, away from her children. In revenge and anger, she vowed to molest and kill newborn babies. She began also to consort with various monsters, producing hundreds of imps daily. Thoroughly demonised for her act of independence, she is said to cause wet dreams by copulating with men while they sleep. Here she appears as succubus or night-hag.

(*Jewish Folktales*, Pinhas Sadeh, translated by Hillel Halkin, London, Collins, 1990, p.80)

4. Daughter of the Moon, Son of the Sun

In Greek mythology Diana, the Moon is also the ultimate witch-goddess and the moon and its associated nocturnal animals are traditionally connected with witches. Thus Niekia, the daughter of the Moon in this story, deserves to be recognized as a witch. An old Tuscan legend tells how Diana sent her daughter, Aradia (apparently a corruption of Herodias), down to Earth in order to establish witchcraft and to become 'the first of witches known'. This legend was published in the form of a strange, but now much-celebrated manuscript known as *Aradia, the Gospel of the Witches*. A nineteenth-century folklorist, Charles Godfrey Leland, was responsible for the translation and publication of the work and claimed to have obtained it from Maddalena, a practising strega, a divining witch. Niekia seems to have the same descent, though her function is different. Like Niekia, Aradia too returns to her mother when her function here on Earth ends.

James Riordan speaks in his introduction of the tough life of the Siberian tribes whose children were set to work as early as seven or eight. Tales told at night around the fire were their only form of recreation and learning. The first collectors of Siberian folklore were the political exiles of the mid-nineteenth century.

(*Siberian Folktales, The Sun Maiden and The Crescent Moon*, James Riordan, Edinburgh, Canongate, 1989, p.202)

5. The Loving Fox

Fox-witches and dog-witches, once well-known in Japan, were said to throng the houses of certain families who controlled them. Often, too, they would promise to aid a shaman or others who showed them kindness and offered them protection. Here the fox-witch sacrifices herself for the man who shows her love and by doing so achieves redemption and a place in heaven. See 'The Goodwife of Laggan' for an English version of a witch attempting redemption. The witch-as-a-beautiful-woman generally tempts her prey with the intention of somehow 'unmanning' him, usually by sapping his energy in some way, or by enslaving him. This beautiful story subverts that concept entirely.

(*The Yanagita Kunio Guide to the Japanese Folktale*, edited and translated by Fanny Hagin Mayer, Bloomington, Indiana University Press, 1948)

6. The Story of Aristomenes

Thessaly was renowned for its immensely powerful witches, notable among them Erichtho the Crone of Thessaly (Lucan's *Pharsalia*). Here, Meroe (drunkenness) and Panthia (the Goddess) are wonderfully wicked, turning a revenge mission into engagingly spiteful revelry.

The references to castration are shocking and amusing but they epitomise some of the primal fears of men – castration, damage to genitalia, transformation into beasts of burden and enslavement by women – particularly old women. Metaphorically, too, Meroe's witch-powers castrate men. In her book *The Golden Ass of Apuleius (p.22)* Jungian analyst Marie-Louise von Franz develops the hypothesis that Apuleius had a mother complex and compares the devouring, castrating nature of a possessive and controlling mother to that of the old witch in this story. She points out the similarities between Lucius, the hero of the book, and Apuleius himself.

(*The Golden Ass*, Lucius Apuleius, translated by Robert Graves, London, Penguin, 1960, p.30)

7. Ala and the Old Hag

In European tales testing of this kind, where a hag asks for a young man's favours, chivalry is rewarded, generally through transformation of the hag into a magical consort such as the story of Diarmuid and the loathly lady and a similar Caellie Bheur tale. This old hag, however, is entirely malicious and needs virile Ala's vitality.

(*Folktales from the Congo*, Jan Knappert, London, Heinemann Educational Books Ltd, 1987, p.24)

8. The Queen's Ring

Another witch with a spinning wheel. This story is a different slant on the Frog Prince and explains the King's transformation. A beautiful woman turning into a hideous old hag is familiar in witch tales.

(*The Book of Curses and Enchantments*, Ruth Mannings-Saunders, London, Magnet Books, 1979, p.36)

Part Four: TRANSFORMATIONS

1. The Grinning Face of the Old Woman

This witch is obviously protecting her water-creatures since she only appears to kill hunters.

(*Japanese Tales*, Royall Tyler, New York, Pantheon, 1987, p.297)

2. The Red Woman

Another of Finn's encounters with a woman of the Sidhe (fairies). The Firlbogs, a race of misshapen giants driven out by the Tuatha de Danaan, were the first inhabitants of Ireland. The Red Woman taunts Finn by offering him refuge from the magical powers of the Firlbogs in her territory, then on his refusal, succeeds in the hunt where he has failed. However, he escapes possible enchantment by refusing to eat fairy-touched food.

(*Gods and Fighting Men*, Lady Gregory, Ireland, John Murray, 1904, p.234)

3. The Woman who Turned her Husband into a Snake

The magic stone providing access to special powers and fairy territories exists in Celtic lore too. (See 'Habetrot').

(*Tales of the Cochiti Indians, Smithsonian Institute Bureau of American Ethnology, Bulletin 98*, Ruth Benedict, Washington, Smithsonian Institute, 1934, p.96)

4. Kertong

Believed to have been told by the poet T'ao Ch'ien (365–472), this must be one of the earliest tales of the Fairy Bride group. In the East, Japan in particular, the reptiles in these tales were usually the grander dragons and great serpents. In European tales they are generally mermaids and in the British Isles seals as well as mermaids. Birds and other animals also marry human husbands all over the world and water-creatures seem to be the commonest. In the Indian epic *Mahabharata* the river goddess Ganges herself marries the king. Whatever the origin of the fairy, the taboos are generally the same – the husband is either forbidden to divulge the supernatural identity of the bride or to question her actions. If he breaks this bond, she returns to her own realm, often leaving her offspring behind. In Ireland mermaid and seal (selchie) brides appear to be held against their will because the husband has hidden away their natural skin. When she finds it, the fairy bride returns to the water.

(*Sweet and Sour Tales From China*, Carol Kendall and Yao Wen Li, London, Bodley Head, 1978, p.66)

5. The Boy And the Hare

This is transcribed from an oral performance by Thomas Cecil in the archives of the Ulster Folk and Transport Museum, Hollywood, Ulster. The story has a robust and realistic feel about it which is peculiar to witch-transformation tales in Ireland and England. They generally originate from rustic concerns such as insufficient milk from cows, caused by witches disguised as hares suckling them in the night. Witches turn into hares or black dogs for sport or gain, here in playful competition. There are some instances of the pursuant shifting shape into a fleet, black dog to gain the advantage. Sadly, in most stories the runaway ends up wounded, with a shot, cut or broken paw or limb, and the injury persists on her return to her original form, giving away the witch's identity. Both motifs are found in a Somerset folktale about Granny Pope and her daughter Kersey.

This story is unusual in that it displays a partisan attitude to the witch since it is told from the little boy's perspective. Happily this mischievous granny comes home intact and the boy is none too alarmed by her dishevelled appearance. The laugh is on the hunters here which is in keeping with today's animal rights ideal and the ecological concerns to which contemporary witches ally themselves.

(Thomas Cecil, Ulster, The Ulster Folk and Transport Museum, 1979 tape ref.)

6. Roland

This is a classical transformation story, like 'The Devil's Daughter', where an escaping pair changes form repeatedly in order to elude a demonic pursuer. Often the couple consist of the daughter of the captor assisting the captive with the aid of her parent's magical implements. The parent may be a devil or a witch. Three drops of blood have always been potent magic. In the Bible Abel's blood speaks from the ground. Blood is used in pacts with the Devil and symbolizes life. Here it speaks for the benefit of the heroine, suggesting that girls and women can summon their inner magic when the need arises.

The True Bride motif also occurs in this tale when the forgetful prince recognizes and marries his true love on the day of his wedding to another.
(*The Brothers Grimm*, London, Chancellor Press, 1989, p.263)

7. The Snake Wife

This fairy-bride, like 'The Loving Fox', makes great sacrifices for a human achieving redemption. Her sacrifice is rewarded with permanent human form – the highest form of life for transmigratory souls.
(*The Yanagita Kunio Guide to the Japanese Folktale*, edited and translated by Fanny Hagin Mayer, Bloomington, Indiana University Press, 1986, p.35)

8. The Old Woman in the Wood

In magical tales the witch often loses her powers when the heroine stands up to her. Psychoanalytically there are connotations here of the individual's determination to confront and integrate the evil witch (in Jungian parlance, the Shadow) within. Having owned the dark aspects of the female principle, the maiden is liberated and free to pursue her destiny. In Jungian theory this represents three significant steps – confronting the Shadow (the dark aspect of the subconscious), going on to integrate the female (anima) and masculine (animus) sides which reside within every individual and reaching the desired stage, individuation or wholeness of the Self. This integration is symbolised by the union of the prince and the maid. Other symbols of the self in the story are the gems and the ring which in Jungian alchemical theory represent the true, higher Self. When the individual comes to accept all sides of herself, she can feel complete. The redeemer in fairytales is most often female. Here too, the maiden liberates the prince after following his advice.
(*The Brothers Grimm*, London, Chancellor Press, 1989, p.208)

9. The Leopard Woman

This tale humorously reinforces the ancient roles of man the hunter and woman the gatherer and grower. The woman shape-shifter conveys that women can clearly fulfil all these roles but the result is a man more fearful and ineffectual than an infant.
(*African Folktales*, Roger Abrahams, New York, Pantheon, 1983, p.148)

10. The Three Crones

This hilarious tale illustrates the power of laughter.
(*Italian Folktales*, Italo Calvino, New York, Harcourt Brace Jovanovitch, 1980, p.80)

Part Five: GUARDIANS OF THE SEASONS AND ELEMENTS

1. The First People and the First Corn

This legend was first recorded by a Penobscot Indian in 1893. Tribes in Maine and Nova Scotia also told versions of it. The myth relates to the origin of tobacco and corn, the latter linking it to Demeter whose mark is the ear of corn. Both are aspects of the Great Mother in her desolate phase, grieving for her offspring. The prayer which concludes the story is reminiscent of the eucharist. The goddess of this tale bears striking parallels with Christ and this form of self-sacrifice for the sake of humankind is, surprisingly, rare among Mother Goddesses.

Many stories exist of the Corn Goddesses, ranging from an old Woman who never dies to the seven or nine Corn-Maidens who appear to bestow corn, then disappear along with their bounty when the people become ungrateful, providing an explanation for failed crops and famine. East Anglia and Germany also have Corn Mother stories.
(*The Penobscot Man: Life History Of A Forest Tribe In Maine*, Frank G. Speck, Philadelphia, University of Penn Press, 1940, p.330)

2. The Mistress of Fire

Many folktales tell of women keepers-of-fire, including those of the Amer-Indian and South Pacific tribes. This old folk tale, though not directly about fire, leads the main protagonist, a treacherous crow, to an old hag as the source of fire.
This story probably refers back to human sacrifice which ensured survival during the deep Siberian winters by keeping the fire-goddess propitiated. Fire as a basic and indispensable element of nature is accorded honour by many races. In this story the guardian of fire demands the same respect.
(*Siberian Folktales, The Sun Maiden and the Crescent Moon*, James Riordan, Edinburgh, Canongate, 1989, p.181)

3. Anancy and the Hide-Away Garden

The Witch-Sister dressed in red denotes fertility and menstruation, the latter being an important element in witch-lore. Anancy the trickster (sometimes spelled Anansi) originates from Africa and brought stories to the world. The trickster is an ambivalent character in folktale, both creative and destructive, noble and base. His negative side is apparent in this story where he succeeds in destroying a thing of beauty for sheer greed. He appears to have decimated the domain of a nature goddess to no avail.
(*Anancy Spiderman*, James Berry, London, Walker Books, and New York, Henry Holt and Company, Inc., 1988, p. 39)

4. Johnny Draw the Knife

This haunting tale, included in an article on seal stories, warns of the dangers of the sea and reiterates that it is owed respect.
(*Seal Stories and Belief on Rathlin Island*, Linda-May Ballard, Ulster Folklife, Vol. 29, 1983, p.40)

5. The Snow-Daughter and the Fire-Son

The incontrovertible nature of the seasons forms the theme of this story (see also 'Caelli Bheur'). Winter (snow) and Summer (sun) destroy each

other. (Andrew Lang credits this tale to *Bukowiner Tales and Legends* by Von Wliolocki). The story also contains the motif of the wish as a prayer fulfilled (cf. 'Snow White' *et al* found around the world). The mother of Snow and the Sun may be Mother Nature herself. Perhaps that is why her children are kept from destroying themselves during her lifetime.
(*The Yellow Fairy Book*, Andrew Lang, London, Longmans, Green & Co., 1894, p.206)

6. Mother Holle

This story from the Brothers Grimm contains the familiar combination of a good girl and a bad girl. In the original version the stepmother of the story was in fact the biological mother of both girls (in fact, this is true of several stories about cruel mothers, including 'Snow White'). In later versions she, like the others, was converted into a stepmother in keeping with the Grimm agenda of indoctrinating children, particularly, it seems, girls. The attempt to ingrain certain social concepts in children is obvious elsewhere in this tale. Spinning, for example was a pastime considered appropriate for women, particularly poor ones. The Grimm's spinning heroines came to be associated with diligence, selflessness and privation (emotional and material). Thankfully, however, other kinds of spinning heroines also survive – the lazy, resourceful spinners who do not dedicate themselves to the service of others without hope of reward. They are the familiar women of the 'Tom Tit Tot'/'Three Aunts' group, who are not averse to a bit of natural deceit in order to avoid being tied forever to the spindle. Such heroines exist also in stories more distinctly of the 'Mother Holle' pattern. An English example is that of 'The Long Leather Bag' in which the heroine sets off to seek her fortune and serves the witch until such time as she finds a leather bag filled with gold and runs off with it pursued by the hag but assisted by various creatures she has earlier helped. In 'The Green Lady', also English, the industrious girl discovers her mistress dancing with a 'bogey', lies blatantly to save her skin and is generously rewarded for keeping the secret. The Grimms' own notes to 'Mother Holle' record a tale in which the heroine demands for her own convenience, certain actions of the creatures and objects she meets, but it suited the brothers to abandon that tale and use (or create) a sanitized, version. Its lesson was more in keeping with their ideals of womanhood.

The truth remains, however, that outward beauty has always been the passport to good fortune in fairytales, though it may well be the case that it symbolizes inner goodness. For in the oldest and most authentic tales it is the inherent goodness of the heroine that is rewarded rather than individual acts. Emotional and material deprivation is also a condition that receives ample compensation as tales develop. The combination of beauty and deprivation is infallible. In 'Mother Holle', the girl is forced into the realm of the Nature Goddess, rather like heaven, permanently green and beautiful, as she is in tales with a parallel witch figure, such as the Baba Yaga. The Goddess does not therefore punish her intrusion but eventually rewards her well. The second sister, however, goes from greed and shows disrespect for the natural order of things by neglecting to create the desired weather. Consequently, she is punished. The daring little girl in the terrifying 'Mother Trude' (Grimm) is chastised by being turned into a block of wood and set aflame to warm the witch. Here the bad girl is covered in pitch. An influence of Christianity, I think.

Note that the Goddess is benign in her manner even when she is associated with creating snow which here is symbolized as soft and feathery – something that the people desire. This is directly opposed to cold clime representations of menacing winter hags, such as the Snow Queen, the Caellie Bheur (p.213) or Black Annis of the Dane Hills, Lancs.
(*The Red Fairy Book*, Andrew Lang, Longmans, Green and Company, London, 1890, p.303)

Part Six: WITCHY DEVICES: CAULDRONS, BROOMSTICKS AND TRYSTS WITH THE DEVIL

1. Hooch for Skye!

Duncan Williamson prefaces the tale by saying that he first heard it from his father when he was four. He adds that the travelling folk have their own way of telling this popular Highlands tale.

The power of flight is often gained through a pass-word and here it works with hats instead of brooms (or a cauldron as in 'The Witches Sabbath'. The old women clearly sublimate their grief over the loss of their brother by rescuing Jack. However, there may be a hidden warning in Maggie's assurance that Jack had been dreaming – and that her brother had dreamed the same dream before he died. Jack colludes in the conspiracy of silence even after establishing the events have actually occurred. This pact of secrecy is not unusual between witches and a human who has discovered their mysteries. The Baba Yaga praises Wasilissa in one variant, for not asking about matters which must remain within the house, and in the English tale of 'The Green Lady', the maiden working for her denies seeing her dancing with a Bogey. Similarly in the Austrian tale of 'The Black Woman' the maiden is rewarded for denying that she has seen the witch slowly turning white as she washes away her sins.
(*The Genie And The Fisherman*, Duncan and Linda Williamson, Cambridge, Cambridge University Press, 1991, p.73)

2. The Cauldron-Born

John and Caitlin Matthews describe Ceridwen as the goddess of inspiration (*The Aquarian Guide to British and Irish Mythology*) and also compare her to the Caelli Bheur (see p. 151). Often known as the Old One, she is closely associated with her cauldron and its magical brew. This story amply illustrates both her shape-shifting ability and her vengefulness. But the self-impregnation and rebirth of Gwion is a tragic experience for her and another example where divine justice takes precedence over emotion. Ceridwen is more feared and honoured than loved, perhaps because of her hideous countenance and her vengeful ways. Her huge pudendum hangs down to her knees and her cauldron is simultaneously a symbol of rebirth and human sacrifice. John Matthews writes in *Taliesin: Shamanism and the Bardic Mysteries in Britain and Ireland* that though no texts refer to her as a goddess, certain Welsh phrases do call her *wrach* (witch) or *gwrach* (sorceress).

(*The Song of Taliesin*, John Matthews, London, The Aquarian Press, 1991, p.25)

3. The Witches Sabbath

This story reflects the views of the medieval church which brought about the hideous witch-persecutions of the Middle Ages. The held belief was that witches worked in close liaison with the Devil and consequently against Christianity. Contamination can apparently come from mere mention of Old Erik's name even when purely elliptical as it is here. In fact, the concept of a horned, goat-footed master is probably closer to the Pan-based horned god of witch-craft. Perhaps this form of the Devil originates with Pan too.

(*Folktales of Norway*, edited by Reidar Christiansen, translated by Pat Shaw Iversen, Chicago, University of Chicago Press, 1964, p.36)

4. The Birch Besom

This truly mysterious tale is told by Alec Stewart. The relaxed interchange between Paddy's wife and the priest suggests that she is neither ghost nor witch. But she has access to some supernatural power in order to redeem her body from the possession of a witch. Or it may be that this story hints at the witch's contention that their religion/cult is *pre*-Christian and not *anti*-Christian.

(*The King o' The Black Art And Other Stories*, collected and introduced by Sheila Douglas, Aberdeen, Aberdeen University Press, 1987, p.33).

5. The Broom is Busy

A cryptic tale underscoring the mysteries of the 'fortune-teller woman'. There is a contented fatalism about the rustic philosophy of Odjo and Boki.

(*Caribbean Tales: The Woe Shirt*, Paule Barton, translated by Howard A. Norman, Washington, Graywolf Press, 1982, p.57)

6. *The Horned Women*

This classic witch-tale, eerie and sinister, contains several witchy elements: the spinning-wheel, evil spells and invasion. The horns symbolize the crescent moon, a reminder of the moon's connection with witches, while thirteen is the typical number of the coven.

(*Ancient Legends, Mystic Charms and Superstitions of Ireland*, Lady Wilde, London, Chatto and Windus, 1925, p.10)

7. *The Goodwife of Laggan*

This story consists of four discrete sections: two contests between cat-witches and witch-hunters; the exposure of the witch's true identity; and the witch's attempt to redeem her soul before the Devil enforces their pact.

(*Nine Lives*, Katherine Briggs, London, Routledge and Kegan Paul Ltd., 1980, p.94)

8. *Baba Yaga*

This variant of the famous Baba Yaga tales emphasises the dual nature of the crone almost more than all the others. Its brevity allows the focus to fall on the Yaga's reactive attitude. Like the famous Mother Holle character from Grimms, the witch rewards goodness and punishes ungraciousness. This behaviour is not unlike that of pagan deities or indeed the God of monotheistic religions where industry and kindness are rewarded and lack of veneration is a punishable sin. The Baba Yaga's other characteristics show she is a nature goddess, her mortar and pestle, for example, echoing Demeter's implements.

Names such as 'Spindle-shanks' are common for witches in England too.
(*Russian Folktales*, Aleksander Afanas'ev, New York, Pantheon, 1973, p.194)

Part Seven: HUNGRY HAGS: CANNIBALS AND BLOODSUCKERS

1. *Vikram and the Dakini*

I have retold this tale from memory. King Vikram frequently turns up in Indian fairytales. He appears to be a composite of the great king Vikramaditya (57BC) and the king who is hero of a sequence of twenty-five stories, 'Vikram and the Vampire', in the *Katha Sarit-Sagar* (*The Ocean of Rivers of Story*) (early 12th C). There are several English translations of this.

All storytellers tended to digress occasionally, particularly when dealing with well-known characters such as Vikram or Kali who have a cumulative fairytale tradition, apart from being part of mythology/history. The tellers also offer little philosophical asides, comments on character, moral judgements, informative bits and pieces, the last not always accurate but providing many insights. All Kshatriyas, for example, are not kings, though Kshatriyas (also called Rajputs) comprise the warrior/princely caste.

Then there were the sections they left out – the chthonic, bloody, sexual bits. The skilled story-tellers took our imaginations to a point where they leapt into anarchic action, visualizing the story for themselves. Those childhood images regularly reproduce themselves in my stories – a variation that the flexibility of fairytales can easily contain. Sometimes those elements are dark, at others they are hilarious – but there is always a certain energy about them which must spring from their originators and their environment.

The goddess Kali is well-known to the western world. The medieval treatise, *Kalika Purana* contains the accounts in this story of her ability to suck in through her vagina, and her 'genital contest' with Shiva. Much of the blood and gore is reminiscent of her demon-slaying and she is the patroness of witches and demonesses among other creatures.

2. *The Old Eagle-Hawk Woman*

The author collected this fertility myth along the Roper River in the Northern Territory of Australia. The motif originates from stories of Kunapipi, the earth-goddess of that region, who consumed and then vomited young men. This image clearly replicates crop harvesting and regrowth. In other versions, the fathers of missing boys track down the witch, kill her, and take over her rituals. Thus the awe-inspiring analogy of the sowing and reaping of the harvest with the swallowing and regurgitating of male children by an aged female serves to demonise the goddess. She becomes a predatory creature deserving execution and her powers pass to the men who slay her. This act of wresting the fertility rituals, the traditional preserve of the goddess, is part of the trend clearly discernible in most mythologies, of the patriarchal take-over and reduction of female power. Many myths bear evidence that men were particularly threatened by the ability of women to reproduce as the earth continually reproduces while their lives were finite. The earliest extant mythology – that of Sumeria – contains both motifs, the confinement of a powerful goddess to the Underworld and her brother's search for immortality.

(*Aboriginal Myths and Legends*, Roland Robinson, Melbourne, Sun Books, 1968, p.131)

3. The Two Children and the Witch

This is a variation on 'Hansel and Gretel'. The abandoning mother, the food-providing cannibal witch and the victorious children all appear. But here the children take over the witch's home. In her contests with children, the witch is often stupid.

(*Portuguese Folk-Tales*, Consiglieri Pedroso, translated by Henriqueta Monteiro, London, Folklore Society, 1882, p.59)

4. My Sweet Witch

The title 'witch-master' here applies to the chief-witch and not the man with control over witches as in 'The Witchmaster's Advice' (p.202). Like the witches in some Ozark communities, however, new initiates here must also kill a relative to be accepted by the coven. They are very much part of a community in both places, practising their rituals in secret.

(*Folktales from the Congo*, Jan Knappert, London, Heinemann Educational Books Ltd, 1987, p.61.

5. The Curse

The author describes the elk as a dwarfish birth-fiend who attacked women in childbirth 'pulling out her liver, strangling both her and her child, or stealing the human child and leaving behind a changeling'. (p.64) She also caused miscarriages and sterility. (See 'Rabbi Joshua and the Witch', p.199)

Witches all over the world are noted for enjoying the livers and hearts of humans.

(*100 Armenian Tales*, Suzie Hoogasian-Villa, Detroit, Wayne University, 1966, p.352)

6. Two Children and a Witch

Many fairytale children are swallowed by ferocious creatures such as monsters and wolves and found whole when the monster's stomach is split. Here it is the mother who enters into a contest with the witch and wins. (Source unknown)

7. El-Muzayyara

The editor notes that water-spirits of different kinds are permitted to consort with mortal men but, like other fairy-brides, they impose secrecy upon their partners. Here, however, Idrees clearly believes the 'jinniya' (female jinn) means to kill him.

(*Folktales of Egypt*, Hasan El-Shamy, Chicago, University of Chicago Press, 1938, p.180)

Part Eight: TRIALS AND CONTESTS

1. The Bewitched Churn

The apotropaic measures taken by the bewitched family here have a powerful effect on the witch. Unlike them though she is unwilling to let bygones be bygones.
(*Legendary Fictions of the Irish Celts*, Patrick Kennedy, London, Macmillan, 1891, p.135)

2. Rabbi Joshua and the Witch

The author's footnote dates this story around 5th C, Babylon. Priests – particularly those of the so-called ethical religions – always seem to defeat the witches. These stories re-enact the ancient match between patriarch and matriarch, pagan and monotheist. They are nearly always written from the point of view of monotheistic religious representatives and seek also to allay the fears of the pious. It is very different from Biddy Early's conflicts with the priest of Feakle.
(*Jewish Folktales and Legends*, David Goldstein, London, Hamlyn, 1980)

3. The Witchmaster's Advice

A witch who 'rides' men in the middle of the night is a familiar figure in Scandinavia and the British Isles. Often the riding is literal – the witch transforms the man into a horse and rides him to her revels with the Devil. There are clear sexual connotations here and the men are always exhausted and sometimes injured when they wake in the morning with no memory of their nocturnal transformation. As in this account, the men usually succeed in avenging themselves and exposing the witch. This story is unusual and all the more enjoyable for its scatalogical twist in the tail. It also pulls together the tale motif and the nightmare notion with the man, for the sake of domestic peace, colluding with the explanation of a bad dream.
(*Ozark Superstitions*, Vance Randolph, New York, Columbia University Press, 1947, p.279)

4. The Son of Seven Queens

Once again a woman redeems the hero.
(*Indian Fairytales*, Joseph Jacobs, London, Constable and Company Ltd, 1892, p.115)

5. The Caillie Bheur

I wrote this version of a delightful story from Skye telling of the origins of the Cuchullin mountains. It is an account of the natural battle which results in Spring or Summer replacing Winter. The Caellie is a winter-hag in the tradition of Black Annis of the Dane Hills. The Caellie has a richly varied background. She is a water-guardian, a mother-goddess and occasionally the Loathly Lady.

6. Hag-Rog

I retold this North American story from memory. My title comes from a recent publication *The Terror That Comes In the Night* which contains a version of it recorded from an informant in Newfoundland. Spells to prevent urination and defecation are also found in India and Africa.

7. Biddy Early, the Priest and the Crow

Biddy early died in 1874. Her contests with the local priest were much celebrated so it was fitting that she should have enjoyed a last one on her death-bed. Her magic bottle was closely associated with her powers, one legend being that she was given it by her dead husband Tom in order to help deal with a landlord bent on evicting her. She could see the future by looking into the bottle and thus prepare herself to deal with the disasters in store. It was said that anyone else who looked in the bottle would go mad and that the bottle would lose its powers if Biddy accepted money for her remedies.

Biddy defies the traditional concept of a community witch by having no fear of priest, church or bible. She was vindicated when the priest visited her deathbed. Lenihan quotes an informant:

'The priest that used to criticise her, he made a sermon in Feakle after Biddy dying, an' he referred to her as being a great, wonderful, charitable, good woman. Anything she ever did was for the good.'
(*In Search of Biddy Early*, Edmund Lenihan, Dublin, The Mercier Press, 1987)

8. Petie-Pete versus Witch Bea-Witch

Italo Calvino notes that he has invented names and nonsense rhymes for his version of this well-known tale among other 'touches' in the narrative. He comments in his introduction on some general characteristics in folktales for children.

... a theme of fear and cruelty, scatalogical or obscene details, lines of verse interpolated into the prose and slipping into nonsense rhymes, characterize the coarseness and cruelty which would be considered wholly unsuitable in children's books today. (p. xxx)

Luckily, although fairytales have been through centuries of purging and sanitization, there is a growing tendency to retain their authentic directness and sometimes extreme courses of action.

Some mythologies abound in scatalogical tales, Africa, the South Pacific, various Amer-Indian tales and many more. Among contemporary writers, Roald Dahl has provided children with a lot of enjoyable entertainment by indulging their taste in that area.

(*Italian Folktales*, Italo Calvino, New York, Harcourt Brace Jovanovitch, 1980, p.110)